THE PERSONAL MEMOIRS OF

U.S. GRANT

Volume One

THE PERSONAL MEMOIRS OF

U.S. GRANT

Volume One

ULYSSES S. GRANT

ÆGYPAN PRESS

The Personal Memoirs of U.S. Grant, Volume One
A publication of
ÆGYPAN PRESS

www.aegypan.com

Preface

"Man proposes and God disposes." There are but few important events in the affairs of men brought about by their own choice.

Although frequently urged by friends to write my memoirs I had determined never to do so, nor to write anything for publication. At the age of nearly sixty-two I received an injury from a fall, which confined me closely to the house while it did not apparently affect my general health. This made study a pleasant pastime. Shortly after, the rascality of a business partner developed itself by the announcement of a failure. This was followed soon after by universal depression of all securities, which seemed to threaten the extinction of a good part of the income still retained, and for which I am indebted to the kindly act of friends. At this juncture the editor of the Century Magazine asked me to write a few articles for him. I consented for the money it gave me; for at that moment I was living upon borrowed money. The work I found congenial, and I determined to continue it. The event is an important one for me, for good or evil; I hope for the former.

In preparing these volumes for the public, I have entered upon the task with the sincere desire to avoid doing injustice to anyone, whether on the National or Confederate side, other than the unavoidable injustice of not making mention often where special mention is due. There must be many errors of omission in this work, because the subject is too large to be treated of in two volumes in such way as to do justice to all the officers and men engaged. There were thousands of instances, during the rebellion, of individual, company, regimental and brigade deeds of heroism which deserve special mention and are not here alluded to. The troops engaged in them will have to look to the detailed reports of their individual commanders for the full history of those deeds.

The first volume, as well as a portion of the second, was written before I had reason to suppose I was in a critical condition of health. Later I was reduced almost to the point of death, and it became impossible for me to attend to anything for weeks. I have, however, somewhat regained my strength, and am able, often, to devote as many hours a day as a person should devote to such work. I would have more hope of satisfying the expectation of the public if I could have allowed myself more time. I have used my best efforts, with the aid of my eldest son, F.D. Grant, assisted by his brothers, to verify from the records every statement of fact given. The comments are my own, and show how I saw the matters treated of whether others saw them in the same light or not.

With these remarks I present these volumes to the public, asking no favor but hoping they will meet the approval of the reader.

U.S. GRANT
MOUNT MACGREGOR, NEW YORK, July 1, 1885

VOLUME ONE

Chapter I

ANCESTRY — BIRTH — BOYHOOD

My family is American, and has been for generations, in all its branches, direct and collateral.

Mathew Grant, the founder of the branch in America, of which I am a descendant, reached Dorchester, Massachusetts, in May, 1630. In 1635 he moved to what is now Windsor, Connecticut, and was the surveyor for that colony for more than forty years. He was also, for many years of the time, town clerk. He was a married man when he arrived at Dorchester, but his children were all born in this country. His eldest son, Samuel, took lands on the east side of the Connecticut River, opposite Windsor, which have been held and occupied by descendants of his to this day.

I am of the eighth generation from Mathew Grant, and seventh from Samuel. Mathew Grant's first wife died a few years after their settlement in Windsor, and he soon after married the widow Rockwell, who, with her first husband, had been fellow-passengers with him and his first wife, on the ship Mary and John, from Dorchester, England, in 1630. Mrs. Rockwell had several children by her first marriage, and others by her second. By intermarriage, two or three generations later, I am descended from both the wives of Mathew Grant.

In the fifth descending generation my great grandfather, Noah Grant, and his younger brother, Solomon, held commissions in the English army, in 1756, in the war against the French and Indians. Both were killed that year.

My grandfather, also named Noah, was then but nine years old. At the breaking out of the war of the Revolution, after the battles of Concord and Lexington, he went with a Connecticut company to join the Continental army, and was present at the battle of Bunker Hill. He served until the fall of Yorktown, or through the entire Revolutionary war. He must, however, have been on furlough part of the time — as I believe most of the soldiers of that period were — for he married in Connecticut during the war, had two children, and was a widower at the close. Soon after this he emigrated to Westmoreland County, Pennsylvania, and settled near the town of Greensburg in that county. He took with him the younger of his two children, Peter Grant. The elder, Solomon, remained with his relatives in Connecticut until old enough to do for himself, when he emigrated to the British West Indies.

Not long after his settlement in Pennsylvania, my grandfather, Captain Noah Grant, married a Miss Kelly, and in 1799 he emigrated again, this time to Ohio, and settled where the town of Deerfield now stands. He had now five children, including Peter, a son by his first marriage. My father, Jesse R. Grant, was the second child — oldest son, by the second marriage.

Peter Grant went early to Maysville, Kentucky, where he was very prosperous, married, had a family of nine children, and was drowned at the mouth of the Kanawha River, Virginia, in 1825, being at the time one of the wealthy men of the West.

My grandmother Grant died in 1805, leaving seven children. This broke up the family. Captain Noah Grant was not thrifty in the way of "laying up stores on earth," and, after the death of his second wife, he went, with the two youngest children, to live with his son Peter, in Maysville. The rest of the family found homes in the neighborhood of Deerfield, my father in the family of judge Tod, the father of the late Governor Tod, of Ohio. His industry and independence of character were such, that I imagine his labor compensated fully for the expense of his maintenance.

There must have been a cordiality in his welcome into the Tod family, for to the day of his death he looked upon judge Tod and his wife, with all the reverence he could have felt if they had been parents instead of benefactors. I have often heard him speak of Mrs. Tod as the most admirable woman he had ever known. He remained with the Tod family only a few years, until old enough to learn a trade. He went first, I believe, with his half-brother, Peter Grant, who, though not a tanner himself, owned a tannery in Maysville, Kentucky. Here he learned his trade, and in a few years returned to Deerfield and worked for, and lived in the family of a Mr. Brown, the father of John Brown — "whose body lies moldering in the grave, while his soul goes marching on." I have often heard my father speak of John Brown, particularly since the events at Harper's Ferry. Brown was a boy when they lived in the same house, but he knew him afterwards, and regarded him as a man of great purity of character, of high moral and physical courage, but a fanatic and extremist in whatever he advocated. It was certainly the act of an insane man to attempt the invasion of the South, and the overthrow of slavery, with less than twenty men.

My father set up for himself in business, establishing a tannery at Ravenna, the county seat of Portage County. In a few years he removed from Ravenna, and set up the same business at Point Pleasant, Clermont County, Ohio.

During the minority of my father, the West afforded but poor facilities for the most opulent of the youth to acquire an education, and the majority were dependent, almost exclusively, upon their own exertions for whatever learning they obtained. I have often heard him say that his time at school was limited to six months, when he was very young, too young, indeed, to learn much, or to appreciate the advantages of an education, and to a "quarter's schooling" afterwards, probably while living with judge Tod. But his thirst for education was intense. He learned rapidly, and was a constant reader up to the day of his death in his eightieth year. Books were scarce in the Western Reserve during his youth, but he read every book he could borrow in the neighborhood where he lived. This scarcity gave him the early habit of studying everything he read, so that when he got through with a book, he knew everything in it. The habit continued through life. Even after reading the daily papers — which he never neglected — he could give all the important information they contained. He made himself an excellent English scholar, and before he was twenty years of age was a constant contributor to Western newspapers, and was also, from that time until he was fifty years old, an able debater in the societies for this purpose, which were common in the West at that time. He always took an active part in politics, but was never a candidate for office, except, I believe, that he was the first Mayor of Georgetown. He supported Jackson for the Presidency; but he was a Whig, a great admirer of Henry Clay, and never voted for any other democrat for high office after Jackson.

My mother's family lived in Montgomery County, Pennsylvania, for several generations. I have little information about her ancestors. Her family took no interest in genealogy, so that my grandfather, who died when I was sixteen years old, knew only back to his grandfather. On the other side, my father took a great interest in the subject, and in his researches, he found that there was an entailed estate in Windsor, Connecticut, belonging to the family, to which his nephew, Lawson Grant — still living — was the heir. He was so much interested in the subject that he got his nephew to empower him to act in the matter, and in 1832 or 1833, when I was a boy ten or eleven years old, he went to Windsor, proved the title beyond dispute, and perfected the claim of the owners for a consideration — three thousand dollars, I think. I remember the circumstance well, and remember, too, hearing him say on his return that he found some widows living on the property, who had little or nothing beyond their homes. From these he refused to receive any recompense.

My mother's father, John Simpson, moved from Montgomery County, Pennsylvania, to Clermont County, Ohio, about the year 1819, taking with him his four children, three daughters and one son. My mother, Hannah Simpson, was the third of these children, and was then over twenty years of age. Her oldest sister was at that time married, and had several children. She still lives in Clermont County at this writing, October 5th, 1884, and is over ninety ears of age. Until her memory failed her, a few years ago, she thought the country ruined beyond recovery when the Democratic party lost control in 1860. Her family, which was large, inherited her views, with the exception of one son who settled in Kentucky before the war. He was the only one of the children who entered the volunteer service to suppress the rebellion.

Her brother, next of age and now past eighty-eight, is also still living in Clermont County, within a few miles of the old homestead, and is as active in mind as ever. He was a supporter of the Government during the war, and remains a firm believer, that national success by the Democratic party means irretrievable ruin.

In June, 1821, my father, Jesse R. Grant, married Hannah Simpson. I was born on the 27th of April, 1822, at Point Pleasant, Clermont County, Ohio. In the fall of 1823 we moved to Georgetown, the county seat of Brown, the adjoining county east. This place remained my home, until at the age of seventeen, in 1839, I went to West Point.

The schools, at the time of which I write, were very indifferent. There were no free schools, and none in which the scholars were classified. They were all supported by subscription, and a single teacher — who was often a man or a woman incapable of teaching much, even if they imparted all they knew — would have thirty or forty scholars, male and female, from the infant learning the A B C's up to the young lady of eighteen and the boy of twenty, studying the highest branches taught — the three R's, "Reading, 'Riting, 'Rithmetic." I never saw an algebra, or other mathematical work higher than the arithmetic, in Georgetown, until after I was appointed to West Point. I then bought a work on algebra in Cincinnati; but having no teacher it was Greek to me.

My life in Georgetown was uneventful. From the age of five or six until seventeen, I attended the subscription schools of the village, except during the winters of 1836-7 and 1838-9. The former period was spent in Maysville, Kentucky, attending the school of Richardson and Rand; the latter in Ripley, Ohio, at a private school. I was not studious in habit, and probably did not make progress enough to compensate for the outlay for board and tuition. At all events both winters were spent in going over the same old arithmetic which I knew every word of before, and repeating: "A noun is the name of a thing," which I had also heard my Georgetown teachers repeat, until I had come to believe it — but I cast no reflections upon my old teacher, Richardson. He turned out bright scholars from his school, many of whom have filled conspicuous places in the service of their States. Two of my contemporaries there — who, I believe, never attended any other institution of learning — have held seats in Congress, and one, if not both, other high offices; these are Wadsworth and Brewster.

My father was, from my earliest recollection, in comfortable circumstances, considering the times, his place of residence, and the community in which he lived. Mindful of his own lack of facilities for acquiring an education, his greatest desire in maturer years was for the education of his children. Consequently, as stated before, I never missed a quarter from school from the time I was old enough to attend till the time of leaving home. This did not exempt me from labor. In my early days, everyone labored more or less, in the region where my youth was spent, and more in proportion to their private means. It was only the very poor who were exempt. While my father carried on the manufacture of leather and worked at the trade himself, he owned and tilled considerable land. I detested the trade, preferring almost any other labor; but I was fond of agriculture, and of all employment in which horses were used. We had, among other lands, fifty acres of forest within a mile of the village. In the fall of the year choppers were employed to cut enough wood to last a twelve-month. When I was seven or eight years of age, I began hauling all the wood used in the house and shops. I could not load it on the wagons, of course, at that time, but I could drive, and the choppers would load, and someone at the house unload. When about eleven years old, I was strong enough to hold a plow. From that age until seventeen I did all the work done with horses, such as breaking up the land, furrowing, plowing corn and potatoes, bringing in the crops when harvested, hauling all the wood, besides tending two or three horses, a cow or two, and sawing wood for stoves, etc., while still attending school. For this I was compensated by the fact that there was never any scolding or punishing by my parents; no objection to rational enjoyments, such as fishing, going to the creek a mile away to swim in summer, taking a horse and visiting my grandparents in the adjoining county, fifteen miles off, skating on the ice in winter, or taking a horse and sleigh when there was snow on the ground.

While still quite young I had visited Cincinnati, forty-five miles away, several times, alone; also Maysville, Kentucky, often, and once Louisville. The journey to Louisville was a big one for a boy of that day. I had also gone once with a two-horse carriage to Chillicothe, about seventy miles, with a neighbor's family, who were removing to Toledo, Ohio, and returned alone; and had gone once, in like manner, to Flat Rock, Kentucky, about seventy miles away. On this latter occasion I was fifteen years of age. While at Flat Rock, at the house of a Mr. Payne, whom I was visiting with his brother, a neighbor of ours in Georgetown, I saw a very fine saddle horse, which I rather coveted, and proposed to Mr. Payne, the owner, to trade him for one of the two I was driving. Payne hesitated to trade with a boy, but asking his brother about it, the latter told him that it would be all right, that I was allowed to do as I pleased with the horses. I was seventy miles from home, with a carriage to take back, and Mr. Payne said he did not know that his horse had ever had a collar on. I asked to have him hitched to a farm wagon and we would soon see whether he would work. It was soon evident that the horse had never worn harness before; but he showed no viciousness, and I expressed a confidence that I could manage him. A trade was at once struck, I receiving ten dollars difference.

The next day Mr. Payne, of Georgetown, and I started on our return. We got along very well for a few miles, when we encountered a ferocious dog that frightened the horses and made them run. The new animal kicked at every jump he made. I got the horses stopped, however, before any damage was done, and without running into anything. After giving them a little rest, to quiet their fears, we started again. That instant the new horse kicked, and started to run once more. The road we were on, struck the turnpike within half a mile of the point where the second runaway commenced, and there there was an embankment twenty or more feet deep on the opposite side of the pike. I got the horses stopped on the very brink of the precipice. My new horse was terribly frightened and trembled like an aspen; but he was not half so badly frightened as my companion, Mr. Payne, who deserted me after this last experience, and took passage on a freight wagon for Maysville. Every time I attempted to start, my new horse would commence to kick. I was in quite a dilemma for a time. Once in Maysville I could borrow a horse from an uncle who lived there; but I was more than a day's travel from that point. Finally I took out my bandanna — the style of handkerchief in universal use then — and with this blindfolded my horse. In this way I reached Maysville safely the next day, no doubt much to the surprise of my friend. Here I borrowed a horse from my uncle, and the following day we proceeded on our journey.

About half my school-days in Georgetown were spent at the school of John D. White, a North Carolinian, and the father of Chilton White who represented the district in Congress for one term during the rebellion. Mr. White was always a Democrat in politics, and Chilton followed his father. He had two older brothers — all three being schoolmates of mine at their father's school — who did not go the same way. The second brother died before the rebellion began; he was a Whig, and afterwards a Republican. His oldest brother was a Republican and brave soldier during the rebellion. Chilton is reported as having told of an earlier horse-trade of mine. As he told the story, there was a Mr. Ralston living within a few miles of the village, who owned a colt which I very much wanted. My father had offered twenty dollars for it, but Ralston wanted twenty-five. I was so anxious to have the colt, that after the owner left, I begged to be allowed to take him at the price demanded. My father yielded, but said twenty dollars was all the horse was worth, and told me to offer that price; if it was not accepted I was to offer twenty-two and a half, and if that would not get him, to give the twenty-five. I at once mounted a horse and went for the colt. When I got to Mr. Ralston's house, I said to him: "Papa says I may offer you twenty dollars for the colt, but if you won't take that, I am to offer twenty-two and a half, and if you won't take that, to give you twenty-five." It would not require a Connecticut man to guess the price finally agreed upon. This story is nearly true. I certainly showed very plainly that I had come for the colt and meant to have him. I could not have been over eight years old at the time. This transaction caused me great heart-burning. The story got out among the boys of the village, and it was a long time before I heard the last of it. Boys enjoy the misery of their companions, at least village boys in that day did, and in later life I have found that all adults are not free from the peculiarity. I kept the horse until he was four years old, when he went blind, and I sold him for twenty dollars. When I went to Maysville to school, in 1836, at the age of fourteen, I recognized my colt as one of the blind horses working on the tread-wheel of the ferry-boat.

I have describes enough of my early life to give an impression of the whole. I did not like to work; but I did as much of it, while young, as grown men can be hired to do in these days, and attended school at the same time. I had as many privileges as any boy in the village, and probably more than most of them. I have no recollection of ever having been punished at home, either by scolding or by the rod. But at school the case was different. The rod was freely used there, and I was not exempt from its influence. I can see John D. White — the school teacher — now, with his long beech switch always in his hand. It was not always the same one, either. Switches were brought in bundles, from a beech wood near the school house, by the boys for whose benefit they were intended. Often a whole bundle would be used up in a single day. I never had any hard feelings against my teacher, either while attending the school, or in later years when reflecting upon my experience. Mr. White was a kindhearted man, and was much respected by the community in which he lived. He only followed the universal custom of the period, and that under which he had received his own education.

Chapter II

WEST POINT — GRADUATION

*I*n the winter of 1838-9 I was attending school at Ripley, only ten miles distant from Georgetown, but spent the Christmas holidays at home. During this vacation my father received a letter from the Honorable Thomas Morris, then United States Senator from Ohio. When he read it he said to me, "Ulysses, I believe you are going to receive the appointment." "What appointment?" I inquired. "To West Point; I have applied for it." "But I won't go," I said. He said he thought I would, *and I thought so too, if he did.* I really had no objection to going to West Point, except that I had a very exalted idea of the acquirements necessary to get through. I did not believe I possessed them, and could not bear the idea of failing. There had been four boys from our village, or its immediate neighborhood, who had been graduated from West Point, and never a failure of anyone appointed from Georgetown, except in the case of the one whose place I was to take. He was the son of Dr. Bailey, our nearest and most intimate neighbor. Young Bailey had been appointed in 1837. Finding before the January examination following, that he could not pass, he resigned and went to a private school, and remained there until the following year, when he was reappointed. Before the next examination he was dismissed. Dr. Bailey was a proud and sensitive man, and felt the failure of his son so keenly that he forbade his return home. There were no telegraphs in those days to disseminate news rapidly, no railroads west of the Alleghenies, and but few east; and above all, there were no reporters prying into other people's private affairs. Consequently it did not become generally known that there was a vacancy at West Point from our district until I was appointed. I presume Mrs. Bailey confided to my mother the fact that Bartlett had been dismissed, and that the doctor had forbidden his son's return home.

The Honorable Thomas L. Hamer, one of the ablest men Ohio ever produced, was our member of Congress at the time, and had the right of nomination. He and my father had been members of the same debating society (where they were generally pitted on opposite sides), and intimate personal friends from their early manhood up to a few years before. In politics they differed. Hamer was a life-long Democrat, while my father was a Whig. They had a warm discussion, which finally became angry — over some act of President Jackson, the removal of the deposit of public moneys, I think — after which they never spoke until after my appointment. I know both of them felt badly over this estrangement, and would have been glad at any time to come to a reconciliation; but neither would make the advance. Under these circumstances my father would not write to Hamer for the appointment, but he wrote to Thomas Morris, United States Senator from Ohio, informing him that there was a vacancy at West Point from our district, and that he would be glad if I could be appointed to fill it. This letter, I presume, was turned over to Mr. Hamer, and, as there was no other applicant, he cheerfully appointed me. This healed the breach between the two, never after reopened.

Besides the argument used by my father in favor of my going to West Point — that "he thought I would go" — there was another very strong inducement. I had always a great desire to travel. I was already the best traveled boy in Georgetown, except the sons of one man, John Walker, who had emigrated to Texas with his family, and immigrated back as soon as he could get the means to do so. In his short stay in Texas he acquired a very different opinion of the country from what one would form going there now.

I had been east to Wheeling, Virginia, and north to the Western Reserve, in Ohio, west to Louisville, and south to Bourbon County, Kentucky, besides having driven or ridden pretty much over the whole country within fifty miles of home. Going to West Point would give me the opportunity of visiting the two great cities of the continent, Philadelphia and New York. This was enough. When these places were visited I would have been glad to have had a steamboat or railroad collision, or any other accident happen, by which I might have received a temporary injury sufficient to make me ineligible, for a time, to enter the Academy. Nothing of the kind occurred, and I had to face the music.

Georgetown has a remarkable record for a western village. It is, and has been from its earliest existence, a democratic town. There was probably no time during the rebellion when, if the opportunity could have been afforded, it would not have voted for Jefferson Davis for President of the United States, over Mr. Lincoln, or any other representative of his party; unless it was immediately after some of John Morgan's men, in his celebrated raid through Ohio, spent a few hours in the village. The rebels helped themselves to whatever they could find, horses, boots and shoes, especially horses, and many ordered meals to be prepared for them by the families. This was no doubt a far pleasanter duty for some families than it would have been to render a like service for Union soldiers. The line between the Rebel and Union element in Georgetown was so marked that it led to divisions even in the churches. There were churches in that part of Ohio where treason was preached regularly, and where, to secure membership, hostility to the government, to the war and to the liberation of the slaves, was far more essential than a belief in the authenticity or credibility of the Bible. There were men in Georgetown who filled all the requirements for membership in these churches.

Yet this far-off western village, with a population, including old and young, male and female, of about one thousand — about enough for the organization of a single regiment if all had been men capable of bearing arms — furnished the Union army four general officers and one colonel, West Point graduates, and nine generals and field officers of Volunteers, that I can think of. Of the graduates from West Point, all had citizenship elsewhere at the breaking out of the rebellion, except possibly General A.V. Kautz, who had remained in the army from his graduation. Two of the colonels also entered the service from other localities. The other seven, General McGroierty, Colonels White, Fyffe, Loudon and Marshall, Majors King and Bailey, were all residents of Georgetown when the war broke out, and all of them, who were alive at the close, returned there. Major Bailey was the cadet who had preceded me at West Point. He was killed in West Virginia, in his first engagement. As far as I know, every boy who has entered West Point from that village since my time has been graduated.

I took passage on a steamer at Ripley, Ohio, for Pittsburg, about the middle of May, 1839. Western boats at that day did not make regular trips at stated times, but would stop anywhere, and for any length of time, for passengers or freight. I have myself been detained two or three days at a place after steam was up, the gang planks, all but one, drawn in, and after the time advertised for starting had expired. On this occasion we had no vexatious delays, and in about three days Pittsburg was reached. From Pittsburg I chose passage by the canal to Harrisburg, rather than by the more expeditious stage. This gave a better opportunity of enjoying the fine scenery of Western Pennsylvania, and I had rather a dread of reaching my destination at all. At that time the canal was much patronized by travelers, and, with the comfortable packets of the period, no mode of conveyance could be more pleasant, when time was not an object. From Harrisburg to Philadelphia there was a railroad, the first I had ever seen, except the one on which I had just crossed the summit of the Allegheny Mountains, and over which canal boats were transported. In traveling by the road from Harrisburg, I thought the perfection of rapid transit had been reached. We traveled at least eighteen miles an hour, when at full speed, and made the whole distance averaging probably as much as twelve miles an hour. This seemed like annihilating space. I stopped five days in Philadelphia, saw about every street in the city, attended the theater, visited Girard College (which was then in course of construction), and got reprimanded from home afterwards, for dallying by the way so long. My sojourn in New York was shorter, but long enough to enable me to see the city very well. I reported at West Point on the 30th or 31st of May, and about two weeks later passed my examination for admission, without difficulty, very much to my surprise.

A military life had no charms for me, and I had not the faintest idea of staying in the army even if I should be graduated, which I did not expect. The encampment which preceded the commencement of academic studies was very wearisome and uninteresting. When the 28th of August came — the date for breaking up camp and going into barracks — I felt as though I had been at West Point always, and that if I staid to graduation, I would have to remain always. I did not take hold of my studies with avidity, in fact I rarely ever read over a lesson the second time during my entire cadetship. I could not sit in my room doing nothing. There is a fine library connected with the Academy from which cadets can get books to read in their quarters. I devoted more time to these, than to books relating to the course of studies. Much of the time, I am sorry to say, was devoted to novels, but not those of a trashy sort. I read all of Bulwer's then published, Cooper's, Marryat's, Scott's, Washington Irving's works, Lever's, and many others that I do not now remember. Mathematics was very easy to me, so that when January came, I passed the examination, taking a good standing in that branch. In French, the only other study at that time in the first year's course, my standing was very low. In fact, if the class had been turned the other end foremost I should have been near head. I never succeeded in getting squarely at either end of my class, in any one study, during the four years. I came near it in French, artillery, infantry and cavalry tactics, and conduct.

Early in the session of the Congress which met in December, 1839, a bill was discussed abolishing the Military Academy. I saw in this an honorable way to obtain a discharge, and read the debates with much interest, but with impatience at the delay in taking action, for I was selfish enough to favor the bill. It never passed, and a year later, although the time hung drearily with me, I would have been sorry to have seen it succeed. My idea then was to get through the course, secure a detail for a few years as assistant professor of mathematics at the Academy, and afterwards obtain a permanent position as professor in some respectable college; but circumstances always did shape my course different from my plans.

At the end of two years the class received the usual furlough, extending from the close of the June examination to the 28th of August. This I enjoyed beyond any other period of my life. My father had sold out his business in Georgetown — where my youth had been spent, and to which my daydreams carried me back as my future home, if I should ever be able to retire on a competency. He had moved to Bethel, only twelve miles away, in the adjoining county of Clermont, and had bought a young horse that had never been in harness, for my special use under the saddle during my furlough. Most of my time was spent among my old school-mates — these ten weeks were shorter than one week at West Point.

Persons acquainted with the Academy know that the corps of cadets is divided into four companies for the purpose of military exercises. These companies are officered from the cadets, the superintendent and commandant selecting the officers for their military bearing and qualifications. The adjutant, quartermaster, four captains and twelve lieutenants are taken from the first, or Senior class; the sergeants from the second, or junior class; and the corporals from the third, or Sophomore class. I had not been "called out" as a corporal, but when I returned from furlough I found myself the last but one — about my standing in all the tactics — of eighteen sergeants. The promotion was too much for me. That year my standing in the class — as shown by the number of demerits of the year — was about the same as it was among the sergeants, and I was dropped, and served the fourth year as a private.

During my first year's encampment General Scott visited West Point, and reviewed the cadets. With his commanding figure, his quite colossal size and showy uniform, I thought him the finest specimen of manhood my eyes had ever beheld, and the most to be envied. I could never resemble him in appearance, but I believe I did have a presentiment for a moment that some day I should occupy his place on review — although I had no intention then of remaining in the army. My experience in a horse-trade ten years before, and the ridicule it caused me, were too fresh in my mind for me to communicate this presentiment to even my most intimate chum. The next summer Martin Van Buren, then President of the United States, visited West Point and reviewed the cadets; he did not impress me with the awe which Scott had inspired. In fact I regarded General Scott and Captain C.F. Smith, the Commandant of Cadets, as the two men most to be envied in the nation. I retained a high regard for both up to the day of their death.

The last two years wore away more rapidly than the first two, but they still seemed about five times as long as Ohio years, to me. At last all the examinations were passed, and the members of the class were called upon to record their choice of arms of service and regiments. I was anxious to enter the cavalry, or dragoons as they were then called, but there was only one regiment of dragoons in the Army at that time, and attached to that, besides the full complement of officers, there were at least four brevet second lieutenants. I recorded therefore my first choice, dragoons; second, 4th infantry; and got the latter. Again there was a furlough — or, more properly speaking, leave of absence for the class were now commissioned officers — this time to the end of September. Again I went to Ohio to spend my vacation among my old school-mates; and again I found a fine saddle horse purchased for my special use, besides a horse and buggy that I could drive — but I was not in a physical condition to enjoy myself quite as well as on the former occasion. For six months before graduation I had had a desperate cough ("Tyler's grip" it was called), and I was very much reduced, weighing but one hundred and seventeen pounds, just my weight at entrance, though I had grown six inches in stature in the meantime. There was consumption in my father's family, two of his brothers having died of that disease, which made my symptoms more alarming. The brother and sister next younger than myself died, during the rebellion, of the same disease, and I seemed the most promising subject for it of the three in 1843.

Having made alternate choice of two different arms of service with different uniforms, I could not get a uniform suit until notified of my assignment. I left my measurement with a tailor, with directions not to make the uniform until I notified him whether it was to be for infantry or dragoons. Notice did not reach me for several weeks, and then it took at least a week to get the letter of instructions to the tailor and two more to make the clothes and have them sent to me. This was a time of great suspense. I was impatient to get on my uniform and see how it looked, and probably wanted my old school-mates, particularly the girls, to see me in it.

The conceit was knocked out of me by two little circumstances that happened soon after the arrival of the clothes, which gave me a distaste for military uniform that I never recovered from. Soon after the arrival of the suit I donned it, and put off for Cincinnati on horseback. While I was riding along a street of that city, imagining that everyone was looking at me, with a feeling akin to mine when I first saw General Scott, a little urchin, bareheaded, footed, with dirty and ragged pants held up by bare a single gallows — that's what suspenders were called then — and a shirt that had not seen a wash-tub for weeks, turned to me and cried: "Soldier! will you work? No, sir — ee; I'll sell my shirt first!!" The horse trade and its dire consequences were recalled to mind.

The other circumstance occurred at home. Opposite our house in Bethel stood the old stage tavern where "man and beast" found accommodation, The stable-man was rather dissipated, but possessed of some humor. On my return I found him parading the streets, and attending in the stable, barefooted, but in a pair of sky-blue nankeen pantaloons — just the color of my uniform trousers — with a strip of white cotton sheeting sewed down the outside seams in imitation of mine. The joke was a huge one in the mind of many of the people, and was much enjoyed by them; but I did not appreciate it so highly.

During the remainder of my leave of absence, my time was spent in visiting friends in Georgetown and Cincinnati, and occasionally other towns in that part of the State.

Chapter III

ARMY LIFE — CAUSES OF THE MEXICAN WAR — CAMP SALUBRITY

On the 30th of September I reported for duty at Jefferson Barracks, St. Louis, with the 4th United States infantry. It was the largest military post in the country at that time, being garrisoned by sixteen companies of infantry, eight of the 3d regiment, the remainder of the 4th. Colonel Steven Kearney, one of the ablest officers of the day, commanded the post, and under him discipline was kept at a high standard, but without vexatious rules or regulations. Every drill and roll-call had to be attended, but in the intervals officers were permitted to enjoy themselves, leaving the garrison, and going where they pleased, without making written application to state where they were going for how long, etc., so that they were back for their next duty. It did seem to me, in my early army days, that too many of the older officers, when they came to command posts, made it a study to think what orders they could publish to annoy their subordinates and render them uncomfortable. I noticed, however, a few years later, when the Mexican war broke out, that most of this class of officers discovered they were possessed of disabilities which entirely incapacitated them for active field service. They had the moral courage to proclaim it, too. They were right; but they did not always give their disease the right name.

At West Point I had a class-mate — in the last year of our studies he was room-mate also — F.T. Dent, whose family resided some five miles west of Jefferson Barracks. Two of his unmarried brothers were living at home at that time, and as I had taken with me from Ohio, my horse, saddle and bridle, I soon found my way out to White Haven, the name of the Dent estate. As I found the family congenial my visits became frequent. There were at home, besides the young men, two daughters, one a school miss of fifteen, the other a girl of eight or nine. There was still an older daughter of seventeen, who had been spending several years at boarding-school in St. Louis, but who, though through school, had not yet returned home. She was spending the winter in the city with connections, the family of Colonel John O'Fallon, well known in St. Louis. In February she returned to her country home. After that I do not know but my visits became more frequent; they certainly did become more enjoyable. We would often take walks, or go on horseback to visit the neighbors, until I became quite well acquainted in that vicinity. Sometimes one of the brothers would accompany us, sometimes one of the younger sisters. If the 4th infantry had remained at Jefferson Barracks it is possible, even probable, that this life might have continued for some years without my finding out that there was anything serious the matter with me; but in the following May a circumstance occurred which developed my sentiment so palpably that there was no mistaking it.

The annexation of Texas was at this time the subject of violent discussion in Congress, in the press, and by individuals. The administration of President Tyler, then in power, was making the most strenuous efforts to effect the annexation, which was, indeed, the great and absorbing question of the day. During these discussions the greater part of the single rifle regiment in the army — the 2d dragoons, which had been dismounted a year or two before, and designated "Dismounted Rifles" — was stationed at Fort Jessup, Louisiana, some twenty-five miles east of the Texas line, to observe the frontier. About the 1st of May the 3d infantry was ordered from Jefferson Barracks to Louisiana, to go into camp in the neighborhood of Fort Jessup, and there await further orders. The troops were embarked on steamers and were on their way down the Mississippi within a few days after the receipt of this order. About the time they started I obtained a leave of absence for twenty days to go to Ohio to visit my parents. I was obliged to go to St. Louis to take a steamer for Louisville or Cincinnati, or the first steamer going up the Ohio River to any point. Before I left St. Louis orders were received at Jefferson Barracks for the 4th infantry to follow the 3d. A messenger was sent after me to stop my leaving; but before he could reach me I was off, totally ignorant of these events. A day or two after my arrival at Bethel I received a letter from a classmate and fellow lieutenant in the 4th, informing me of the circumstances related above, and advising me not to open any letter post marked St. Louis or Jefferson Barracks, until the expiration of my leave, and saying that he would pack up my things and take them along for me. His advice was not necessary, for no other letter was sent to me. I now discovered that I was exceedingly anxious to get back to Jefferson Barracks, and I understood the reason without explanation from anyone. My leave of absence required me to report for duty, at Jefferson Barracks, at the end of twenty days. I knew my regiment had gone up the Red River, but I was not disposed to break the letter of my leave; besides, if I had proceeded to Louisiana direct, I could not have reached there until after the expiration of my leave. Accordingly, at the end of the twenty days, I reported for duty to Lieutenant Ewell, commanding at Jefferson Barracks, handing him at the same time my leave of absence. After noticing the phraseology of the order — leaves of absence were generally worded, "at the end of which time he will report for duty with his proper command" — he said he would give me an order to join my regiment in Louisiana. I then asked for a few days' leave before starting, which he readily granted. This was the same Ewell who acquired considerable reputation as a Confederate general during the rebellion. He was a man much esteemed, and deservedly so, in the old army, and proved himself a gallant and efficient officer in two wars — both in my estimation unholy.

I immediately procured a horse and started for the country, taking no baggage with me, of course. There is an insignificant creek — the Gravois — between Jefferson Barracks and the place to which I was going, and at that day there was not a bridge over it from its source to its mouth. There is not water enough in the creek at ordinary stages to run a coffee mill, and at low water there is none running whatever. On this occasion it had been raining heavily, and, when the creek was reached, I found the banks full to overflowing, and the current rapid. I looked at it a moment to consider what to do. One of my superstitions had always been when I started to go anywhere, or to do anything, not to turn back, or stop until the thing intended was accomplished. I have frequently started to go to places where I had never been and to which I did not know the way, depending upon making inquiries on the road, and if I got past the place without knowing it, instead of turning back, I would go on until a road was found turning in the right direction, take that, and come in by the other side. So I struck into the stream, and in an instant the horse was swimming and I being carried down by the current. I headed the horse towards the other bank and soon reached it, wet through and without other clothes on that side of the stream. I went on, however, to my destination and borrowed a dry suit from my — future — brother-in-law. We were not of the same size, but the clothes answered every purpose until I got more of my own.

Before I returned I mustered up courage to make known, in the most awkward manner imaginable, the discovery I had made on learning that the 4th infantry had been ordered away from Jefferson Barracks. The young lady afterwards admitted that she too, although until then she had never looked upon me other than as a visitor whose company was agreeable to her, had experienced a depression of spirits she could not account for when the regiment left. Before separating it was definitely understood that at a convenient time we would join our fortunes, and not let the removal of a regiment trouble us. This was in May, 1844. It was the 22d of August, 1848, before the fulfillment of this agreement. My duties kept me on the frontier of Louisiana with the Army of Observation during the pendency of Annexation; and afterwards I was absent through the war with Mexico, provoked by the action of the army, if not by the annexation itself During that time there was a constant correspondence between Miss Dent and myself, but we only met once in the period of four years and three months. In May, 1845, I procured a leave for twenty days, visited St. Louis, and obtained the consent of the parents for the union, which had not been asked for before.

As already stated, it was never my intention to remain in the army long, but to prepare myself for a professorship in some college. Accordingly, soon after I was settled at Jefferson Barracks, I wrote a letter to Professor Church — Professor of Mathematics at West Point — requesting him to ask my designation as his assistant, when next a detail had to be made. Assistant professors at West Point are all officers of the army, supposed to be selected for their special fitness for the particular branch of study they are assigned to teach. The answer from Professor Church was entirely satisfactory, and no doubt I should have been detailed a year or two later but for the Mexican War coming on. Accordingly I laid out for myself a course of studies to be pursued in garrison, with regularity, if not persistency. I reviewed my West Point course of mathematics during the seven months at Jefferson Barracks, and read many valuable historical works, besides an occasional novel. To help my memory I kept a book in which I would write up, from time to time, my recollections of all I had read since last posting it. When the regiment was ordered away, I being absent at the time, my effects were packed up by Lieutenant Haslett, of the 4th infantry, and taken along. I never saw my journal after, nor did I ever keep another, except for a portion of the time while traveling abroad. Often since a fear has crossed my mind lest that book might turn up yet, and fall into the hands of some malicious person who would publish it. I know its appearance would cause me as much heart-burning as my youthful horse-trade, or the later rebuke for wearing uniform clothes.

The 3d infantry had selected camping grounds on the reservation at Fort Jessup, about midway between the Red River and the Sabine. Our orders required us to go into camp in the same neighborhood, and await further instructions. Those authorized to do so selected a place in the pine woods, between the old town of Natchitoches and Grand Ecore, about three miles from each, and on high ground back from the river. The place was given the name of Camp Salubrity, and proved entitled to it. The camp was on a high, sandy, pine ridge, with spring branches in the valley, in front and rear. The springs furnished an abundance of cool, pure water, and the ridge was above the flight of mosquitoes, which abound in that region in great multitudes and of great voracity. In the valley they swarmed in myriads, but never came to the summit of the ridge. The regiment occupied this camp six months before the first death occurred, and that was caused by an accident.

There was no intimation given that the removal of the 3d and 4th regiments of infantry to the western border of Louisiana was occasioned in any way by the prospective annexation of Texas, but it was generally understood that such was the case. Ostensibly we were intended to prevent filibustering into Texas, but really as a menace to Mexico in case she appeared to contemplate war. Generally the officers of the army were indifferent whether the annexation was consummated or not; but not so all of them. For myself, I was bitterly opposed to the measure, and to this day regard the war, which resulted, as one of the most unjust ever waged by a stronger against a weaker nation. It was an instance of a republic following the bad example of European monarchies, in not considering justice in their desire to acquire additional territory. Texas was originally a state belonging to the republic of Mexico. It extended from the Sabine River on the east to the Rio Grande on the west, and from the Gulf of Mexico on the south and east to the territory of the United States and New Mexico — another Mexican state at that time — on the north and west. An empire in territory, it had but a very sparse population, until settled by Americans who had received authority from Mexico to colonize. These colonists paid very little attention to the supreme government, and introduced slavery into the state almost from the start, though the constitution of Mexico did not, nor does it now, sanction that institution. Soon they set up an independent government of their own, and war existed, between Texas and Mexico, in name from that time until 1836, when active hostilities very nearly ceased upon the capture of Santa Anna, the Mexican President. Before long, however, the same people — who with permission of Mexico had colonized Texas, and afterwards set up slavery there, and then seceded as soon as they felt strong enough to do so — offered themselves and the State to the United States, and in 1845 their offer was accepted. The occupation, separation and annexation were, from the inception of the movement to its final consummation, a conspiracy to acquire territory out of which slave states might be formed for the American Union.

Even if the annexation itself could be justified, the manner in which the subsequent war was forced upon Mexico cannot. The fact is, annexationists wanted more territory than they could possibly lay any claim to, as part of the new acquisition. Texas, as an independent State, never had exercised jurisdiction over the territory between the Nueces River and the Rio Grande. Mexico had never recognized the independence of Texas, and maintained that, even if independent, the State had no claim south of the Nueces. I am aware that a treaty, made by the Texans with Santa Anna while he was under duress, ceded all the territory between the Nueces and the Rio Grande —, but he was a prisoner of war when the treaty was made, and his life was in jeopardy. He knew, too, that he deserved execution at the hands of the Texans, if they should ever capture him. The Texans, if they had taken his life, would have only followed the example set by Santa Anna himself a few years before, when he executed the entire garrison of the Alamo and the villagers of Goliad.

In taking military possession of Texas after annexation, the army of occupation, under General Taylor, was directed to occupy the disputed territory. The army did not stop at the Nueces and offer to negotiate for a settlement of the boundary question, but went beyond, apparently in order to force Mexico to initiate war. It is to the credit of the American nation, however, that after conquering Mexico, and while practically holding the country in our possession, so that we could have retained the whole of it, or made any terms we chose, we paid a round sum for the additional territory taken; more than it was worth, or was likely to be, to Mexico. To us it was an empire and of incalculable value; but it might have been obtained by other means. The Southern rebellion was largely the outgrowth of the Mexican war. Nations, like individuals, are punished for their transgressions. We got our punishment in the most sanguinary and expensive war of modern times.

The 4th infantry went into camp at Salubrity in the month of May, 1844, with instructions, as I have said, to await further orders. At first, officers and men occupied ordinary tents. As the summer heat increased these were covered by sheds to break the rays of the sun. The summer was whiled away in social enjoyments among the officers, in visiting those stationed at, and near, Fort Jessup, twenty-five miles away, visiting the planters on the Red River, and the citizens of Natchitoches and Grand Ecore. There was much pleasant intercourse between the inhabitants and the officers of the army. I retain very agreeable recollections of my stay at Camp Salubrity, and of the acquaintances made there, and no doubt my feeling is shared by the few officers living who were there at the time. I can call to mind only two officers of the 4th infantry, besides myself, who were at Camp Salubrity with the regiment, who are now alive.

With a war in prospect, and belonging to a regiment that had an unusual number of officers detailed on special duty away from the regiment, my hopes of being ordered to West Point as instructor vanished. At the time of which I now write, officers in the quartermaster's, commissary's and adjutant — general's departments were appointed from the line of the army, and did not vacate their regimental commissions until their regimental and staff commissions were for the same grades. Generally lieutenants were appointed to captaincies to fill vacancies in the staff corps. If they should reach a captaincy in the line before they arrived at a majority in the staff, they would elect which commission they would retain. In the 4th infantry, in 1844, at least six line officers were on duty in the staff, and therefore permanently detached from the regiment. Under these circumstances I gave up everything like a special course of reading, and only read thereafter for my own amusement, and not very much for that, until the war was over. I kept a horse and rode, and staid out of doors most of the time by day, and entirely recovered from the cough which I had carried from West Point, and from all indications of consumption. I have often thought that my life was saved, and my health restored, by exercise and exposure, enforced by an administrative act, and a war, both of which I disapproved.

As summer wore away, and cool days and colder nights came upon us, the tents We were occupying ceased to afford comfortable quarters; and "further orders" not reaching us, we began to look about to remedy the hardship. Men were put to work getting out timber to build huts, and in a very short time all were comfortably housed — privates as well as officers. The outlay by the government in accomplishing this was nothing, or nearly nothing. The winter was spent more agreeably than the summer had been. There were occasional parties given by the planters along the "coast" — as the bottom lands on the Red River were called. The climate was delightful.

Near the close of the short session of Congress of 1844-5, the bill for the annexation of Texas to the United States was passed. It reached President Tyler on the 1st of March, 1845, and promptly received his approval. When the news reached us we began to look again for "further orders." They did not arrive promptly, and on the 1st of May following I asked and obtained a leave of absence for twenty days, for the purpose of visiting — St. Louis. The object of this visit has been before stated.

Early in July the long expected orders were received, but they only took the regiment to New Orleans Barracks. We reached there before the middle of the month, and again waited weeks for still further orders. The yellow fever was raging in New Orleans during the time we remained there, and the streets of the city had the appearance of a continuous well-observed Sunday. I recollect but one occasion when this observance seemed to be broken by the inhabitants. One morning about daylight I happened to be awake, and, hearing the discharge of a rifle not far off, I looked out to ascertain where the sound came from. I observed a couple of clusters of men near by, and learned afterwards that "it was nothing; only a couple of gentlemen deciding a difference of opinion with rifles, at twenty paces." I do not remember if either was killed, or even hurt, but no doubt the question of difference was settled satisfactorily, and "honorably," in the estimation of the parties engaged. I do not believe I ever would have the courage to fight a duel. If any man should wrong me to the extent of my being willing to kill him, I would not be willing to give him the choice of weapons with which it should be done, and of the time, place and distance separating us, when I executed him. If I should do another such a wrong as to justify him in killing me, I would make any reasonable atonement within my power, if convinced of the wrong done. I place my opposition to dueling on higher grounds than here stated. No doubt a majority of the duels fought have been for want of moral courage on the part of those engaged to decline.

At Camp Salubrity, and when we went to New Orleans Barracks, the 4th infantry was commanded by Colonel Vose, then an old gentleman who had not commanded on drill for a number of years. He was not a man to discover infirmity in the presence of danger. It now appeared that war was imminent, and he felt that it was his duty to brush up his tactics. Accordingly, when we got settled down at our new post, he took command of the regiment at a battalion drill. Only two or three evolutions had been gone through when he dismissed the battalion, and, turning to go to his own quarters, dropped dead. He had not been complaining of ill health, but no doubt died of heart disease. He was a most estimable man, of exemplary habits, and by no means the author of his own disease.

Chapter IV

CORPUS CHRISTI — MEXICAN SMUGGLING — SPANISH RULE IN MEXICO — SUPPLYING TRANSPORTATION

*E*arly in September the regiment left New Orleans for Corpus Christi, now in Texas. Ocean steamers were not then common, and the passage was made in sailing vessels. At that time there was not more than three feet of water in the channel at the outlet of Corpus Christi Bay; the debarkation, therefore, had to take place by small steamers, and at an island in the channel called Shell Island, the ships anchoring some miles out from shore. This made the work slow, and as the army was only supplied with one or two steamers, it took a number of days to effect the landing of a single regiment with its stores, camp and garrison equipage, etc. There happened to be pleasant weather while this was going on, but the land-swell was so great that when the ship and steamer were on opposite sides of the same wave they would be at considerable distance apart. The men and baggage were let down to a point higher than the lower deck of the steamer, and when ship and steamer got into the trough between the waves, and were close together, the load would be drawn over the steamer and rapidly run down until it rested on the deck.

After I had gone ashore, and had been on guard several days at Shell Island, quite six miles from the ship, I had occasion for some reason or other to return on board. While on the Suviah — I think that was the name of our vessel — I heard a tremendous racket at the other end of the ship, and much and excited sailor language, such as "damn your eyes," etc. In a moment or two the captain, who was an excitable little man, dying with consumption, and not weighing much over a hundred pounds, came running out, carrying a saber nearly as large and as heavy as he was, and crying, that his men had mutinied. It was necessary to sustain the captain without question, and in a few minutes all the sailors charged with mutiny were in irons. I rather felt for a time a wish that I had not gone aboard just then. As the men charged with mutiny submitted to being placed in irons without resistance, I always doubted if they knew that they had mutinied until they were told.

By the time I was ready to leave the ship again I thought I had learned enough of the working of the double and single pulley, by which passengers were let down from the upper deck of the ship to the steamer below, and determined to let myself down without assistance. Without saying anything of my intentions to anyone, I mounted the railing, and taking hold of the center rope, just below the upper block, I put one foot on the hook below the lower block, and stepped off just as I did so someone called out "hold on." It was too late. I tried to "hold on" with all my might, but my heels went up, and my head went down so rapidly that my hold broke, and I plunged head foremost into the water, some twenty-five feet below, with such velocity that it seemed to me I never would stop. When I came to the surface again, being a fair swimmer, and not having lost my presence of mind, I swam around until a bucket was let down for me, and I was drawn up without a scratch or injury. I do not believe there was a man on board who sympathized with me in the least when they found me uninjured. I rather enjoyed the joke myself The captain of the Suviah died of his disease a few months later, and I believe before the mutineers were tried. I hope they got clear, because, as before stated, I always thought the mutiny was all in the brain of a very weak and sick man.

After reaching shore, or Shell Island, the labor of getting to Corpus Christi was slow and tedious. There was, if my memory serves me, but one small steamer to transport troops and baggage when the 4th infantry arrived. Others were procured later. The distance from Shell Island to Corpus Christi was some sixteen or eighteen miles. The channel to the bay was so shallow that the steamer, small as it was, had to be dragged over the bottom when loaded. Not more than one trip a day could be effected. Later this was remedied, by deepening the channel and increasing the number of vessels suitable to its navigation.

Corpus Christi is near the head of the bay of the same name, formed by the entrance of the Nueces River into tide-water, and is on the west bank of that bay. At the time of its first occupancy by United States troops there was a small Mexican hamlet there, containing probably less than one hundred souls. There was, in addition, a small American trading post, at which goods were sold to Mexican smugglers. All goods were put up in compact packages of about one hundred pounds each, suitable for loading on pack mules. Two of these packages made a load for an ordinary Mexican mule, and three for the larger ones. The bulk of the trade was in leaf tobacco, and domestic cotton-cloths and calicoes.

The Mexicans had, before the arrival of the army, but little to offer in exchange except silver. The trade in tobacco was enormous, considering the population to be supplied. Almost every Mexican above the age of ten years, and many much younger, smoked the cigarette. Nearly every Mexican carried a pouch of leaf tobacco, powdered by rolling in the hands, and a roll of corn husks to make wrappers. The cigarettes were made by the smokers as they used them.

Up to the time of which I write, and for years afterwards — I think until the administration of President Juarez — the cultivation, manufacture and sale of tobacco constituted a government monopoly, and paid the bulk of the revenue collected from internal sources. The price was enormously high, and made successful smuggling very profitable. The difficulty of obtaining tobacco is probably the reason why everybody, male and female, used it at that time. I know from my own experience that when I was at West Point, the fact that tobacco, in every form, was prohibited, and the mere possession of the weed severely punished, made the majority of the cadets, myself included, try to acquire the habit of using it. I failed utterly at the time and for many years afterward; but the majority accomplished the object of their youthful ambition.

Under Spanish rule Mexico was prohibited from producing anything that the mother-country could supply. This rule excluded the cultivation of the grape, olive and many other articles to which the soil and climate were well adapted. The country was governed for "revenue only;" and tobacco, which cannot be raised in Spain, but is indigenous to Mexico, offered a fine instrumentality for securing this prime object of government. The native population had been in the habit of using "the weed" from a period, back of any recorded history of this continent. Bad habits — if not restrained by law or public opinion — spread more rapidly and universally than good ones, and the Spanish colonists adopted the use of tobacco almost as generally as the natives. Spain, therefore, in order to secure the largest revenue from this source, prohibited the cultivation, except in specified localities — and in these places farmed out the privilege at a very high price. The tobacco when raised could only be sold to the government, and the price to the consumer was limited only by the avarice of the authorities, and the capacity of the people to pay.

All laws for the government of the country were enacted in Spain, and the officers for their execution were appointed by the Crown, and sent out to the New El Dorado. The Mexicans had been brought up ignorant of how to legislate or how to rule. When they gained their independence, after many years of war, it was the most natural thing in the world that they should adopt as their own the laws then in existence. The only change was, that Mexico became her own executor of the laws and the recipient of the revenues. The tobacco tax, yielding so large a revenue under the law as it stood, was one of the last, if not the very last, of the obnoxious imposts to be repealed. Now, the citizens are allowed to cultivate any crops the soil will yield. Tobacco is cheap, and every quality can be produced. Its use is by no means so general as when I first visited the country.

Gradually the "Army of Occupation" assembled at Corpus Christi. When it was all together it consisted of seven companies of the 2d regiment of dragoons, four companies of light artillery, five regiments of infantry — the 3d, 4th, 5th, 7th and 8th — and one regiment of artillery acting as infantry — not more than three thousand men in all. General Zachary Taylor commanded the whole. There were troops enough in one body to establish a drill and discipline sufficient to fit men and officers for all they were capable of in case of battle. The rank and file were composed of men who had enlisted in time of peace, to serve for seven dollars a month, and were necessarily inferior as material to the average volunteers enlisted later in the war expressly to fight, and also to the volunteers in the war for the preservation of the Union. The men engaged in the Mexican war were brave, and the officers of the regular army, from highest to lowest, were educated in their profession. A more efficient army for its number and armament, I do not believe ever fought a battle than the one commanded by General Taylor in his first two engagements on Mexican — or Texan soil.

The presence of United States troops on the edge of the disputed territory furthest from the Mexican settlements, was not sufficient to provoke hostilities. We were sent to provoke a fight, but it was essential that Mexico should commence it. It was very doubtful whether Congress would declare war; but if Mexico should attack our troops, the Executive could announce, "Whereas, war exists by the acts of, etc.," and prosecute the contest with vigor. Once initiated there were but few public men who would have the courage to oppose it. Experience proves that the man who obstructs a war in which his nation is engaged, no matter whether right or wrong, occupies no enviable place in life or history. Better for him, individually, to advocate "war, pestilence, and famine," than to act as obstructionist to a war already begun. The history of the defeated rebel will be honorable hereafter, compared with that of the Northern man who aided him by conspiring against his government while protected by it. The most favorable posthumous history the stay-at-home traitor can hope for is — oblivion.

Mexico showing no willingness to come to the Nueces to drive the invaders from her soil, it became necessary for the "invaders" to approach to within a convenient distance to be struck. Accordingly, preparations were begun for moving the army to the Rio Grande, to a point near Matamoras. It was desirable to occupy a position near the largest center of population possible to reach, without absolutely invading territory to which we set up no claim whatever.

The distance from Corpus Christi to Matamoras is about one hundred and fifty miles. The country does not abound in fresh water, and the length of the marches had to be regulated by the distance between water supplies. Besides the streams, there were occasional pools, filled during the rainy season, some probably made by the traders, who traveled constantly between Corpus Christi and the Rio Grande, and some by the buffalo. There was not at that time a single habitation, cultivated field, or herd of domestic animals, between Corpus Christi and Matamoras. It was necessary, therefore, to have a wagon train sufficiently large to transport the camp and garrison equipage, officers' baggage, rations for the army, and part rations of grain for the artillery horses and all the animals taken from the north, where they had been accustomed to having their forage furnished them. The army was but indifferently supplied with transportation. Wagons and harness could easily be supplied from the north but mules and horses could not so readily be brought. The American traders and Mexican smugglers came to the relief. Contracts were made for mules at from eight to eleven dollars each. The smugglers furnished the animals, and took their pay in goods of the description before mentioned. I doubt whether the Mexicans received in value from the traders five dollars per head for the animals they furnished, and still more, whether they paid anything but their own time in procuring them. Such is trade; such is war. The government paid in hard cash to the contractor the stipulated price.

Between the Rio Grande and the Nueces there was at that time a large band of wild horses feeding; as numerous, probably, as the band of buffalo roaming further north was before its rapid extermination commenced. The Mexicans used to capture these in large numbers and bring them into the American settlements and sell them. A picked animal could be purchased at from eight to twelve dollars, but taken at wholesale, they could be bought for thirty-six dollars a dozen. Some of these were purchased for the army, and answered a most useful purpose. The horses were generally very strong, formed much like the Norman horse, and with very heavy manes and tails. A number of officers supplied themselves with these, and they generally rendered as useful service as the northern animal in fact they were much better when grazing was the only means of supplying forage.

There was no need for haste, and some months were consumed in the necessary preparations for a move. In the meantime the army was engaged in all the duties pertaining to the officer and the soldier. Twice, that I remember, small trains were sent from Corpus Christi, with cavalry escorts, to San Antonio and Austin, with paymasters and funds to pay off small detachments of troops stationed at those places. General Taylor encouraged officers to accompany these expeditions. I accompanied one of them in December, 1845. The distance from Corpus Christi to San Antonio was then computed at one hundred and fifty miles. Now that roads exist it is probably less. From San Antonio to Austin we computed the distance at one hundred and ten miles, and from the latter place back to Corpus Christi at over two hundred miles. I know the distance now from San Antonio to Austin is but little over eighty miles, so that our computation was probably too high.

There was not at the time an individual living between Corpus Christi and San Antonio until within about thirty miles of the latter point, where there were a few scattering Mexican settlements along the San Antonio River. The people in at least one of these hamlets lived underground for protection against the Indians. The country abounded in game, such as deer and antelope, with abundance of wild turkeys along the streams and where there were nut-bearing woods. On the Nueces, about twenty-five miles up from Corpus Christi, were a few log cabins, the remains of a town called San Patricio, but the inhabitants had all been massacred by the Indians, or driven away.

San Antonio was about equally divided in population between Americans and Mexicans. From there to Austin there was not a single residence except at New Braunfels, on the Guadalupe River. At that point was a settlement of Germans who had only that year come into the State. At all events they were living in small huts, about such as soldiers would hastily construct for temporary occupation. From Austin to Corpus Christi there was only a small settlement at Bastrop, with a few farms along the Colorado River; but after leaving that, there were no settlements except the home of one man, with one female slave, at the old town of Goliad. Some of the houses were still standing. Goliad had been quite a village for the period and region, but some years before there had been a Mexican massacre, in which every inhabitant had been killed or driven away. This, with the massacre of the prisoners in the Alamo, San Antonio, about the same time, more than three hundred men in all, furnished the strongest justification the Texans had for carrying on the war with so much cruelty. In fact, from that time until the Mexican. war, the hostilities between Texans and Mexicans was so great that neither was safe in the neighborhood of the other who might be in superior numbers or possessed of superior arms. The man we found living there seemed like an old friend; he had come from near Fort

Jessup, Louisiana, where the officers of the 3d and 4th infantry and the 2d dragoons had known him and his family. He had emigrated in advance of his family to build up a home for them.

Chapter V

TRIP TO AUSTIN — PROMOTION TO FULL SECOND LIEUTENANT — ARMY OF OCCUPATION

*W*hen our party left Corpus Christi it was quite large, including the cavalry escort, Paymaster, Major Dix, his clerk and the officers who, like myself, were simply on leave; but all the officers on leave, except Lieutenant Benjamin — afterwards killed in the valley of Mexico — Lieutenant, now General, Augur, and myself, concluded to spend their allotted time at San Antonio and return from there. We were all to be back at Corpus Christi by the end of the month. The paymaster was detained in Austin so long that, if we had waited for him, we would have exceeded our leave. We concluded, therefore, to start back at once with the animals we had, and having to rely principally on grass for their food, it was a good six days' journey. We had to sleep on the prairie every night, except at Goliad, and possibly one night on the Colorado, without shelter and with only such food as we carried with us, and prepared ourselves. The journey was hazardous on account of Indians, and there were white men in Texas whom I would not have cared to meet in a secluded place. Lieutenant Augur was taken seriously sick before we reached Goliad and at a distance from any habitation. To add to the complication, his horse — a mustang that had probably been captured from the band of wild horses before alluded to, and of un-doubted longevity at his capture — gave out. It was absolutely necessary to get forward to Goliad to find a shelter for our sick companion. By dint of patience and exceedingly slow movements, Goliad was at last reached, and a shelter and bed secured for our patient. We remained over a day, hoping that Augur might recover sufficiently to resume his travels. He did not, however, and knowing that Major Dix would be along in a few days, with his wagon-train, now empty, and escort, we arranged with our Louisiana friend to take the best of care of the sick lieutenant until thus relieved, and went on.

I had never been a sportsman in my life; had scarcely ever gone in search of game, and rarely seen any when looking for it. On this trip there was no minute of time while traveling between San Patricio and the settlements on the San Antonio River, from San Antonio to Austin, and again from the Colorado River back to San Patricio, when deer or antelope could not be seen in great numbers. Each officer carried a shot-gun, and every evening, after going into camp, some would go out and soon return with venison and wild turkeys enough for the entire camp. I, however, never went out, and had no occasion to fire my gun; except, being detained over a day at Goliad, Benjamin and I concluded to go down to the creek — which was fringed with timber, much of it the pecan — and bring back a few turkeys. We had scarcely reached the edge of the timber when I heard the flutter of wings overhead, and in an instant I saw two or three turkeys flying away. These were soon followed by more, then more, and more, until a flock of twenty or thirty had left from just over my head. All this time I stood watching the turkeys to see where they flew — with my gun on my shoulder, and never once thought of leveling it at the birds. When I had time to reflect upon the matter, I came to the conclusion that as a sportsman I was a failure, and went back to the house. Benjamin remained out, and got as many turkeys as he wanted to carry back.

After the second night at Goliad, Benjamin and I started to make the remainder of the journey alone. We reached Corpus Christi just in time to avoid "absence without leave." We met no one not even an Indian — during the remainder of our journey, except at San Patricio. A new settlement had been started there in our absence of three weeks, induced possibly by the fact that there were houses already built, while the proximity of troops gave protection against the Indians. On the evening of the first day out from Goliad we heard the most unearthly howling of wolves, directly in our front. The prairie grass was tall and we could not see the beasts, but the sound indicated that they were near. To my ear it appeared that there must have been enough of them to devour our party, horses and all, at a single meal. The part of Ohio that I hailed from was not thickly settled, but wolves had been driven out long before I left. Benjamin was from Indiana, still less populated, where the wolf yet roamed over the prairies. He understood the nature of the animal and the capacity of a few to make believe there was an unlimited number of them. He kept on towards the noise, unmoved. I followed in his trail, lacking moral courage to turn back and join our sick companion. I have no doubt that if Benjamin had proposed returning to Goliad, I would not only have "seconded the motion" but have suggested that it was very hard-hearted in us to leave Augur sick there in the first place; but Benjamin did not propose turning back. When he did speak it was to ask: "Grant, how many wolves do you think there are in that pack?" Knowing where he was from, and suspecting that he thought I would overestimate the number, I determined to show my acquaintance with the animal by putting the estimate below what possibly could be correct, and answered: "Oh, about twenty," very indifferently. He smiled and rode on. In a minute we were close upon them, and before they saw us. There were just *two* of them. Seated upon their haunches, with their mouths close together, they had made all the noise we had been hearing for the past ten minutes. I have often thought of this incident since when I have heard the noise of a few disappointed politicians who had deserted their associates. There are always more of them before they are counted.

A week or two before leaving Corpus Christi on this trip, I had been promoted from brevet second-lieutenant, 4th infantry, to full second-lieutenant, 7th infantry. Frank Gardner,* of the 7th, was promoted to the 4th in the same orders. We immediately made application to be transferred, so as to get back to our old regiments. On my return, I found that our application had been approved at Washington. While in the 7th infantry I was in the company of Captain Holmes, afterwards a Lieutenant-general in the Confederate army. I never came in contact with him in the war of the Rebellion, nor did he render any very conspicuous service in his high rank. My transfer carried me to the company of Captain McCall, who resigned from the army after the Mexican war and settled in Philadelphia. He was prompt, however, to volunteer when the rebellion broke out, and soon rose to the rank of major-general in the Union army. I was not fortunate enough to meet him after he resigned. In the old army he was esteemed very highly as a soldier and gentleman. Our relations were always most pleasant.

The preparations at Corpus Christi for an advance progressed as rapidly in the absence of some twenty or more lieutenants as if we had been there. The principal business consisted in securing mules, and getting them broken to harness. The process was slow but amusing. The animals sold to the government were all young and unbroken, even to the saddle, and were quite as wild as the wild horses of the prairie. Usually a number would be brought in by a company of Mexicans,

---

* Afterwards General Gardner, C.S.A.

partners in the delivery. The mules were first driven into a stockade, called a corral, enclosing an acre or more of ground. The Mexicans, — who were all experienced in throwing the lasso, — would go into the corral on horseback, with their lassos attached to the pommels of their saddles. Soldiers detailed as teamsters and black smiths would also enter the corral, the former with ropes to serve as halters, the latter with branding irons and a fire to keep the irons heated. A lasso was then thrown over the neck of a mule, when he would immediately go to the length of his tether, first one end, then the other in the air. While he was thus plunging and gyrating, another lasso would be thrown by another Mexican, catching the animal by a fore-foot. This would bring the mule to the ground, when he was seized and held by the teamsters while the blacksmith put upon him, with hot irons, the initials "U.S." Ropes were then put about the neck, with a slipnoose which would tighten around the throat if pulled. With a man on each side holding these ropes, the mule was released from his other bindings and allowed to rise. With more or less difficulty he would be conducted to a picket rope outside and fastened there. The delivery of that mule was then complete. This process was gone through with every mule and wild horse with the army of occupation.

The method of breaking them was less cruel and much more amusing. It is a well-known fact that where domestic animals are used for specific purposes from generation to generation, the descendants are easily, as a rule, subdued to the same uses. At that time in Northern Mexico the mule, or his ancestors, the horse and the ass, was seldom used except for the saddle or pack. At all events the Corpus Christi mule resisted the new use to which he was being put. The treatment he was subjected to in order to overcome his prejudices was summary and effective.

The soldiers were principally foreigners who had enlisted in our large cities, and, with the exception of a chance drayman among them, it is not probable that any of the men who reported themselves as competent teamsters had ever driven a mule-team in their lives, or indeed that many had had any previous experience in driving any animal whatever to harness. Numbers together can accomplish what twice their number acting individually could not perform. Five mules were allotted to each wagon. A teamster would select at the picket rope five animals of nearly the same color and general appearance for his team. With a full corps of assistants, other teamsters, he would then proceed to get his mules together. In two's the men would approach each animal selected, avoiding as far as possible its heels. Two ropes would be put about the neck of each animal, with a slip noose, so that he could be choked if too unruly. They were then led out, harnessed by force and hitched to the wagon in the position they had to keep ever after. Two men remained on either side of the leader, with the lassos about its neck, and one man retained the same restraining influence over each of the others. All being ready, the hold would be slackened and the team started. The first motion was generally five mules in the air at one time, backs bowed, hind feet extended to the rear. After repeating this movement a few times the leaders would start to run. This would bring the breeching tight against the mules at the wheels, which these last seemed to regard as a most unwarrantable attempt at coercion and would resist by taking a seat, sometimes going so far as to lie down. In time all were broken in to do their duty submissively if not cheerfully, but there never was a time during the war when it was safe to let a Mexican mule get entirely loose. Their drivers were all teamsters by the time they got through.

I recollect one case of a mule that had worked in a team under the saddle, not only for some time at Corpus Christi, where he was broken, but all the way to the point opposite Matamoras, then to Camargo, where he got loose from his fastenings during the night. He did not run away at first, but staid in the neighborhood for a day or two, coming up sometimes to the feed trough even; but on the approach of the teamster he always got out of the way. At last, growing tired of the constant effort to catch him, he disappeared altogether. Nothing short of a Mexican with his lasso could have caught him. Regulations would not have warranted the expenditure of a dollar in hiring a man with a lasso to catch that mule; but they did allow the expenditure "of the mule," on a certificate that he had run away without any fault of the quartermaster on whose returns he was borne, and also the purchase of another to take his place. I am a competent witness, for I was regimental quartermaster at the time.

While at Corpus Christi all the officers who had a fancy for riding kept horses. The animals cost but little in the first instance, and when picketed they would get their living without any cost. I had three not long before the army moved, but a sad accident bereft me of them all at one time. A colored boy who gave them all the attention they got — besides looking after my tent and that of a class-mate and fellow-lieutenant and cooking for us, all for about eight dollars per month, was riding one to water and leading the other two. The led horses pulled him from his seat and all three ran away. They never were heard of afterwards. Shortly after that someone told Captain Bliss, General Taylor's Adjutant-General, of my misfortune. "Yes; I heard Grant lost five or six dollars' worth of horses the other day," he replied. That was a slander; they were broken to the saddle when I got them and cost nearly twenty dollars. I never suspected the colored boy of malicious intent in letting them get away, because, if they had not escaped, he could have had one of them to ride on the long march then in prospect.

Chapter VI

ADVANCE OF THE ARMY — CROSSING THE COLORADO — THE RIO GRANDE

*A*t last the preparations were complete and orders were issued for the advance to begin on the 8th of March. General Taylor had an army of not more than three thousand men. One battery, the siege guns and all the convalescent troops were sent on by water to Brazos Santiago, at the mouth of the Rio Grande. A guard was left back at Corpus Christi to look after public property and to take care of those who were too sick to be removed. The remainder of the army, probably not more than twenty five hundred men, was divided into three brigades, with the cavalry independent. Colonel Twiggs, with seven companies of dragoons and a battery of light artillery, moved on the 8th. He was followed by the three infantry brigades, with a day's interval between the commands. Thus the rear brigade did not move from Corpus Christi until the 11th of March. In view of the immense bodies of men moved on the same day over narrow roads, through dense forests and across large streams, in our late war, it seems strange now that a body of less than three thousand men should have been broken into four columns, separated by a day's march.

General Taylor was opposed to anything like plundering by the troops, and in this instance, I doubt not, he looked upon the enemy as the aggrieved party and was not willing to injure them further than his instructions from Washington demanded. His orders to the troops enjoined scrupulous regard for the rights of all peaceable persons and the payment of the highest price for all supplies taken for the use of the army.

All officers of foot regiments who had horses were permitted to ride them on the march when it did not interfere with their military duties. As already related, having lost my "five or six dollars' worth of horses" but a short time before I determined not to get another, but to make the journey on foot. My company commander, Captain McCall, had two good American horses, of considerably more value in that country, where native horses were cheap, than they were in the States. He used one himself and wanted the other for his servant. He was quite anxious to know whether I did not intend to get me another horse before the march began. I told him No; I belonged to a foot regiment. I did not understand the object of his solicitude at the time, but, when we were about to start, he said: "There, Grant, is a horse for you." I found that he could not bear the idea of his servant riding on a long march while his lieutenant went a-foot. He had found a mustang, a three-year old colt only recently captured, which had been purchased by one of the colored servants with the regiment for the sum of three dollars. It was probably the only horse at Corpus Christi that could have been purchased just then for any reasonable price. Five dollars, sixty-six and two-thirds percent advance, induced the owner to part with the mustang. I was sorry to take him, because I really felt that, belonging to a foot regiment, it was my duty to march with the men. But I saw the Captain's earnestness in the matter, and accepted the horse for the trip. The day we started was the first time the horse had ever been under saddle. I had, however, but little difficulty in breaking him, though for the first day there were frequent disagreements between us as to which way we should go, and sometimes whether we should go at all. At no time during the day could I choose exactly the part of the column I would march with; but after that, I had as tractable a horse as any with the army, and there was none that stood the trip better. He never ate a mouthful of food on the journey except the grass he could pick within the length of his picket rope.

A few days out from Corpus Christi, the immense herd of wild horses that ranged at that time between the Nueces and the Rio Grande was seen directly in advance of the head of the column and but a few miles off. It was the very band from which the horse I was riding had been captured but a few weeks before. The column was halted for a rest, and a number of officers, myself among them, rode out two or three miles to the right to see the extent of the herd. The country was a rolling prairie, and, from the higher ground, the vision was obstructed only by the earth's curvature. As far as the eye could reach to our right, the herd extended. To the left, it extended equally. There was no estimating the number of animals in it; I have no idea that they could all have been corralled in the State of Rhode Island, or Delaware, at one time. If they had been, they would have been so thick that the pasturage would have given out the first day. People who saw the Southern herd of buffalo, fifteen or twenty years ago, can appreciate the size of the Texas band of wild horses in 1846.

At the point where the army struck the Little Colorado River, the stream was quite wide and of sufficient depth for navigation. The water was brackish and the banks were fringed with timber. Here the whole army concentrated before attempting to cross. The army was not accompanied by a pontoon train, and at that time the troops were not instructed in bridge building. To add to the embarrassment of the situation, the army was here, for the first time, threatened with opposition. Buglers, concealed from our view by the brush on the opposite side, sounded the "assembly," and other military calls. Like the wolves before spoken of, they gave the impression that there was a large number of them and that, if the troops were in proportion to the noise, they were sufficient to devour General Taylor and his army. There were probably but few troops, and those engaged principally in watching the movements of the "invader." A few of our cavalry dashed in, and forded and swam the stream, and all opposition was soon dispersed. I do not remember that a single shot was fired.

The troops waded the stream, which was up to their necks in the deepest part. Teams were crossed by attaching a long rope to the end of the wagon tongue passing it between the two swing mules and by the side of the leader, hitching his bridle as well as the bridle of the mules in rear to it, and carrying the end to men on the opposite shore. The bank down to the water was steep on both sides. A rope long enough to cross the river, therefore, was attached to the back axle of the wagon, and men behind would hold the rope to prevent the wagon "beating" the mules into the water. This latter rope also served the purpose of bringing the end of the forward one back, to be used over again. The water was deep enough for a short distance to swim the little Mexican mules which the army was then using, but they, and the wagons, were pulled through so fast by the men at the end of the rope ahead, that no time was left them to show their obstinacy. In this manner the artillery and transportation of the "army of occupation" crossed the Colorado River.

About the middle of the month of March the advance of the army reached the Rio Grande and went into camp near the banks of the river, opposite the city of Matamoras and almost under the guns of a small fort at the lower end of the town. There was not at that time a single habitation from Corpus Christi until the Rio Grande was reached.

The work of fortifying was commenced at once. The fort was laid out by the engineers, but the work was done by the soldiers under the supervision of their officers, the chief engineer retaining general directions. The Mexicans now became so incensed at our near approach that some of their troops crossed the river above us, and made it unsafe for small bodies of men to go far beyond the limits of camp. They captured two companies of dragoons, commanded by Captains Thornton and Hardee. The latter figured as a general in the late war, on the Confederate side, and was author of the tactics first used by both armies. Lieutenant Theodric Porter, of the 4th infantry, was killed while out with a small detachment; and Major Cross, the assistant quartermaster-general, had also been killed not far from camp.

There was no base of supplies nearer than Point Isabel, on the coast, north of the mouth of the Rio Grande and twenty-five miles away. The enemy, if the Mexicans could be called such at this time when no war had been declared, hovered about in such numbers that it was not safe to send a wagon train after supplies with any escort that could be spared. I have already said that General Taylor's whole command on the Rio Grande numbered less than three thousand men. He had, however, a few more troops at Point Isabel or Brazos Santiago. The supplies brought from Corpus Christi in wagons were running short. Work was therefore pushed with great vigor on the defenses, to enable the minimum number of troops to hold the fort. All the men who could be employed, were kept at work from early dawn until darkness closed the labors of the day. With all this the fort was not completed until the supplies grew so short that further delay in obtaining more could not be thought of. By the latter part of April the work was in a partially defensible condition, and the 7th infantry, Major Jacob Brown commanding, was marched in to garrison it, with some few pieces of artillery. All the supplies on hand, with the exception of enough to carry the rest of the army to Point Isabel, were left with the garrison, and the march was commenced with the remainder of the command, every wagon being taken with the army. Early on the second day after starting the force reached its destination, without opposition from the Mexicans. There was some delay in getting supplies ashore from vessels at anchor in the open roadstead.

Chapter VII

THE MEXICAN WAR — THE BATTLE OF PALO
ALTO — THE BATTLE OF RESACA DE LA PALMA
— ARMY OF INVASION — GENERAL TAYLOR —
MOVEMENT ON CAMARGO

*W*hile General Taylor was away with the bulk of his army, the little garrison up the river was besieged. As we lay in our tents upon the seashore, the artillery at the fort on the Rio Grande could be distinctly heard.

The war had begun.

There were no possible means of obtaining news from the garrison, and information from outside could not be otherwise than unfavorable. What General Taylor's feelings were during this suspense I do not know; but for myself, a young second-lieutenant who had never heard a hostile gun before, I felt sorry that I had enlisted. A great many men, when they smell battle afar off, chafe to get into the fray. When they say so themselves they generally fail to convince their hearers that they are as anxious as they would like to make believe, and as they approach danger they become more subdued. This rule is not universal, for I have known a few men who were always aching for a fight when there was no enemy near, who were as good as their word when the battle did come. But the number of such men is small.

On the 7th of May the wagons were all loaded and General Taylor started on his return, with his army reinforced at Point Isabel, but still less than three thousand strong, to relieve the garrison on the Rio Grande. The road from Point Isabel to Matamoras is over an open, rolling, treeless prairie, until the timber that borders the bank of the Rio Grande is reached. This river, like the Mississippi, flows through a rich alluvial valley in the most meandering manner, running towards all points of the compass at times within a few miles. Formerly the river ran by Resaca de la Palma, some four or five miles east of the present channel. The old bed of the river at Resaca had become filled at places, leaving a succession of little lakes. The timber that had formerly grown upon both banks, and for a considerable distance out, was still standing. This timber was struck six or eight miles out from the besieged garrison, at a point known as Palo Alto — "Tall trees" or "woods."

Early in the forenoon of the 8th of May as Palo Alto was approached, an army, certainly outnumbering our little force, was seen, drawn up in line of battle just in front of the timber. Their bayonets and spearheads glistened in the sunlight formidably. The force was composed largely of cavalry armed with lances. Where we were the grass was tall, reaching nearly to the shoulders of the men, very stiff, and each stock was pointed at the top, and hard and almost as sharp as a darning-needle. General Taylor halted his army before the head of column came in range of the artillery of the Mexicans. He then formed a line of battle, facing the enemy. His artillery, two batteries and two eighteen-pounder iron guns, drawn by oxen, were placed in position at intervals along the line. A battalion was thrown to the rear, commanded by Lieutenant-Colonel Childs, of the artillery, as reserves. These preparations completed, orders were given for a platoon of each company to stack arms and go to a stream off to the right of the command, to fill their canteens and also those of the rest of their respective companies. When the men were all back in their places in line, the command to advance was given. As I looked down that long line of about three thousand armed men, advancing towards a larger force also armed, I thought what a fearful responsibility General Taylor must feel, commanding such a host and so far away from friends. The Mexicans immediately opened fire upon us, first with artillery and then with infantry. At first their shots did not reach us, and the advance was continued. As we got nearer, the cannon balls commenced going through the ranks. They hurt no one, however, during this advance, because they would strike the ground long before they reached our line, and ricocheted through the tall grass so slowly that the men would see them and open ranks and let them pass. When we got to a point where the artillery could be used with effect, a halt was called, and the battle opened on both sides.

The infantry under General Taylor was armed with flint-lock muskets, and paper cartridges charged with powder, buck-shot and ball. At the distance of a few hundred yards a man might fire at you all day without your finding it out. The artillery was generally six-pounder brass guns throwing only solid shot; but General Taylor had with him three or four twelve-pounder howitzers throwing shell, besides his eighteen-pounders before spoken of, that had a long range. This made a powerful armament. The Mexicans were armed about as we were so far as their infantry was concerned, but their artillery only fired solid shot. We had greatly the advantage in this arm.

The artillery was advanced a rod or two in front of the line, and opened fire. The infantry stood at order arms as spectators, watching the effect of our shots upon the enemy, and watching his shots so as to step out of their way. It could be seen that the eighteen-pounders and the howitzers did a great deal of execution. On our side there was little or no loss while we occupied this position. During the battle Major Ringgold, an accomplished and brave artillery officer, was mortally wounded, and Lieutenant Luther, also of the artillery, was struck. During the day several advances were made, and just at dusk it became evident that the Mexicans were falling back. We again advanced, and occupied at the close of the battle substantially the ground held by the enemy at the beginning. In this last move there was a brisk fire upon our troops, and some execution was done. One cannon-ball passed through our ranks, not far from me. It took off the head of an enlisted man, and the under jaw of Captain Page of my regiment, while the splinters from the musket of the killed soldier, and his brains and bones, knocked down two or three others, including one officer, Lieutenant Wallen, — hurting them more or less. Our casualties for the day were nine killed and forty-seven wounded.

At the break of day on the 9th, the army under Taylor was ready to renew the battle; but an advance showed that the enemy had entirely left our front during the night. The chaparral before us was impenetrable except where there were roads or trails, with occasionally clear or bare spots of small dimensions. A body of men penetrating it might easily be ambushed. It was better to have a few men caught in this way than the whole army, yet it was necessary that the garrison at the river should be relieved. To get to them the chaparral had to be passed. Thus I assume General Taylor reasoned. He halted the army not far in advance of the ground occupied by the Mexicans the day before, and selected Captain C.F. Smith, of the artillery, and Captain McCall, of my company, to take one hundred and fifty picked men each and find where the enemy had gone. This left me in command of the company, an honor and responsibility I thought very great.

Smith and McCall found no obstruction in the way of their advance until they came up to the succession of ponds, before describes, at Resaca. The Mexicans had passed them and formed their lines on the opposite bank. This position they had strengthened a little by throwing up dead trees and brush in their front, and by placing artillery to cover the approaches and open places. Smith and McCall deployed on each side of the road as well as they could, and engaged the enemy at long

range. Word was sent back, and the advance of the whole army was at
once commenced. As we came up we were deployed in like manner. I
was with the right wing, and led my company through the thicket
wherever a penetrable place could be found, taking advantage of any
clear spot that would carry me towards the enemy. At last I got pretty
close up without knowing it. The balls commenced to whistle very thick
overhead, cutting the limbs of the chaparral right and left. We could
not see the enemy, so I ordered my men to lie down, an order that did
not have to be enforced. We kept our position until it became evident
that the enemy were not firing at us, and then withdrew to find better
ground to advance upon.

By this time some progress had been made on our left. A section of
artillery had been captured by the cavalry, and some prisoners had been
taken. The Mexicans were giving way all along the line, and many of
them had, no doubt, left early. I at last found a clear space separating
two ponds. There seemed to be a few men in front and I charged upon
them with my company.

There was no resistance, and we captured a Mexican colonel, who had
been wounded, and a few men. Just as I was sending them to the rear
with a guard of two or three men, a private came from the front bringing
back one of our officers, who had been badly wounded in advance of
where I was. The ground had been charged over before. My exploit was
equal to that of the soldier who boasted that he had cut off the leg of
one of the enemy. When asked why he did not cut off his head, he
replied: "Someone had done that before." This left no doubt in my mind
but that the battle of Resaca de la Palma would have been won, just as
it was, if I had not been there. There was no further resistance. The
evening of the 9th the army was encamped on its old ground near the
Fort, and the garrison was relieved. The siege had lasted a number of
days, but the casualties were few in number. Major Jacob Brown, of the
7th infantry, the commanding officer, had been killed, and in his honor
the fort was named. Since then a town of considerable importance has
sprung up on the ground occupied by the fort and troops, which has
also taken his name.

The battles of Palo Alto and Resaca de la Palma seemed to us engaged,
as pretty important affairs; but we had only a faint conception of their
magnitude until they were fought over in the North by the Press and
the reports came back to us. At the same time, or about the same time,
we learned that war existed between the United States and Mexico, by
the acts of the latter country. On learning this fact General Taylor
transferred our camps to the south or west bank of the river, and
Matamoras was occupied. We then became the "Army of Invasion."

Up to this time Taylor had none but regular troops in his command; but now that invasion had already taken place, volunteers for one year commenced arriving. The army remained at Matamoras until sufficiently reinforced to warrant a movement into the interior. General Taylor was not an officer to trouble the administration much with his demands, but was inclined to do the best he could with the means given him. He felt his responsibility as going no further. If he had thought that he was sent to perform an impossibility with the means given him, he would probably have informed the authorities of his opinion and left them to determine what should be done. If the judgment was against him he would have gone on and done the best he could with the means at hand without parading his grievance before the public. No soldier could face either danger or responsibility more calmly than he. These are qualities more rarely found than genius or physical courage.

General Taylor never made any great show or parade, either of uniform or retinue. In dress he was possibly too plain, rarely wearing anything in the field to indicate his rank, or even that he was an officer; but he was known to every soldier in his army, and was respected by all. I can call to mind only one instance when I saw him in uniform, and one other when I heard of his wearing it, On both occasions he was unfortunate. The first was at Corpus Christi. He had concluded to review his army before starting on the march and gave orders accordingly. Colonel Twiggs was then second in rank with the army, and to him was given the command of the review. Colonel and Brevet Brigadier-General Worth, a far different soldier from Taylor in the use of the uniform, was next to Twiggs in rank, and claimed superiority by virtue of his brevet rank when the accidents of service threw them where one or the other had to command. Worth declined to attend the review as subordinate to Twiggs until the question was settled by the highest authority. This broke up the review, and the question was referred to Washington for final decision.

General Taylor was himself only a colonel, in real rank, at that time, and a brigadier-general by brevet. He was assigned to duty, however, by the President, with the rank which his brevet gave him. Worth was not so assigned, but by virtue of commanding a division he must, under the army regulations of that day, have drawn the pay of his brevet rank. The question was submitted to Washington, and no response was received until after the army had reached the Rio Grande. It was decided against General Worth, who at once tendered his resignation and left the army, going north, no doubt, by the same vessel that carried it. This kept him out of the battles of Palo Alto and Resaca de la Palma. Either the resignation was not accepted, or General Worth withdrew it before action had been taken. At all events he returned to the army in time to command his division in the battle of Monterey, and served with it to the end of the war.

The second occasion on which General Taylor was said to have donned his uniform, was in order to receive a visit from the Flag Officer of the naval squadron off the mouth of the Rio Grande. While the army was on that river the Flag Officer sent word that he would call on the General to pay his respects on a certain day. General Taylor, knowing that naval officers habitually wore all the uniform the "law allowed" on all occasions of ceremony, thought it would be only civil to receive his guest in the same style. His uniform was therefore got out, brushed up, and put on, in advance of the visit. The Flag Officer, knowing General Taylor's aversion to the wearing of the uniform, and feeling that it would be regarded as a compliment should he meet him in civilian's dress, left off his uniform for this occasion. The meeting was said to have been embarrassing to both, and the conversation was principally apologetic.

The time was whiled away pleasantly enough at Matamoras, while we were waiting for volunteers. It is probable that all the most important people of the territory occupied by our army left their homes before we got there, but with those remaining the best of relations apparently existed. It was the policy of the Commanding General to allow no pillaging, no taking of private property for public or individual use without satisfactory compensation, so that a better market was afforded than the people had ever known before.

Among the troops that joined us at Matamoras was an Ohio regiment, of which Thomas L. Hamer, the Member of Congress who had given me my appointment to West Point, was major. He told me then that he could have had the colonelcy, but that as he knew he was to be appointed a brigadier-general, he preferred at first to take the lower grade. I have said before that Hamer was one of the ablest men Ohio ever produced. At that time he was in the prime of life, being less than fifty years of age, and possessed an admirable physique, promising long life. But he was taken sick before Monterey, and died within a few days. I have always believed that had his life been spared, he would have been President of the United States during the term filled by President Pierce. Had Hamer filled that office his partiality for me was such, there is but little doubt I should have been appointed to one of the staff corps of the army — the Pay Department probably — and would therefore now be preparing to retire. Neither of these speculations is unreasonable, and they are mentioned to show how little men control their own destiny.

Reinforcements having arrived, in the month of August the movement commenced from Matamoras to Camargo, the head of navigation on the Rio Grande. The line of the Rio Grande was all that was necessary to hold, unless it was intended to invade Mexico from the North. In that case the most natural route to take was the one which General Taylor selected. It entered a pass in the Sierra Madre Mountains, at Monterey, through which the main road runs to the City of Mexico. Monterey itself was a good point to hold, even if the line of the Rio Grande covered all the territory we desired to occupy at that time. It is built on a plain two thousand feet above tide water, where the air is bracing and the situation healthy.

On the 19th of August the army started for Monterey, leaving a small garrison at Matamoras. The troops, with the exception of the artillery, cavalry, and the brigade to which I belonged, were moved up the river to Camargo on steamers. As there were but two or three of these, the boats had to make a number of trips before the last of the troops were up. Those who marched did so by the south side of the river. Lieutenant-Colonel Garland, of the 4th infantry, was the brigade commander, and on this occasion commanded the entire marching force. One day out convinced him that marching by day in that latitude, in the month of August, was not a beneficial sanitary measure, particularly for Northern men. The order of marching was changed and night marches were substituted with the best results.

When Camargo was reached, we found a city of tents outside the Mexican hamlet. I was detailed to act as quartermaster and commissary to the regiment. The teams that had proven abundantly sufficient to transport all supplies from Corpus Christi to the Rio Grande over the level prairies of Texas, were entirely inadequate to the needs of the reinforced army in a mountainous country. To obviate the deficiency, pack mules were hired, with Mexicans to pack and drive them. I had charge of the few wagons allotted to the 4th infantry and of the pack train to supplement them. There were not men enough in the army to manage that train without the help of Mexicans who had learned how. As it was the difficulty was great enough. The troops would take up their march at an early hour each day. After they had started, the tents and cooking utensils had to be made into packages, so that they could be lashed to the backs of the mules. Sheet-iron kettles, tent-poles and mess chests were inconvenient articles to transport in that way. It took several hours to get ready to start each morning, and by the time we were ready some of the mules first loaded would be tired of standing so long with their loads on their backs. Sometimes one would start to run, bowing his back and kicking up until he scattered his load; others would lie down and try to disarrange their loads by attempting to get on the top of them by rolling on them; others with tent-poles for part of their loads would manage to run a tent-pole on one side of a sapling while they would take the other. I am not aware of ever having used a profane expletive in my life; but I would have the charity to excuse those who may have done so, if they were in charge of a train of Mexican pack mules at the time.

Chapter VIII

ADVANCE ON MONTEREY — THE BLACK FORT —
THE BATTLE OF MONTEREY — SURRENDER OF
THE CITY

*T*he advance from Camargo was commenced on the 5th of September. The army was divided into four columns, separated from each other by one day's march. The advance reached Cerralvo in four days and halted for the remainder of the troops to come up. By the 13th the rear-guard had arrived, and the same day the advance resumed its march, followed as before, a day separating the divisions. The forward division halted again at Marin, twenty-four miles from Monterey. Both this place and Cerralvo were nearly deserted, and men, women and children were seen running and scattered over the hills as we approached; but when the people returned they found all their abandoned property safe, which must have given them a favorable opinion of Los Grengos — "the Yankees." From Marin the movement was in mass. On the 19th General Taylor, with is army, was encamped at Walnut Springs, within three miles of Monterey.

The town is on a small stream coming out of the mountain-pass, and is backed by a range of hills of moderate elevation. To the north, between the city and Walnut Springs, stretches an extensive plain. On this plain, and entirely outside of the last houses of the city, stood a strong fort, enclosed on all sides, to which our army gave the name of "Black Fort." Its guns commanded the approaches to the city to the full extent of their range. There were two detached spurs of hills or mountains to the north and northwest of the city, which were also fortified. On one of these stood the Bishop's Palace. The road to Saltillo leaves the upper or western end of the city under the fire of the guns from these heights. The lower or eastern end was defended by two or three small detached works, armed with artillery and infantry. To the south was the mountain stream before mentioned, and back of that the range of foot-hills. The plaza in the center of the city was the citadel, properly speaking. All the streets leading from it were swept by artillery, cannon being entrenched behind temporary parapets. The house-tops near the plaza were converted into infantry fortifications by the use of sand-bags for parapets. Such were the defenses of Monterey in September, 1847. General Ampudia, with a force of certainly ten thousand men, was in command.

General Taylor's force was about six thousand five hundred strong, in three divisions, under Generals Butler, Twiggs and Worth. The troops went into camp at Walnut Springs, while the engineer officers, under Major Mansfield — a General in the late war — commenced their reconnaissance. Major Mansfield found that it would be practicable to get troops around, out of range of the Black Fort and the works on the detached hills to the northwest of the city, to the Saltillo road. With this road in our possession, the enemy would be cut off from receiving further supplies, if not from all communication with the interior. General Worth, with his division somewhat reinforced, was given the task of gaining possession of the Saltillo road, and of carrying the detached works outside the city, in that quarter. He started on his march early in the afternoon of the 20th. The divisions under Generals Butler and Twiggs were drawn up to threaten the east and north sides of the city and the works on those fronts, in support of the movement under General Worth. Worth's was regarded as the main attack on Monterey, and all other operations were in support of it. His march this day was uninterrupted; but the enemy was seen to reinforce heavily about the Bishop's Palace and the other outside fortifications on their left. General Worth reached a defensible position just out of range of the enemy's guns on the heights northwest of the city, and bivouacked for the night. The engineer officers with him — Captain Sanders and Lieutenant George G. Meade, afterwards the commander of the victorious National army at the battle of Gettysburg — made a reconnaissance to the Saltillo road under cover of night.

During the night of the 20th General Taylor had established a battery, consisting of two twenty-four-pounder howitzers and a ten inch mortar, at a point from which they could play upon Black Fort. A natural depression in the plain, sufficiently deep to protect men standing in it from the fire from the fort, was selected and the battery established on the crest nearest the enemy. The 4th infantry, then consisting of but six reduced companies, was ordered to support the artillerists while they were entrenching themselves and their guns. I was regimental quartermaster at the time and was ordered to remain in charge of camp and the public property at Walnut Springs. It was supposed that the regiment would return to its camp in the morning.

The point for establishing the siege battery was reached and the work performed without attracting the attention of the enemy. At daylight the next morning fire was opened on both sides and continued with, what seemed to me at that day, great fury. My curiosity got the better of my judgment, and I mounted a horse and rode to the front to see what was going on. I had been there but a short time when an order to charge was given, and lacking the moral courage to return to camp — where I had been ordered to stay — I charged with the regiment As soon as the troops were out of the depression they came under the fire of Black Fort. As they advanced they got under fire from batteries guarding the east, or lower, end of the city, and of musketry. About one-third of the men engaged in the charge were killed or wounded in the space of a few minutes. We retreated to get out of fire, not backward, but eastward and perpendicular to the direct road running into the city from Walnut Springs. I was, I believe, the only person in the 4th infantry in the charge who was on horseback. When we got to a lace of safety the regiment halted and drew itself together — what was left of it. The adjutant of the regiment, Lieutenant Hoskins, who was not in robust health, found himself very much fatigued from running on foot in the charge and retreat, and, seeing me on horseback, expressed a wish that he could be mounted also. I offered him my horse and he accepted the offer. A few minutes later I saw a soldier, a quartermaster's man, mounted, not far away. I ran to him, took his horse and was back with the regiment in a few minutes. In a short time we were off again; and the next place of safety from the shots of the enemy that I recollect of being in, was a field of cane or corn to the northeast of the lower batteries. The adjutant to whom I had loaned my horse was killed, and I was designated to act in his place.

This charge was ill-conceived, or badly executed. We belonged to the brigade commanded by Lieutenant-Colonel Garland, and he had received orders to charge the lower batteries of the city, and carry them if he could without too much loss, for the purpose of creating a diversion in favor of Worth, who was conducting the movement which it was intended should be decisive. By a movement by the left flank Garland could have led his men beyond the range of the fire from Black Fort and advanced towards the northeast angle of the city, as well covered from fire as could be expected. There was no undue loss of life in reaching the lower end of Monterey, except that sustained by Garland's command.

Meanwhile Quitman's brigade, conducted by an officer of engineers, had reached the eastern end of the city, and was placed under cover of the houses without much loss. Colonel Garland's brigade also arrived at the suburbs, and, by the assistance of some of our troops that had reached house-tops from which they could fire into a little battery covering the approaches to the lower end of the city, the battery was speedily captured and its guns were turned upon another work of the enemy. An entrance into the east end of the city was now secured, and the houses protected our troops so long as they were inactive. On the west General Worth had reached the Saltillo road after some fighting but without heavy loss. He turned from his new position and captured the forts on both heights in that quarter. This gave him possession of the upper or west end of Monterey. Troops from both Twiggs's and Butler's divisions were in possession of the east end of the town, but the Black Fort to the north of the town and the plaza in the center were still in the possession of the enemy. Our camps at Walnut Springs, three miles away, were guarded by a company from each regiment. A regiment of Kentucky volunteers guarded the mortars and howitzers engaged against Black Fort. Practically Monterey was invested.

There was nothing done on the 22d by the United States troops; but the enemy kept up a harmless fire upon us from Black Fort and the batteries still in their possession at the east end of the city. During the night they evacuated these; so that on the morning of the 23d we held undisputed possession of the east end of Monterey.

Twiggs's division was at the lower end of the city, and well covered from the fire of the enemy. But the streets leading to the plaza — all Spanish or Spanish-American towns have near their centers a square called a plaza — were commanded from all directions by artillery. The houses were flat-roofed and but one or two stories high, and about the plaza the roofs were manned with infantry, the troops being protected from our fire by parapets made of sand-bags. All advances into the city were thus attended with much danger. While moving along streets which did not lead to the plaza, our men were protected from the fire, and from the view, of the enemy except at the crossings; but at these a volley of musketry and a discharge of grape-shot were invariably encountered. The 3d and 4th regiments of infantry made an advance nearly to the plaza in this way and with heavy loss. The loss of the 3d infantry in commissioned officers was especially severe. There were only five companies of the regiment and not over twelve officers present, and five of these officers were killed. When within a square of the plaza this small command, ten companies in all, was brought to a halt. Placing themselves under cover from the shots of the enemy, the men would watch to detect a head above the sand-bags on the neighboring houses. The exposure of a single head would bring a volley from our soldiers.

We had not occupied this position long when it was discovered that our ammunition was growing low. I volunteered to go back* to the point we had started from, report our position to General Twiggs, and ask for ammunition to be forwarded. We were at this time occupying ground off from the street, in rear of the houses. My ride back was an exposed one. Before starting I adjusted myself on the side of my horse furthest from the enemy, and with only one foot holding to the cantle of the saddle, and an arm over the neck of the horse exposed, I started at full run. It was only at street crossings that my horse was under fire, but these I crossed at such a flying rate that generally I was past and under cover of the next block of houses before the enemy fired. I got out safely without a scratch.

At one place on my ride, I saw a sentry walking in front of a house, and stopped to inquire what he was doing there. Finding that the house was full of wounded American officers and soldiers, I dismounted and went in. I found there Captain Williams, of the Engineer Corps, wounded in the head, probably fatally, and Lieutenant Territt, also badly wounded his bowels protruding from his wound. There were quite a number of soldiers also. Promising them to report their situation, I left, readjusted myself to my horse, recommenced the run, and was soon with the troops at the east end. Before ammunition could be collected, the two regiments I had been with were seen returning, running the same gauntlet in getting out that they had passed in going in, but with comparatively little loss. The movement was countermanded and the troops were withdrawn. The poor wounded officers and men I had found, fell into the hands of the enemy during the night, and died.

While this was going on at the east, General Worth, with a small division of troops, was advancing towards the plaza from the opposite end of the city. He resorted to a better expedient for getting to the plaza — the citadel — than we did on the east. Instead of moving by the open streets, he advanced through the houses, cutting passageways from one to another. Without much loss of life, he got so near the plaza during

---

* General Garland expressed a wish to get a message back to General Twiggs, his division commander, or General Taylor, to the effect that he was nearly out of ammunition and must have more sent to him, or otherwise be reinforced. Deeming the return dangerous he did not like to order anyone to carry it, so he called for a volunteer. Lieutenant Grant offered his services, which were accepted. — PUBLISHERS.

the night that before morning, Ampudia, the Mexican commander, made overtures for the surrender of the city and garrison. This stopped all further hostilities. The terms of surrender were soon agreed upon. The prisoners were paroled and permitted to take their horses and personal property with them.

My pity was aroused by the sight of the Mexican garrison of Monterey marching out of town as prisoners, and no doubt the same feeling was experienced by most of our army who witnessed it. Many of the prisoners were cavalry, armed with lances, and mounted on miserable little half-starved horses that did not look as if they could carry their riders out of town. The men looked in but little better condition. I thought how little interest the men before me had in the results of the war, and how little knowledge they had of "what it was all about."

After the surrender of the garrison of Monterey a quiet camp life was led until midwinter. As had been the case on the Rio Grande, the people who remained at their homes fraternized with the "Yankees" in the pleasantest manner. In fact, under the humane policy of our commander, I question whether the great majority of the Mexican people did not regret our departure as much as they had regretted our coming. Property and person were thoroughly protected, and a market was afforded for all the products of the country such as the people had never enjoyed before. The educated and wealthy portion of the population here, as elsewhere, abandoned their homes and remained away from them as long as they were in the possession of the invaders; but this class formed a very small percentage of the whole population.

Chapter IX

POLITICAL INTRIGUE — BUENA VISTA — MOVEMENT AGAINST VERA CRUZ — SIEGE AND CAPTURE OF VERA CRUZ

*T*he Mexican war was a political war, and the administration conducting it desired to make party capital out of it. General Scott was at the head of the army, and, being a soldier of acknowledged professional capacity, his claim to the command of the forces in the field was almost indisputable and does not seem to have been denied by President Polk, or Marcy, his Secretary of War. Scott was a Whig and the administration was democratic. General Scott was also known to have political aspirations, and nothing so popularizes a candidate for high civil positions as military victories. It would not do therefore to give him command of the "army of conquest." The plans submitted by Scott for a campaign in Mexico were disapproved by the administration, and he replied, in a tone possibly a little disrespectful, to the effect that, if a soldier's plans were not to be supported by the administration, success could not be expected. This was on the 27th of May, 1846. Four days later General Scott was notified that he need not go to Mexico. General Gaines was next in rank, but he was too old and feeble to take the field. Colonel Zachary Taylor — a brigadier-general by brevet — was therefore left in command. He, too, was a Whig, but was not supposed to entertain any political ambitions; nor did he; but after the fall of Monterey, his third battle and third complete victory, the Whig papers at home began to speak of him as the candidate of their party for the Presidency. Something had to be done to neutralize his growing popularity. He could not be relieved from duty in the field where all his battles had been victories: the design would have been too transparent. It was finally decided to send General Scott to Mexico in chief command, and to authorize him to carry out his own original plan: that is, capture Vera Cruz and march upon the capital of the country. It was no doubt supposed that Scott's ambition would lead him to slaughter Taylor or destroy his chances for the Presidency, and yet it was hoped that he would not make sufficient capital himself to secure the prize.

The administration had indeed a most embarrassing problem to solve. It was engaged in a war of conquest which must be carried to a successful issue, or the political object would be unattained. Yet all the capable officers of the requisite rank belonged to the opposition, and the man selected for his lack of political ambition had himself become a prominent candidate for the Presidency. It was necessary to destroy his chances promptly. The problem was to do this without the loss of conquest and without permitting another general of the same political party to acquire like popularity. The fact is, the administration of Mr. Polk made every preparation to disgrace Scott, or, to speak more correctly, to drive him to such desperation that he would disgrace himself.

General Scott had opposed conquest by the way of the Rio Grande, Matamoras and Saltillo from the first. Now that he was in command of all the forces in Mexico, he withdrew from Taylor most of his regular troops and left him only enough volunteers, as he thought, to hold the line then in possession of the invading army. Indeed Scott did not deem it important to hold anything beyond the Rio Grande, and authorized Taylor to fall back to that line if he chose. General Taylor protested against the depletion of his army, and his subsequent movement upon Buena Vista would indicate that he did not share the views of his chief in regard to the unimportance of conquest beyond the Rio Grande.

Scott had estimated the men and material that would be required to capture Vera Cruz and to march on the capital of the country, two hundred and sixty miles in the interior. He was promised all he asked and seemed to have not only the confidence of the President, but his sincere good wishes. The promises were all broken. Only about half the troops were furnished that had been pledged, other war material was withheld and Scott had scarcely started for Mexico before the President undertook to supersede him by the appointment of Senator Thomas H. Benton as lieutenant-general. This being refused by Congress, the President asked legislative authority to place a junior over a senior of the same grade, with the view of appointing Benton to the rank of major-general and then placing him in command of the army, but Congress failed to accede to this proposition as well, and Scott remained in command: but every general appointed to serve under him was politically opposed to the chief, and several were personally hostile.

General Scott reached Brazos Santiago or Point Isabel, at the mouth of the Rio Grande, late in December, 1846, and proceeded at once up the river to Camargo, where he had written General Taylor to meet him. Taylor, however, had gone to, or towards Tampico, for the purpose of establishing a post there. He had started on this march before he was aware of General Scott being in the country. Under these circumstances Scott had to issue his orders designating the troops to be withdrawn from Taylor, without the personal consultation he had expected to hold with his subordinate.

General Taylor's victory at Buena Vista, February 22d, 23d, and 24th, 1847, with an army composed almost entirely of volunteers who had not been in battle before, and over a vastly superior force numerically, made his nomination for the Presidency by the Whigs a foregone conclusion. He was nominated and elected in 1848. I believe that he sincerely regretted this turn in his fortunes, preferring the peace afforded by a quiet life free from abuse to the honor of filling the highest office in the gift of any people, the Presidency of the United States.

When General Scott assumed command of the army of invasion, I was in the division of General David Twiggs, in Taylor's command; but under the new orders my regiment was transferred to the division of General William Worth, in which I served to the close of the war. The troops withdrawn from Taylor to form part of the forces to operate against Vera Cruz, were assembled at the mouth of the Rio Grande preparatory to embarkation for their destination. I found General Worth a different man from any I had before served directly under. He was nervous, impatient and restless on the march, or when important or responsible duty confronted him. There was not the least reason for haste on the march, for it was known that it would take weeks to assemble shipping enough at the point of our embarkation to carry the army, but General Worth moved his division with a rapidity that would have been commendable had he been going to the relief of a beleaguered garrison. The length of the marches was regulated by the distances between places affording a supply of water for the troops, and these distances were sometimes long and sometimes short. General Worth on one occasion at least, after having made the full distance intended for the day, and after the troops were in camp and preparing their food, ordered tents struck and made the march that night which had been intended for the next day. Some commanders can move troops so as to get the maximum distance out of them without fatigue, while others can wear them out in a few days without accomplishing so much. General Worth belonged to this latter class. He enjoyed, however, a fine reputation for his fighting qualities, and thus attached his officers and men to him.

The army lay in camp upon the sand-beach in the neighborhood of the mouth of the Rio Grande for several weeks, awaiting the arrival of transports to carry it to its new field of operations. The transports were all sailing vessels. The passage was a tedious one, and many of the troops were on shipboard over thirty days from the embarkation at the mouth of the Rio Grande to the time of debarkation south of Vera Cruz. The trip was a comfortless one for officers and men. The transports used were built for carrying freight and possessed but limited accommodations for passengers, and the climate added to the discomfort of all.

The transports with troops were assembled in the harbor of Anton Lizardo, some sixteen miles south of Vera Cruz, as they arrived, and there awaited the remainder of the fleet, bringing artillery, ammunition and supplies of all kinds from the North. With the fleet there was a little steam propeller dispatch-boat — the first vessel of the kind I had ever seen, and probably the first of its kind ever seen by anyone then with the army. At that day ocean steamers were rare, and what there were were sidewheelers. This little vessel, going through the fleet so fast, so noiselessly and with its propeller under water out of view, attracted a great deal of attention. I recollect that Lieutenant Sidney Smith, of the 4th infantry, by whom I happened to be standing on the deck of a vessel when this propeller was passing, exclaimed, "Why, the thing looks as if it was propelled by the force of circumstances."

Finally on the 7th of March, 1847, the little army of ten or twelve thousand men, given Scott to invade a country with a population of seven or eight millions, a mountainous country affording the greatest possible natural advantages for defense, was all assembled and ready to commence the perilous task of landing from vessels lying in the open sea.

The debarkation took place inside of the little island of Sacrificios, some three miles south of Vera Cruz. The vessels could not get anywhere near shore, so that everything had to be landed in lighters or surf-boats; General Scott had provided these before leaving the North. The breakers were sometimes high, so that the landing was tedious. The men were got ashore rapidly, because they could wade when they came to shallow water; but the camp and garrison equipage, provisions, ammunition and all stores had to be protected from the salt water, and therefore their landing took several days. The Mexicans were very kind to us, however, and threw no obstacles in the way of our landing except an occasional shot from their nearest fort. During the debarkation one shot took off the head of Major Albertis. No other, I believe, reached anywhere near the same distance. On the 9th of March the troops were landed and the investment of Vera Cruz, from the Gulf of Mexico south of the city to the Gulf again on the north, was soon and easily effected. The landing of stores was continued until everything was got ashore.

Vera Cruz, at the time of which I write and up to 1880, was a walled city. The wall extended from the water's edge south of the town to the water again on the north. There were fortifications at intervals along the line and at the angles. In front of the city, and on an island half a mile out in the Gulf, stands San Juan de Ulloa, an enclosed fortification of large dimensions and great strength for that period. Against artillery of the present day the land forts and walls would prove elements of weakness rather than strength. After the invading army had established their camps out of range of the fire from the city, batteries were established, under cover of night, far to the front of the line where the troops lay. These batteries were entrenched and the approaches sufficiently protected. If a sortie had been made at any time by the Mexicans, the men serving the batteries could have been quickly reinforced without great exposure to the fire from the enemy's main line. No serious attempt was made to capture the batteries or to drive our troops away.

The siege continued with brisk firing on our side till the 27th of March, by which time a considerable breach had been made in the wall surrounding the city. Upon this General Morales, who was Governor of both the city and of San Juan de Ulloa, commenced a correspondence with General Scott looking to the surrender of the town, forts and garrison. On the 29th Vera Cruz and San Juan de Ulloa were occupied by Scott's army. About five thousand prisoners and four hundred pieces of artillery, besides large amounts of small arms and ammunition, fell into the hands of the victorious force. The casualties on our side during the siege amounted to sixty-four officers and men, killed and wounded.

Chapter X

MARCH TO JALAPA — BATTLE OF CERRO GORDO — PEROTE — PUEBLA — SCOTT AND TAYLOR

General Scott had less than twelve thousand men at Vera Cruz. He had been promised by the administration a very much larger force, or claimed that he had, and he was a man of veracity. Twelve thousand was a very small army with which to penetrate two hundred and sixty miles into an enemy's country, and to besiege the capital; a city, at that time, of largely over one hundred thousand inhabitants. Then, too, any line of march that could be selected led through mountain passes easily defended. In fact, there were at that time but two roads from Vera Cruz to the City of Mexico that could be taken by an army; one by Jalapa and Perote, the other by Cordova and Orizaba, the two coming together on the great plain which extends to the City of Mexico after the range of mountains is passed.

It was very important to get the army away from Vera Cruz as soon as possible, in order to avoid the yellow fever, or vomito, which usually visits that city early in the year, and is very fatal to persons not acclimated; but transportation, which was expected from the North, was arriving very slowly. It was absolutely necessary to have enough to supply the army to Jalapa, sixty-five miles in the interior and above the fevers of the coast. At that point the country is fertile, and an army of the size of General Scott's could subsist there for an indefinite period. Not counting the sick, the weak and the garrisons for the captured city and fort, the moving column was now less than ten thousand strong. This force was composed of three divisions, under Generals Twiggs, Patterson, and Worth. The importance of escaping the vomito was so great that as soon as transportation enough could be got together to move a division the advance was commenced. On the 8th of April, Twiggs's division started for Jalapa. He was followed very soon by Patterson, with his division. General Worth was to bring up the rear with his command as soon as transportation enough was assembled to carry six days' rations for his troops with the necessary ammunition and camp and garrison equipage. It was the 13th of April before this division left Vera Cruz.

The leading division ran against the enemy at Cerro Gordo, some fifty miles west, on the road to Jalapa, and went into camp at Plan del Rio, about three miles from the fortifications. General Patterson reached Plan del Rio with his division soon after Twiggs arrived. The two were then secure against an attack from Santa Anna, who commanded the Mexican forces. At all events they confronted the enemy without reinforcements and without molestation, until the 18th of April. General Scott had remained at Vera Cruz to hasten preparations for the field; but on the 12th, learning the situation at the front, he hastened on to take personal supervision. He at once commenced his preparations for the capture of the position held by Santa Anna and of the troops holding it.

Cerro Gordo is one of the higher spurs of the mountains some twelve to fifteen miles east of Jalapa, and Santa Anna had selected this point as the easiest to defend against an invading army. The road, said to have been built by Cortez, zigzags around the mountainside and was defended at every turn by artillery. On either side were deep chasms or mountain walls. A direct attack along the road was an impossibility. A flank movement seemed equally impossible. After the arrival of the commanding-general upon the scene, reconnaissances were sent out to find, or to make, a road by which the rear of the enemy's works might be reached without a front attack. These reconnaissances were made under the supervision of Captain Robert E. Lee, assisted by Lieutenants P.G.T. Beauregard, Isaac I. Stevens, Z.B. Tower, G.W. Smith, George B. McClellan, and J.G. Foster, of the corps of engineers, all officers who attained rank and fame, on one side or the other, in the great conflict for the preservation of the unity of the nation. The reconnaissance was completed, and the labor of cutting out and making roads by the flank of the enemy was effected by the 17th of the month. This was accomplished without the knowledge of Santa Anna or his army, and over ground where he supposed it impossible. On the same day General Scott issued his order for the attack on the 18th.

The attack was made as ordered, and perhaps there was not a battle of the Mexican war, or of any other, where orders issued before an engagement were nearer being a correct report of what afterwards took place. Under the supervision of the engineers, roadways had been opened over chasms to the right where the walls were so steep that men could barely climb them. Animals could not. These had been opened under cover of night, without attracting the notice of the enemy. The engineers, who had directed the opening, led the way and the troops followed. Artillery was let down the steep slopes by hand, the men engaged attaching a strong rope to the rear axle and letting the guns down, a piece at a time, while the men at the ropes kept their ground on top, paying out gradually, while a few at the front directed the course of the piece. In like manner the guns were drawn by hand up the opposite slopes. In this way Scott's troops reached their assigned position in rear of most of the entrenchments of the enemy, unobserved. The attack was made, the Mexican reserves behind the works beat a hasty retreat, and those occupying them surrendered. On the left General Pillow's command made a formidable demonstration, which doubtless held a part of the enemy in his front and contributed to the victory. I am not pretending to give full details of all the battles fought, but of the portion that I saw. There were troops engaged on both sides at other points in which both sustained losses; but the battle was won as here narrated.

The surprise of the enemy was complete, the victory overwhelming; some three thousand prisoners fell into Scott's hands, also a large amount of ordnance and ordnance stores. The prisoners were paroled, the artillery parked and the small arms and ammunition destroyed. The battle of Buena Vista was probably very important to the success of General Scott at Cerro Gordo and in his entire campaign from Vera Cruz to the great plains reaching to the City of Mexico. The only army Santa Anna had to protect his capital and the mountain passes west of Vera Cruz, was the one he had with him confronting General Taylor. It is not likely that he would have gone as far north as Monterey to attack the United States troops when he knew his country was threatened with invasion further south. When Taylor moved to Saltillo and then advanced on to Buena Vista, Santa Anna crossed the desert confronting the invading army, hoping no doubt to crush it and get back in time to meet General Scott in the mountain passes west of Vera Cruz. His attack on Taylor was disastrous to the Mexican army, but, notwithstanding this, he marched his army to Cerro Gordo, a distance not much short of one thousand miles by the line he had to travel, in time to entrench himself well before Scott got there. If he had been successful at Buena Vista his troops would no doubt have made a more stubborn resistance at Cerro Gordo. Had the battle of Buena Vista not been fought Santa Anna would have had time to move leisurely to meet the invader further south and with an army not demoralized nor depleted by defeat.

After the battle the victorious army moved on to Jalapa, where it was in a beautiful, productive and healthy country, far above the fevers of the coast. Jalapa, however, is still in the mountains, and between there and the great plain the whole line of the road is easy of defense. It was important, therefore, to get possession of the great highway between the seacoast and the capital up to the point where it leaves the mountains, before the enemy could have time to re-organize and fortify in our front. Worth's division was selected to go forward to secure this result. The division marched to Perote on the great plain, not far from where the road debouches from the mountains. There is a low, strong fort on the plain in front of the town, known as the Castle of Perote. This, however, offered no resistance and fell into our hands, with its armament.

General Scott having now only nine or ten thousand men west of Vera Cruz, and the time of some four thousand of them being about to expire, a long delay was the consequence. The troops were in a healthy climate, and where they could subsist for an indefinite period even if their line back to Vera Cruz should be cut off. It being ascertained that the men whose time would expire before the City of Mexico could possibly fall into the hands of the American army, would not remain beyond the term for which they had volunteered, the commanding-general determined to discharge them at once, for a delay until the expiration of their time would have compelled them to pass through Vera Cruz during the season of the vomito. This reduced Scott's force in the field to about five thousand men.

Early in May, Worth, with his division, left Perote and marched on to Puebla. The roads were wide and the country open except through one pass in a spur of mountains coming up from the south, through which the road runs. Notwithstanding this the small column was divided into two bodies, moving a day apart. Nothing occurred on the march of special note, except that while lying at the town of Amozoque — an easy day's march east of Puebla — a body of the enemy's cavalry, two or three thousand strong, was seen to our right, not more than a mile away. A battery or two, with two or three infantry regiments, was sent against them and they soon disappeared. On the 15th of May we entered the city of Puebla.

General Worth was in command at Puebla until the latter end of May, when General Scott arrived. Here, as well as on the march up, his restlessness, particularly under responsibilities, showed itself. During his brief command he had the enemy hovering around near the city, in vastly superior numbers to his own. The brigade to which I was attached changed quarters three different times in about a week, occupying at first quarters near the plaza, in the heart of the city; then at the western entrance; then at the extreme east. On one occasion General Worth had the troops in line, under arms, all day, with three days' cooked rations in their haversacks. He galloped from one command to another proclaiming the near proximity of Santa Anna with an army vastly superior to his own. General Scott arrived upon the scene the latter part of the month, and nothing more was heard of Santa Anna and his myriads. There were, of course, bodies of mounted Mexicans hovering around to watch our movements and to pick up stragglers, or small bodies of troops, if they ventured too far out. These always withdrew on the approach of any considerable number of our soldiers. After the arrival of General Scott I was sent, as quartermaster, with a large train of wagons, back two days' march at least, to procure forage. We had less than a thousand men as escort, and never thought of danger. We procured full loads for our entire train at two plantations, which could easily have furnished as much more.

There had been great delay in obtaining the authority of Congress for the raising of the troops asked for by the administration. A bill was before the National Legislature from early in the session of 1846-7, authorizing the creation of ten additional regiments for the war to be attached to the regular army, but it was the middle of February before it became a law. Appointments of commissioned officers had then to be made; men had to be enlisted, the regiments equipped and the whole transported to Mexico. It was August before General Scott received reinforcement sufficient to warrant an advance. His moving column, not even now more than ten thousand strong, was in four divisions, commanded by Generals Twiggs, Worth, Pillow and Quitman. There was also a cavalry corps under General Harney, composed of detachments of the 1st, 2d, and 3d dragoons. The advance commenced on the 7th of August with Twiggs's division in front. The remaining three divisions followed, with an interval of a day between. The marches were short, to make concentration easier in case of attack.

I had now been in battle with the two leading commanders conducting armies in a foreign land. The contrast between the two was very marked. General Taylor never wore uniform, but dressed himself entirely for comfort. He moved about the field in which he was operating to see through his own eyes the situation. Often he would be without staff officers, and when he was accompanied by them there was no prescribed order in which they followed. He was very much given to sit his horse side-ways — with both feet on one side — particularly on the battlefield. General Scott was the reverse in all these particulars. He always wore all the uniform prescribed or allowed by law when he inspected his lines; word would be sent to all division and brigade commanders in advance, notifying them of the hour when the commanding general might be expected. This was done so that all the army might be under arms to salute their chief as he passed. On these occasions he wore his dress uniform, cocked hat, aiguillettes, saber and spurs. His staff proper, besides all officers constructively on his staff — engineers, inspectors, quartermasters, etc., that could be spared — followed, also in uniform and in prescribed order. Orders were prepared with great care and evidently with the view that they should be a history of what followed.

In their modes of expressing thought, these two generals contrasted quite as strongly as in their other characteristics. General Scott was precise in language, cultivated a style peculiarly his own; was proud of his rhetoric; not averse to speaking of himself, often in the third person, and he could bestow praise upon the person he was talking about without the least embarrassment. Taylor was not a conversationalist, but on paper he could put his meaning so plainly that there could be no mistaking it. He knew how to express what he wanted to say in the fewest well-chosen words, but would not sacrifice meaning to the construction of high-sounding sentences. But with their opposite characteristics both were great and successful soldiers; both were true, patriotic and upright in all their dealings. Both were pleasant to serve under — Taylor was pleasant to serve with. Scott saw more through the eyes of his staff officers than through his own. His plans were deliberately prepared, and fully expressed in orders. Taylor saw for himself, and gave orders to meet the emergency without reference to how they would read in history.

Chapter XI

ADVANCE ON THE CITY OF MEXICO — BATTLE OF CONTRERAS — ASSAULT AT CHURUBUSCO — NEGOTIATIONS FOR PEACE — BATTLE OF MOLINO DEL REY — STORMING OF CHAPULTEPEC — SAN COSME — EVACUATION OF THE CITY — HALLS OF THE MONTEZUMAS

*T*he route followed by the army from Puebla to the City of Mexico was over Rio Frio mountain, the road leading over which, at the highest point, is about eleven thousand feet above tide water. The pass through this mountain might have been easily defended, but it was not; and the advanced division reached the summit in three days after leaving Puebla. The City of Mexico lies west of Rio Frio mountain, on a plain backed by another mountain six miles farther west, with others still nearer on the north and south. Between the western base of Rio Frio and the City of Mexico there are three lakes, Chalco and Xochimilco on the left and Texcoco on the right, extending to the east end of the City of Mexico. Chalco and Texcoco are divided by a narrow strip of land over which the direct road to the city runs. Xochimilco is also to the left of the road, but at a considerable distance south of it, and is connected with Lake Chalco by a narrow channel. There is a high rocky mound, called El Penon, on the right of the road, springing up from the low flat ground dividing the lakes. This mound was strengthened by entrenchments at its base and summit, and rendered a direct attack impracticable.

Scott's army was rapidly concentrated about Ayotla and other points near the eastern end of Lake Chalco. Reconnaissances were made up to within gun-shot of El Penon, while engineers were seeking a route by the south side of Lake Chalco to flank the city, and come upon it from the south and southwest. A way was found around the lake, and by the 18th of August troops were in St. Augustin Tlalpam, a town about eleven miles due south from the plaza of the capital. Between St. Augustin Tlalpam and the city lie the hacienda of San Antonio and the village of Churubusco, and southwest of them is Contreras. All these points, except St. Augustin Tlalpam, were entrenched and strongly garrisoned. Contreras is situated on the side of a mountain, near its base, where volcanic rocks are piled in great confusion, reaching nearly to San Antonio. This made the approach to the city from the south very difficult.

The brigade to which I was attached — Garland's, of Worth's division — was sent to confront San Antonio, two or three miles from St. Augustin Tlalpam, on the road to Churubusco and the City of Mexico. The ground on which San Antonio stands is completely in the valley, and the surface of the land is only a little above the level of the lakes, and, except to the southwest, it was cut up by deep ditches filled with water. To the southwest is the Pedregal — the volcanic rock before spoken of — over which cavalry or artillery could not be passed, and infantry would make but poor progress if confronted by an enemy. From the position occupied by Garland's brigade, therefore, no movement could be made against the defenses of San Antonio except to the front, and by a narrow causeway, over perfectly level ground, every inch of which was commanded by the enemy's artillery and infantry. If Contreras, some three miles west and south, should fall into our hands, troops from there could move to the right flank of all the positions held by the enemy between us and the city. Under these circumstances General Scott directed the holding of the front of the enemy without making an attack until further orders.

On the 18th of August, the day of reaching San Augustin Tlalpam, Garland's brigade secured a position within easy range of the advanced entrenchments of San Antonio, but where his troops were protected by an artificial embankment that had been thrown up for some other purpose than defense. General Scott at once set his engineers reconnoitering the works about Contreras, and on the 19th movements were commenced to get troops into positions from which an assault could be made upon the force occupying that place. The Pedregal on the north and northeast, and the mountain on the south, made the passage by either flank of the enemy's defenses difficult, for their work stood exactly between those natural bulwarks; but a road was completed during the day and night of the 19th, and troops were got to the north and west of the enemy.

This affair, like that of Cerro Gordo, was an engagement in which the officers of the engineer corps won special distinction. In fact, in both cases, tasks which seemed difficult at first sight were made easier for the troops that had to execute them than they would have been on an ordinary field. The very strength of each of these positions was, by the skill of the engineers, converted into a defense for the assaulting parties while securing their positions for final attack. All the troops with General Scott in the valley of Mexico, except a part of the division of General Quitman at San Augustin Tlalpam and the brigade of Garland (Worth's division) at San Antonio, were engaged at the battle of Contreras, or were on their way, in obedience to the orders of their chief, to reinforce those who were engaged. The assault was made on the morning of the 20th, and in less than half an hour from the sound of the advance the position was in our hands, with many prisoners and large quantities of ordnance and other stores. The brigade commanded by General Riley was from its position the most conspicuous in the final assault, but all did well, volunteers and regulars.

From the point occupied by Garland's brigade we could see the progress made at Contreras and the movement of troops toward the flank and rear of the enemy opposing us. The Mexicans all the way back to the city could see the same thing, and their conduct showed plainly that they did not enjoy the sight. We moved out at once, and found them gone from our immediate front. Clarke's brigade of Worth's division now moved west over the point of the Pedregal, and after having passed to the north sufficiently to clear San Antonio, turned east and got on the causeway leading to Churubusco and the City of Mexico. When he approached Churubusco his left, under Colonel Hoffman, attacked a tête-de-pont at that place and brought on an engagement. About an hour after, Garland was ordered to advance directly along the causeway, and got up in time to take part in the engagement. San Antonio was found evacuated, the evacuation having probably taken place immediately upon the enemy seeing the stars and stripes waving over Contreras.

The troops that had been engaged at Contreras, and even then on their way to that battlefield, were moved by a causeway west of, and parallel to the one by way of San Antonio and Churubusco. It was expected by the commanding general that these troops would move north sufficiently far to flank the enemy out of his position at Churubusco, before turning east to reach the San Antonio road, but they did not succeed in this, and Churubusco proved to be about the severest battle fought in the valley of Mexico. General Scott coming upon the battlefield about this juncture, ordered two brigades, under Shields, to move north and turn the right of the enemy. This Shields did, but not without hard fighting and heavy loss. The enemy finally gave way, leaving in our hands prisoners, artillery and small arms. The balance of the causeway held by the enemy, up to the very gates of the city, fell in like manner. I recollect at this place that some of the gunners who had stood their ground, were deserters from General Taylor's army on the Rio Grande.

Both the strategy and tactics displayed by General Scott in these various engagements of the 20th of August, 1847, were faultless as I look upon them now, after the lapse of so many years. As before stated, the work of the engineer officers who made the reconnaissances and led the different commands to their destinations, was so perfect that the chief was able to give his orders to his various subordinates with all the precision he could use on an ordinary march. I mean, up to the points from which the attack was to commence. After that point is reached the enemy often induces a change of orders not before contemplated. The enemy outside the city outnumbered our soldiery quite three to one, but they had become so demoralized by the succession of defeats this day, that the City of Mexico could have been entered without much further bloodshed. In fact, Captain Philip Kearney — afterwards a general in the war of the rebellion — rode with a squadron of cavalry to the very gates of the city, and would no doubt have entered with his little force, only at that point he was badly wounded, as were several of his officers. He had not heard the call for a halt.

General Franklin Pierce had joined the army in Mexico, at Puebla, a short time before the advance upon the capital commenced. He had consequently not been in any of the engagements of the war up to the battle of Contreras. By an unfortunate fall of his horse on the afternoon of the 19th he was painfully injured. The next day, when his brigade, with the other troops engaged on the same field, was ordered against the flank and rear of the enemy guarding the different points of the road from San Augustin Tlalpam to the city, General Pierce attempted to accompany them. He was not sufficiently recovered to do so, and fainted. This circumstance gave rise to exceedingly unfair and unjust criticisms of him when he became a candidate for the Presidency. Whatever General Pierce's qualifications may have been for the Presidency, he was a gentleman and a man of courage. I was not a supporter of him politically, but I knew him more intimately than I did any other of the volunteer generals.

General Scott abstained from entering the city at this time, because Mr. Nicholas P. Trist, the commissioner on the part of the United States to negotiate a treaty of peace with Mexico, was with the army, and either he or General Scott thought — probably both of them — that a treaty would be more possible while the Mexican government was in possession of the capital than if it was scattered and the capital in the hands of an invader. Be this as it may, we did not enter at that time. The army took up positions along the slopes of the mountains south of the city, as far west as Tacubaya. Negotiations were at once entered into with Santa Anna, who was then practically *the government* and the immediate commander of all the troops engaged in defense of the country. A truce was signed which denied to either party the right to strengthen its position, or to receive reinforcements during the continuance of the armistices, but authorized General Scott to draw supplies for his army from the city in the meantime.

Negotiations were commenced at once and were kept up vigorously between Mr. Trist and the commissioners appointed on the part of Mexico, until the 2d of September. At that time Mr. Trist handed in his ultimatum. Texas was to be given up absolutely by Mexico, and New Mexico and California ceded to the United States for a stipulated sum to be afterwards determined. I do not suppose Mr. Trist had any discretion whatever in regard to boundaries. The war was one of conquest, in the interest of an institution, and the probabilities are that private instructions were for the acquisition of territory out of which new States might be carved. At all events the Mexicans felt so outraged at the terms proposed that they commenced preparations for defense, without giving notice of the termination of the armistice. The terms of the truce had been violated before, when teams had been sent into the city to bring out supplies for the army. The first train entering the city was very severely threatened by a mob. This, however, was apologized for by the authorities and all responsibility for it denied; and thereafter, to avoid exciting the Mexican people and soldiery, our teams with their escorts were sent in at night, when the troops were in barracks and the citizens in bed. The circumstance was overlooked and negotiations continued. As soon as the news reached General Scott of the second violation of the armistice, about the 4th of September, he wrote a vigorous note to President Santa Anna, calling his attention to it, and, receiving an unsatisfactory reply, declared the armistice at an end.

General Scott, with Worth's division, was now occupying Tacubaya, a village some four miles southwest of the City of Mexico, and extending from the base up the mountainside for the distance of half a mile. More than a mile west, and also a little above the plain, stands Molino del Rey. The mill is a long stone structure, one story high and several hundred feet in length. At the period of which I speak General Scott supposed a portion of the mill to be used as a foundry for the casting of guns. This, however, proved to be a mistake. It was valuable to the Mexicans because of the quantity of grain it contained. The building is flat roofed, and a line of sand-bags over the outer walls rendered the top quite a formidable defense for infantry. Chapultepec is a mound springing up from the plain to the height of probably three hundred feet, and almost in a direct line between Molino del Rey and the western part of the city. It was fortified both on the top and on the rocky and precipitous sides.

The City of Mexico is supplied with water by two aqueducts, resting on strong stone arches. One of these aqueducts draws its supply of water from a mountain stream coming into it at or near Molino del Rey, and runs north close to the west base of Chapultepec; thence along the center of a wide road, until it reaches the road running east into the city by the Garita San Cosme; from which point the aqueduct and road both run east to the city. The second aqueduct starts from the east base of Chapultepec, where it is fed by a spring, and runs northeast to the city. This aqueduct, like the other, runs in the middle of a broad road-way, thus leaving a space on each side. The arches supporting the aqueduct afforded protection for advancing troops as well as to those engaged defensively. At points on the San Cosme road parapets were thrown across, with an embrasure for a single piece of artillery in each. At the point where both road and aqueduct turn at right angles from north to east, there was not only one of these parapets supplied by one gun and infantry supports, but the houses to the north of the San Cosme road, facing south and commanding a view of the road back to Chapultepec, were covered with infantry, protected by parapets made of sandbags. The roads leading to garitas (the gates) San Cosme and Belen, by which these aqueducts enter the city, were strongly entrenched. Deep, wide ditches, filled with water, lined the sides of both roads. Such were the defenses of the City of Mexico in September, 1847, on the routes over which General Scott entered.

Prior to the Mexican war General Scott had been very partial to General Worth — indeed he continued so up to the close of hostilities — but, for some reason, Worth had become estranged from his chief. Scott evidently took this coldness somewhat to heart. He did not retaliate, however, but on the contrary showed every disposition to appease his subordinate. It was understood at the time that he gave Worth authority to plan and execute the battle of Molino del Rey without dictation or interference from anyone, for the very purpose of restoring their former relations. The effort failed, and the two generals remained ever after cold and indifferent towards each other, if not actually hostile.

The battle of Molino del Rey was fought on the 8th of September. The night of the 7th, Worth sent for his brigade and regimental commanders, with their staffs, to come to his quarters to receive instructions for the morrow. These orders contemplated a movement up to within striking distance of the Mills before daylight. The engineers had reconnoitered the ground as well as possible, and had acquired all the information necessary to base proper orders both for approach and attack.

By daylight on the morning of the 8th, the troops to be engaged at Molino were all at the places designated. The ground in front of the Mills, to the south, was commanded by the artillery from the summit of Chapultepec as well as by the lighter batteries at hand; but a charge was made, and soon all was over. Worth's troops entered the Mills by every door, and the enemy beat a hasty retreat back to Chapultepec. Had this victory been followed up promptly, no doubt Americans and Mexicans would have gone over the defenses of Chapultepec so near together that the place would have fallen into our hands without further loss. The defenders of the works could not have fired upon us without endangering their own men. This was not done, and five days later more valuable lives were sacrificed to carry works which had been so nearly in our possession on the 8th. I do not criticize the failure to capture Chapultepec at this time. The result that followed the first assault could not possibly have been foreseen, and to profit by the unexpected advantage, the commanding general must have been on the spot and given the necessary instructions at the moment, or the troops must have kept on without orders. It is always, however, in order to follow a retreating foe, unless stopped or otherwise directed. The loss on our side at Molino del Rey was severe for the numbers engaged. It was especially so among commissioned officers.

I was with the earliest of the troops to enter the Mills. In passing through to the north side, looking towards Chapultepec, I happened to notice that there were armed Mexicans still on top of the building, only a few feet from many of our men. Not seeing any stairway or ladder reaching to the top of the building, I took a few soldiers, and had a cart that happened to be standing near brought up, and, placing the shafts against the wall and chocking the wheels so that the cart could not back, used the shafts as a sort of ladder extending to within three or four feet of the top. By this I climbed to the roof of the building, followed by a few men, but found a private soldier had preceded me by some other way. There were still quite a number of Mexicans on the roof, among them a major and five or six officers of lower grades, who had not succeeded in getting away before our troops occupied the building. They still had their arms, while the soldier before mentioned was walking as sentry, guarding the prisoners he had *surrounded,* all by himself. I halted the sentinel, received the swords from the commissioned officers, and proceeded, with the assistance of the soldiers now with me, to disable the muskets by striking them against the edge of the wall, and throw them to the ground below.

Molino del Rey was now captured, and the troops engaged, with the exception of an appropriate guard over the captured position and property, were marched back to their quarters in Tacubaya. The engagement did not last many minutes, but the killed and wounded were numerous for the number of troops engaged.

During the night of the 11th batteries were established which could play upon the fortifications of Chapultepec. The bombardment commenced early on the morning of the 12th, but there was no further engagement during this day than that of the artillery. General Scott assigned the capture of Chapultepec to General Pillow, but did not leave the details to his judgment. Two assaulting columns, two hundred and fifty men each, composed of volunteers for the occasion, were formed. They were commanded by Captains McKinzie and Casey respectively. The assault was successful, but bloody.

In later years, if not at the time, the battles of Molino del Rey and Chapultepec have seemed to me to have been wholly unnecessary. When the assaults upon the garitas of San Cosme and Belen were determined upon, the road running east to the former gate could have been reached easily, without an engagement, by moving along south of the Mills until west of them sufficiently far to be out of range, thence north to the road above mentioned; or, if desirable to keep the two attacking columns nearer together, the troops could have been turned east so as to come on the aqueduct road out of range of the guns from Chapultepec. In like manner, the troops designated to act against Belen could have kept east of Chapultepec, out of range, and come on to the aqueduct, also out of range of Chapultepec. Molino del Rey and Chapultepec would both have been necessarily evacuated if this course had been pursued, for they would have been turned.

General Quitman, a volunteer from the State of Mississippi, who stood well with the army both as a soldier and as a man, commanded the column acting against Belen. General Worth commanded the column against San Cosme. When Chapultepec fell the advance commenced along the two aqueduct roads. I was on the road to San Cosme, and witnessed most that took place on that route. When opposition was encountered our troops sheltered themselves by keeping under the arches supporting the aqueduct, advancing an arch at a time. We encountered no serious obstruction until within gun-shot of the point where the road we were on intersects that running east to the city, the point where the aqueduct turns at a right angle. I have described the defenses of this position before. There were but three commissioned officers besides myself, that I can now call to mind, with the advance when the above position was reached. One of these officers was a Lieutenant Semmes, of the Marine Corps. I think Captain Gore, and Lieutenant Judah, of the 4th infantry, were the others. Our progress was stopped for the time by the single piece of artillery at the angle of the roads and the infantry occupying the house-tops back from it.

West of the road from where we were, stood a house occupying the southwest angle made by the San Cosme road and the road we were moving upon. A stone wall ran from the house along each of these roads for a considerable distance and thence back until it joined, enclosing quite a yard about the house. I watched my opportunity and skipped across the road and behind the south wall. Proceeding cautiously to the west corner of the enclosure, I peeped around and seeing nobody, continued, still cautiously, until the road running east and west was reached. I then returned to the troops, and called for volunteers. All that were close to me, or that heard me, about a dozen, offered their services. Commanding them to carry their arms at a trail, I watched our opportunity and got them across the road and under cover of the wall beyond, before the enemy had a shot at us. Our men under cover of the arches kept a close watch on the entrenchments that crossed our path and the house-tops beyond, and whenever a head showed itself above the parapets they would fire at it. Our crossing was thus made practicable without loss.

When we reached a safe position I instructed my little command again to carry their arms at a trail, not to fire at the enemy until they were ordered, and to move very cautiously following me until the San Cosme road was reached; we would then be on the flank of the men serving the gun on the road, and with no obstruction between us and them. When we reached the southwest corner of the enclosure before described, I saw some United States troops pushing north through a shallow ditch near by, who had come up since my reconnaissance. This was the company of Captain Horace Brooks, of the artillery, acting as infantry. I explained to Brooks briefly what I had discovered and what I was about to do. He said, as I knew the ground and he did not, I might go on and he would follow. As soon as we got on the road leading to the city the troops serving the gun on the parapet retreated, and those on the house-tops near by followed; our men went after them in such close pursuit — the troops we had left under the arches joining — that a second line across the road, about half-way between the first and the garita, was carried. No reinforcements had yet come up except Brooks's company, and the position we had taken was too advanced to be held by so small a force. It was given up, but retaken later in the day, with some loss.

Worth's command gradually advanced to the front now open to it. Later in the day in reconnoitering I found a church off to the south of the road, which looked to me as if the belfry would command the ground back of the garita San Cosme. I got an officer of the voltigeurs, with a mountain howitzer and men to work it, to go with me. The road being in possession of the enemy, we had to take the field to the south to reach the church. This took us over several ditches breast deep in water and grown up with water plants. These ditches, however, were not over eight or ten feet in width. The howitzer was taken to pieces and carried by the men to its destination. When I knocked for admission a priest came to the door who, while extremely polite, declined to admit us. With the little Spanish then at my command, I explained to him that he might save property by opening the door, and he certainly would save himself from becoming a prisoner, for a time at least; and besides, I intended to go in whether he consented or not. He began to see his duty in the same light that I did, and opened the door, though he did not look as if it gave him special pleasure to do so. The gun was carried to the belfry and put together. We were not more than two or three hundred yards from San Cosme. The shots from our little gun dropped in upon the enemy and created great confusion. Why they did not send out a small party and capture us, I do not know. We had no infantry or other defenses besides our one gun.

The effect of this gun upon the troops about the gate of the city was so marked that General Worth saw it from his position.* He was so pleased that he sent a staff officer, Lieutenant Pemberton — later Lieutenant-General commanding the defenses of Vicksburg — to bring me to him. He expressed his gratification at the services the howitzer in the church steeple was doing, saying that every shot was effective, and ordered a captain of voltigeurs to report to me with another howitzer to be placed along with the one already rendering so much service. I could not tell the General that there was not room enough in the steeple for another gun, because he probably would have looked upon such a statement as a contradiction from a second lieutenant. I took the captain with me, but did not use his gun.

The night of the 13th of September was spent by the troops under General Worth in the houses near San Cosme, and in line confronting the general line of the enemy across to Belen. The troops that I was with were in the houses north of the road leading into the city, and were engaged during the night in cutting passage-ways from one house to another towards the town. During the night Santa Anna, with his army — except the deserters — left the city. He liberated all the convicts confined in the town, hoping, no doubt, that they would inflict upon us some injury before daylight; but several hours after Santa Anna was out of the way, the city authorities sent a delegation to General Scott to ask — if not demand — an armistice, respecting church property, the rights of citizens and the supremacy of the city government in the management of municipal affairs. General Scott declined to trammel himself with conditions, but gave assurances that those who chose to remain within our lines would be protected so long as they behaved themselves properly.

General Quitman had advanced along his line very successfully on the 13th, so that at night his command occupied nearly the same position at Belen that Worth's troops did about San Cosme. After the interview above related between General Scott and the city council, orders were issued for the cautious entry of both columns in the morning. The troops under Worth were to stop at the Alameda, a park near the west end of the city. Quitman was to go directly to the Plaza, and take possession of the Palace — a mass of buildings on the east side in which Congress has its sessions, the national courts are held, the

---

* Mentioned in the reports of Major Lee, Colonel Garland and General Worth. — PUBLISHERS.

public offices are all located, the President resides, and much room is left for museums, receptions, etc. This is the building generally designated as the "Halls of the Montezumas."

Chapter XII

PROMOTION TO FIRST LIEUTENANT — CAPTURE OF THE CITY OF MEXICO — THE ARMY — MEXICAN SOLDIERS — PEACE NEGOTIATIONS

O n entering the city the troops were fired upon by the released convicts, and possibly by deserters and hostile citizens. The streets were deserted, and the place presented the appearance of a "city of the dead," except for this firing by unseen persons from house-tops, windows, and around corners. In this firing the lieutenant-colonel of my regiment, Garland, was badly wounded, Lieutenant Sidney Smith, of the 4th infantry, was also wounded mortally. He died a few days after, and by his death I was promoted to the grade of first lieutenant.* I had gone

---

* *Note.* — It had been a favorite idea with General Scott for a great many years before the Mexican war to have established in the United States a soldiers' home, patterned after something of the kind abroad, particularly, I believe, in France. He recommended this uniformly, or at least frequently, in his annual reports to the Secretary of War, but never got any hearing. Now, as he had conquered the state, he made assessments upon the different large towns and cities occupied by our troops, in proportion to their capacity to pay, and appointed officers to receive the money. In addition to the sum thus realized he had derived, through capture at Cerro Gordo, sales of captured government tobacco, etc., sums which swelled the fund to a total of about $220,000. Portions of this fund were distributed among the rank and file, given to the wounded in hospital, or applied in other ways, leaving a balance of some $118,000 remaining unapplied at the close of the war. After the war was over and the troops all home, General Scott applied to have this money, which had never been turned into the Treasury of the United States, expended in establishing such homes as he had previously recommended. This fund was the foundation of the Soldiers' Home at Washington City, and also one at Harrodsburgh, Kentucky.

into the battle of Palo Alto in May, 1846, a second lieutenant, and I entered the city of Mexico sixteen months later with the same rank, after having been in all the engagements possible for any one man and in a regiment that lost more officers during the war than it ever had present at any one engagement. My regiment lost four commissioned officers, all senior to me, by steamboat explosions during the Mexican war. The Mexicans were not so discriminating. They sometimes picked off my juniors.

General Scott soon followed the troops into the city, in state. I wonder that he was not fired upon, but I believe he was not; at all events he was not hurt. He took quarters at first in the "Halls of the Montezumas," and from there issued his wise and discreet orders for the government of a conquered city, and for suppressing the hostile acts of liberated convicts already spoken of — orders which challenge the respect of all who study them. Lawlessness was soon suppressed, and the City of Mexico settled down into a quiet, law-abiding place. The people began to make their appearance upon the streets without fear of the invaders. Shortly afterwards the bulk of the troops were sent from the city to the villages at the foot of the mountains, four or five miles to the south and southwest.

Whether General Scott approved of the Mexican war and the manner in which it was brought about, I have no means of knowing. His orders to troops indicate only a soldierly spirit, with probably a little regard for the perpetuation of his own fame. On the other hand, General Taylor's, I think, indicate that he considered the administration accountable for the war, and felt no responsibility resting on himself further than for the faithful performance of his duties. Both generals deserve the commendations of their countrymen and to live in the grateful memory of this people to the latest generation.

Earlier in this narrative I have stated that the plain, reached after passing the mountains east of Perote, extends to the cities of Puebla and Mexico. The route traveled by the army before reaching Puebla, goes over a pass in a spur of mountain coming up from the south. This pass is very susceptible of defense by a smaller against a larger force. Again, the highest point of the road-bed between Vera Cruz and the City of Mexico is over Rio Frio mountain, which also might have been successfully defended by an inferior against a superior force. But by moving north of the mountains, and about thirty miles north of Puebla, both of these passes would have been avoided. The road from Perote to the City of Mexico, by this latter route, is as level as the prairies in our West.

The latter went into disuse many years ago. In fact it never had many soldiers in it, and was, I believe, finally sold.

Arriving due north from Puebla, troops could have been detached to take possession of that place, and then proceeding west with the rest of the army no mountain would have been encountered before reaching the City of Mexico. It is true this road would have brought troops in by Guadalupe — a town, church and detached spur of mountain about two miles north of the capital, all bearing the same general name — and at this point Lake Texcoco comes near to the mountain, which was fortified both at the base and on the sides: but troops could have passed north of the mountain and come in only a few miles to the northwest, and so flanked the position, as they actually did on the south.

It has always seemed to me that this northern route to the City of Mexico, would have been the better one to have taken. But my later experience has taught me two lessons: first, that things are seen plainer after the events have occurred; second, that the most confident critics are generally those who know the least about the matter criticized. I know just enough about the Mexican war to approve heartily of most of the generalship, but to differ with a little of it. It is natural that an important city like Puebla should not have been passed with contempt; it may be natural that the direct road to it should have been taken; but it could have been passed, its evacuation insured and possession acquired without danger of encountering the enemy in intricate mountain defiles. In this same way the City of Mexico could have been approached without any danger of opposition, except in the open field.

But General Scott's successes are an answer to all criticism. He invaded a populous country, penetrating two hundred and sixty miles into the interior, with a force at no time equal to one-half of that opposed to him; he was without a base; the enemy was always entrenched, always on the defensive; yet he won every battle, he captured the capital, and conquered the government. Credit is due to the troops engaged, it is true, but the plans and the strategy were the general's.

I had now made marches and been in battle under both General Scott and General Taylor. The former divided his force of 10,500 men into four columns, starting a day apart, in moving from Puebla to the capital of the nation, when it was known that an army more than twice as large as his own stood ready to resist his coming. The road was broad and the country open except in crossing the Rio Frio mountain. General Taylor pursued the same course in marching toward an enemy. He moved even in smaller bodies. I never thought at the time to doubt the infallibility of these two generals in all matters pertaining to their profession. I supposed they moved in small bodies because more men could not be passed over a single road on the same day with their artillery and necessary trains. Later I found the fallacy of this belief. The rebellion, which followed as a sequence to the Mexican war, never could have been suppressed if larger bodies of men could not have been moved at the same time than was the custom under Scott and Taylor.

The victories in Mexico were, in every instance, over vastly superior numbers. There were two reasons for this. Both General Scott and General Taylor had such armies as are not often got together. At the battles of Palo Alto and Resaca-de-la-Palma, General Taylor had a small army, but it was composed exclusively of regular troops, under the best of drill and discipline. Every officer, from the highest to the lowest, was educated in his profession, not at West Point necessarily, but in the camp, in garrison, and many of them in Indian wars. The rank and file were probably inferior, as material out of which to make an army, to the volunteers that participated in all the later battles of the war; but they were brave men, and then drill and discipline brought out all there was in them. A better army, man for man, probably never faced an enemy than the one commanded by General Taylor in the earliest two engagements of the Mexican war. The volunteers who followed were of better material, but without drill or discipline at the start. They were associated with so many disciplined men and professionally educated officers, that when they went into engagements it was with a confidence they would not have felt otherwise. They became soldiers themselves almost at once. All these conditions we would enjoy again in case of war.

The Mexican army of that day was hardly an organization. The private soldier was picked up from the lower class of the inhabitants when wanted; his consent was not asked; he was poorly clothed, worse fed, and seldom paid. He was turned adrift when no longer wanted. The officers of the lower grades were but little superior to the men. With all this I have seen as brave stands made by some of these men as I have ever seen made by soldiers. Now Mexico has a standing army larger than that of the United States. They have a military school modeled after West Point. Their officers are educated and, no doubt, generally brave. The Mexican war of 1846–8 would be an impossibility in this generation.

The Mexicans have shown a patriotism which it would be well if we would imitate in part, but with more regard to truth. They celebrate the anniversaries of Chapultepec and Molino del Rey as of very great victories. The anniversaries are recognized as national holidays. At these two battles, while the United States troops were victorious, it was at very great sacrifice of life compared with what the Mexicans suffered. The Mexicans, as on many other occasions, stood up as well as any troops ever did. The trouble seemed to be the lack of experience among the officers, which led them after a certain time to simply quit, without being particularly whipped, but because they had fought enough. Their authorities of the present day grow enthusiastic over their theme when telling of these victories, and speak with pride of the large sum of money they forced us to pay in the end. With us, now twenty years after the close of the most stupendous war ever known, we have writers — who profess devotion to the nation — engaged in trying to prove that the Union forces were not victorious; practically, they say, we were slashed around from Donelson to Vicksburg and to Chattanooga; and in the East from Gettysburg to Appomattox, when the physical rebellion gave out from sheer exhaustion. There is no difference in the amount of romance in the two stories.

I would not have the anniversaries of our victories celebrated, nor those of our defeats made fast days and spent in humiliation and prayer; but I would like to see truthful history written. Such history will do full credit to the courage, endurance and soldierly ability of the American citizen, no matter what section of the country he hailed from, or in what ranks he fought. The justice of the cause which in the end prevailed, will, I doubt not, come to be acknowledged by every citizen of the land, in time. For the present, and so long as there are living witnesses of the great war of sections, there will be people who will not be consoled for the loss of a cause which they believed to be holy. As time passes, people, even of the South, will begin to wonder how it was possible that their ancestors ever fought for or justified institutions which acknowledged the right of property in man.

After the fall of the capital and the dispersal of the government of Mexico, it looked very much as if military occupation of the country for a long time might be necessary. General Scott at once began the preparation of orders, regulations and laws in view of this contingency. He contemplated making the country pay all the expenses of the occupation, without the army becoming a perceptible burden upon the people. His plan was to levy a direct tax upon the separate states, and collect, at the ports left open to trade, a duty on all imports. From the beginning of the war private property had not been taken, either for the use of the army or of individuals, without full compensation. This policy was to be pursued. There were not troops enough in the valley of Mexico to occupy many points, but now that there was no organized army of the enemy of any size, reinforcements could be got from the Rio Grande, and there were also new volunteers arriving from time to time, all by way of Vera Cruz. Military possession was taken of Cuernavaca, fifty miles south of the City of Mexico; of Toluca, nearly as far west, and of Pachuca, a mining town of great importance, some sixty miles to the northeast. Vera Cruz, Jalapa, Orizaba, and Puebla were already in our possession.

Meanwhile the Mexican government had departed in the person of Santa Anna, and it looked doubtful for a time whether the United States commissioner, Mr. Trist, would find anybody to negotiate with. A temporary government, however, was soon established at Queretaro, and Trist began negotiations for a conclusion of the war. Before terms were finally agreed upon he was ordered back to Washington, but General Scott prevailed upon him to remain, as an arrangement had been so nearly reached, and the administration must approve his acts if he succeeded in making such a treaty as had been contemplated in his instructions. The treaty was finally signed the 2d of February, 1848, and accepted by the government at Washington. It is that known as the "Treaty of Guadalupe Hidalgo," and secured to the United States the Rio Grande as the boundary of Texas, and the whole territory then included in New Mexico and Upper California, for the sum of $15,000,000.

Soon after entering the city of Mexico, the opposition of Generals Pillow, Worth and Colonel Duncan to General Scott became very marked. Scott claimed that they had demanded of the President his removal. I do not know whether this is so or not, but I do know of their unconcealed hostility to their chief. At last he placed them in arrest, and preferred charges against them of insubordination and disrespect. This act brought on a crisis in the career of the general commanding. He had asserted from the beginning that the administration was hostile to him; that it had failed in its promises of men and war material; that the President himself had shown duplicity if not treachery in the endeavor to procure the appointment of Benton: and the administration now gave open evidence of its enmity. About the middle of February orders came convening a court of inquiry, composed of Brevet Brigadier-General Towson, the paymaster-general of the army, Brigadier-General Cushing and Colonel Belknap, to inquire into the conduct of the accused and the accuser, and shortly afterwards orders were received from Washington, relieving Scott of the command of the army in the field and assigning Major-General William O. Butler of Kentucky to the place. This order also released Pillow, Worth and Duncan from arrest.

If a change was to be made the selection of General Butler was agreeable to everyone concerned, so far as I remember to have heard expressions on the subject. There were many who regarded the treatment of General Scott as harsh and unjust. It is quite possible that the vanity of the General had led him to say and do things that afforded a plausible pretext to the administration for doing just what it did and what it had wanted to do from the start. The court tried the accuser quite as much as the accused. It was adjourned before completing its labors, to meet in Frederick, Maryland. General Scott left the country, and never after had more than the nominal command of the army until early in 1861. He certainly was not sustained in his efforts to maintain discipline in high places.

The efforts to kill off politically the two successful generals, made them both candidates for the Presidency. General Taylor was nominated in 1848, and was elected. Four years later General Scott received the nomination but was badly beaten, and the party nominating him died with his defeat.*

Chapter XIII

TREATY OF PEACE — MEXICAN BULL FIGHTS — REGIMENTAL QUARTERMASTER — TRIP TO POPOCATAPETL — TRIP TO THE CAVES OF MEXICO

*T*he treaty of peace between the two countries was signed by the commissioners of each side early in February, 1848. It took a considerable time for it to reach Washington, receive the approval of the administration, and be finally ratified by the Senate. It was naturally

---

* The Mexican war made three presidential candidates, Scott, Taylor and Pierce — and any number of aspirants for that high office. It made also governors of States, members of the cabinet, foreign ministers and other officers of high rank both in state and nation. The rebellion, which contained more war in a single day, at some critical periods, than the whole Mexican war in two years, has not been so fruitful of political results to those engaged on the Union side. On the other side, the side of the South, nearly every man who holds office of any sort whatever, either in the state or in the nation, was a Confederate soldier, but this is easily accounted for from the fact that the South was a military camp, and there were very few people of a suitable age to be in the army who were not in it.

supposed by the army that there would be no more fighting, and officers and men were of course anxious to get home, but knowing there must be delay they contented themselves as best they could. Every Sunday there was a bull fight for the amusement of those who would pay their fifty cents. I attended one of them — just one — not wishing to leave the country without having witnessed the national sport. The sight to me was sickening. I could not see how human beings could enjoy the sufferings of beasts, and often of men, as they seemed to do on these occasions.

At these sports there are usually from four to six bulls sacrificed. The audience occupies seats around the ring in which the exhibition is given, each seat but the foremost rising higher than the one in front, so that everyone can get a full view of the sport. When all is ready a bull is turned into the ring. Three or four men come in, mounted on the merest skeletons of horses blind or blind folded and so weak that they could not make a sudden turn with their riders without danger of falling down. The men are armed with spears having a point as sharp as a needle. Other men enter the arena on foot, armed with red flags and explosives about the size of a musket cartridge. To each of these explosives is fastened a barbed needle which serves the purpose of attaching them to the bull by running the needle into the skin. Before the animal is turned loose a lot of these explosives are attached to him. The pain from the pricking of the skin by the needles is exasperating; but when the explosions of the cartridges commence the animal becomes frantic. As he makes a lunge towards one horseman, another runs a spear into him. He turns towards his last tormentor when a man on foot holds out a red flag; the bull rushes for this and is allowed to take it on his horns. The flag drops and covers the eyes of the animal so that he is at a loss what to do; it is jerked from him and the torment is renewed. When the animal is worked into an uncontrollable frenzy, the horsemen withdraw, and the matadores — literally murderers — enter, armed with knives having blades twelve or eighteen inches long, and sharp. The trick is to dodge an attack from the animal and stab him to the heart as he passes. If these efforts fail the bull is finally lassoed, held fast and killed by driving a knife blade into the spinal column just back of the horns. He is then dragged out by horses or mules, another is let into the ring, and the same performance is renewed.

On the occasion when I was present one of the bulls was not turned aside by the attacks in the rear, the presentations of the red flag, etc., etc., but kept right on, and placing his horns under the flanks of a horse threw him and his rider to the ground with great force. The horse was killed and the rider lay prostrate as if dead. The bull was then lassoed and killed in the manner above described. Men came in and carried the dead man off in a litter. When the slaughtered bull and horse were dragged out, a fresh bull was turned into the ring. Conspicuous among the spectators was the man who had been carried out on a litter but a few minutes before. He was only dead so far as that performance went; but the corpse was so lively that it could not forego the chance of witnessing the discomfiture of some of his brethren who might not be so fortunate. There was a feeling of disgust manifested by the audience to find that he had come to life again. I confess that I felt sorry to see the cruelty to the bull and the horse. I did not stay for the conclusion of the performance; but while I did stay, there was not a bull killed in the prescribed way.

Bull fights are now prohibited in the Federal District — embracing a territory around the City of Mexico, somewhat larger than the District of Columbia — and they are not an institution in any part of the country. During one of my recent visits to Mexico, bull fights were got up in my honor at Puebla and at Pachuca. I was not notified in advance so as to be able to decline and thus prevent the performance; but in both cases I civilly declined to attend.

Another amusement of the people of Mexico of that day, and one which nearly all indulged in, male and female, old and young, priest and layman, was Monte playing. Regular feast weeks were held every year at what was then known as St. Augustin Tlalpam, eleven miles out of town. There were dealers to suit every class and condition of people. In many of the booths tlackos — the copper coin of the country, four of them making six and a quarter cents of our money — were piled up in great quantities, with some silver, to accommodate the people who could not bet more than a few pennies at a time. In other booths silver formed the bulk of the capital of the bank, with a few doubloons to be changed if there should be a run of luck against the bank. In some there was no coin except gold. Here the rich were said to bet away their entire estates in a single day. All this is stopped now.

For myself, I was kept somewhat busy during the winter of 1847-8. My regiment was stationed in Tacubaya. I was regimental quartermaster and commissary. General Scott had been unable to get clothing for the troops from the North. The men were becoming — well, they needed clothing. Material had to be purchased, such as could be obtained, and people employed to make it up into "Yankee uniforms." A quartermaster in the city was designated to attend to this special duty; but clothing was so much needed that it was seized as fast as made up. A regiment was glad to get a dozen suits at a time. I had to look after this matter for the 4th infantry. Then our regimental fund had run down and some of the musicians in the band had been without their extra pay for a number of months.

The regimental bands at that day were kept up partly by pay from the government, and partly by pay from the regimental fund. There was authority of law for enlisting a certain number of men as musicians. So many could receive the pay of non-commissioned officers of the various grades, and the remainder the pay of privates. This would not secure a band leader, nor good players on certain instruments. In garrison there are various ways of keeping up a regimental fund sufficient to give extra pay to musicians, establish libraries and ten-pin alleys, subscribe to magazines and furnish many extra comforts to the men. The best device for supplying the fund is to issue bread to the soldiers instead of flour. The ration used to be eighteen ounces per day of either flour or bread; and one hundred pounds of flour will make one hundred and forty pounds of bread. This saving was purchased by the commissary for the benefit of the fund. In the emergency the 4th infantry was laboring under, I rented a bakery in the city, hired bakers — Mexicans — bought fuel and whatever was necessary, and I also got a contract from the chief commissary of the army for baking a large amount of hard bread. In two months I made more money for the fund than my pay amounted to during the entire war. While stationed at Monterey I had relieved the post fund in the same way. There, however, was no profit except in the saving of flour by converting it into bread.

In the spring of 1848 a party of officers obtained leave to visit Popocatapetl, the highest volcano in America, and to take an escort. I went with the party, many of whom afterwards occupied conspicuous positions before the country. Of those who "went south," and attained high rank, there was Lieutenant Richard Anderson, who commanded a corps at Spottsylvania; Captain Sibley, a major-general, and, after the war, for a number of years in the employ of the Khedive of Egypt; Captain George Crittenden, a rebel general; S.B. Buckner, who surrendered Fort Donelson; and Mansfield Lovell, who commanded at New Orleans before that city fell into the hands of the National troops. Of those who remained on our side there were Captain Andrew Porter, Lieutenant C.P. Stone and Lieutenant Z.B. Tower. There were quite a number of other officers, whose names I cannot recollect.

At a little village (Ozumba) near the base of Popocatapetl, where we purposed to commence the ascent, we procured guides and two pack mules with forage for our horses. High up on the mountain there was a deserted house of one room, called the Vaqueria, which had been occupied years before by men in charge of cattle ranging on the mountain. The pasturage up there was very fine when we saw it, and there were still some cattle, descendants of the former domestic herd, which had now become wild. It was possible to go on horseback as far as the Vaqueria, though the road was somewhat hazardous in places. Sometimes it was very narrow with a yawning precipice on one side, hundreds of feet down to a roaring mountain torrent below, and almost perpendicular walls on the other side. At one of these places one of our mules loaded with two sacks of barley, one on each side, the two about as big as he was, struck his load against the mountainside and was precipitated to the bottom. The descent was steep but not perpendicular. The mule rolled over and over until the bottom was reached, and we supposed of course the poor animal was dashed to pieces. What was our surprise, not long after we had gone into bivouac, to see the lost mule, cargo and owner coming up the ascent. The load had protected the animal from serious injury; and his owner had gone after him and found a way back to the path leading up to the hut where we were to stay.

The night at the Vaqueria was one of the most unpleasant I ever knew. It was very cold and the rain fell in torrents. A little higher up the rain ceased and snow began. The wind blew with great velocity. The log-cabin we were in had lost the roof entirely on one side, and on the other it was hardly better then a sieve. There was little or no sleep that night. As soon as it was light the next morning, we started to make the ascent to the summit. The wind continued to blow with violence and the weather was still cloudy, but there was neither rain nor snow. The clouds, however, concealed from our view the country below us, except at times a momentary glimpse could be got through a clear space between them. The wind carried the loose snow around the mountainsides in such volumes as to make it almost impossible to stand up against it. We labored on and on, until it became evident that the top could not be reached before night, if at all in such a storm, and we concluded to return. The descent was easy and rapid, though dangerous, until we got below the snow line. At the cabin we mounted our horses, and by night were at Ozumba.

The fatigues of the day and the loss of sleep the night before drove us to bed early. Our beds consisted of a place on the dirt-floor with a blanket under us. Soon all were asleep; but long before morning first one and then another of our party began to cry out with excruciating pain in the eyes. Not one escaped it. By morning the eyes of half the party were so swollen that they were entirely closed. The others suffered pain equally. The feeling was about what might be expected from the prick of a sharp needle at a white heat. We remained in quarters until the afternoon bathing our eyes in cold water. This relieved us very much, and before night the pain had entirely left. The swelling, however, continued, and about half the party still had their eyes entirely closed; but we concluded to make a start back, those who could see a little leading the horses of those who could not see at all. We moved back to the village of Ameca Ameca, some six miles, and stopped again for the night. The next morning all were entirely well and free from pain. The weather was clear and Popocatapetl stood out in all its beauty, the top looking as if not a mile away, and inviting us to return. About half the party were anxious to try the ascent again, and concluded to do so. The remainder — I was with the remainder — concluded that we had got all the pleasure there was to be had out of mountain climbing, and that we would visit the great caves of Mexico, some ninety miles from where we then were, on the road to Acapulco.

The party that ascended the mountain the second time succeeded in reaching the crater at the top, with but little of the labor they encountered in their first attempt. Three of them — Anderson, Stone and Buckner — wrote accounts of their journey, which were published at the time. I made no notes of this excursion, and have read nothing about it since, but it seems to me that I can see the whole of it as vividly as if it were but yesterday. I have been back at Ameca Ameca, and the village beyond, twice in the last five years. The scene had not changed materially from my recollection of it.

The party which I was with moved south down the valley to the town of Cuantla, some forty miles from Ameca Ameca. The latter stands on the plain at the foot of Popocatapetl, at an elevation of about eight thousand feet above tide water. The slope down is gradual as the traveler moves south, but one would not judge that, in going to Cuantla, descent enough had been made to occasion a material change in the climate and productions of the soil; but such is the case. In the morning we left a temperate climate where the cereals and fruits are those common to the United States, we halted in the evening in a tropical climate where the orange and banana, the coffee and the sugar-cane were flourishing. We had been traveling, apparently, on a plain all day, but in the direction of the flow of water.

Soon after the capture of the City of Mexico an armistice had been agreed to, designating the limits beyond which troops of the respective armies were not to go during its continuance. Our party knew nothing about these limits. As we approached Cuantla bugles sounded the assembly, and soldiers rushed from the guard-house in the edge of the town towards us. Our party halted, and I tied a white pocket handkerchief to a stick and, using it as a flag of truce, proceeded on to the town. Captains Sibley and Porter followed a few hundred yards behind. I was detained at the guard-house until a messenger could be dispatched to

the quarters of the commanding general, who authorized that I should
be conducted to him. I had been with the general but a few minutes
when the two officers following announced themselves. The Mexican
general reminded us that it was a violation of the truce for us to be
there. However, as we had no special authority from our own commanding general, and as we knew nothing about the terms of the truce, we
were permitted to occupy a vacant house outside the guard for the night,
with the promise of a guide to put us on the road to Cuernavaca the
next morning.

Cuernavaca is a town west of Guantla. The country through which
we passed, between these two towns, is tropical in climate and productions and rich in scenery. At one point, about half-way between the two
places, the road goes over a low pass in the mountains in which there
is a very quaint old town, the inhabitants of which at that day were
nearly all full-blooded Indians. Very few of them even spoke Spanish.
The houses were built of stone and generally only one story high. The
streets were narrow, and had probably been paved before Cortez visited
the country. They had not been graded, but the paving had been done
on the natural surface. We had with us one vehicle, a cart, which was
probably the first wheeled vehicle that had ever passed through that
town.

On a hill overlooking this town stands the tomb of an ancient king;
and it was understood that the inhabitants venerated this tomb very
highly, as well as the memory of the ruler who was supposed to be buried
in it. We ascended the mountain and surveyed the tomb; but it showed
no particular marks of architectural taste, mechanical skill or advanced
civilization. The next day we went into Cuernavaca.

After a day's rest at Cuernavaca our party set out again on the journey
to the great caves of Mexico. We had proceeded but a few miles when
we were stopped, as before, by a guard and notified that the terms of
the existing armistice did not permit us to go further in that direction.
Upon convincing the guard that we were a mere party of pleasure seekers
desirous of visiting the great natural curiosities of the country which
we expected soon to leave, we were conducted to a large hacienda near
by, and directed to remain there until the commanding general of that
department could be communicated with and his decision obtained as
to whether we should be permitted to pursue our journey. The guard
promised to send a messenger at once, and expected a reply by night.
At night there was no response from the commanding general, but the
captain of the guard was sure he would have a reply by morning. Again
in the morning there was no reply. The second evening the same thing
happened, and finally we learned that the guard had sent no message

or messenger to the department commander. We determined therefore to go on unless stopped by a force sufficient to compel obedience.

After a few hours' travel we came to a town where a scene similar to the one at Cuantia occurred. The commanding officer sent a guide to conduct our party around the village and to put us upon our road again. This was the last interruption: that night we rested at a large coffee plantation, some eight miles from the cave we were on the way to visit. It must have been a Saturday night; the peons had been paid off, and spent part of the night in gambling away their scanty week's earnings. Their coin was principally copper, and I do not believe there was a man among them who had received as much as twenty-five cents in money. They were as much excited, however, as if they had been staking thousands. I recollect one poor fellow, who had lost his last tlacko, pulled off his shirt and, in the most excited manner, put that up on the turn of a card. Monte was the game played, the place out of doors, near the window of the room occupied by the officers of our party.

The next morning we were at the mouth of the cave at an early hour, provided with guides, candles and rockets. We explored to a distance of about three miles from the entrance, and found a succession of chambers of great dimensions and of great beauty when lit up with our rockets. Stalactites and stalagmites of all sizes were discovered. Some of the former were many feet in diameter and extended from ceiling to floor; some of the latter were but a few feet high from the floor; but the formation is going on constantly, and many centuries hence these stalagmites will extend to the ceiling and become complete columns. The stalagmites were all a little concave, and the cavities were filled with water. The water percolates through the roof, a drop at a time — often the drops several minutes apart — and more or less charged with mineral matter. Evaporation goes on slowly, leaving the mineral behind. This in time makes the immense columns, many of them thousands of tons in weight, which serve to support the roofs over the vast chambers. I recollect that at one point in the cave one of these columns is of such huge proportions that there is only a narrow passage left on either side of it. Some of our party became satisfied with their explorations before we had reached the point to which the guides were accustomed to take explorers, and started back without guides. Coming to the large column spoken of, they followed it entirely around, and commenced retracing their steps into the bowels of the mountain, without being aware of the fact. When the rest of us had completed our explorations, we started out with our guides, but had not gone far before we saw the torches of an approaching party. We could not conceive who these could be, for all of us had come in together, and there were none but ourselves at the entrance when we started in. Very soon we found it was our friends. It took them some time to conceive how they had got where they were. They were sure they had kept straight on for the mouth of the cave, and had gone about far enough to have reached it.

Chapter XIV

RETURN OF THE ARMY — MARRIAGE — ORDERED TO THE PACIFIC COAST — CROSSING THE ISTHMUS — ARRIVAL AT SAN FRANCISCO

*M*y experience in the Mexican war was of great advantage to me afterwards. Besides the many practical lessons it taught, the war brought nearly all the officers of the regular army together so as to make them personally acquainted. It also brought them in contact with volunteers, many of whom served in the war of the rebellion afterwards. Then, in my particular case, I had been at West Point at about the right time to meet most of the graduates who were of a suitable age at the breaking out of the rebellion to be trusted with large commands. Graduating in 1843, I was at the military academy from one to four years with all cadets who graduated between 1840 and 1846 — seven classes. These classes embraced more than fifty officers who afterwards became generals on one side or the other in the rebellion, many of them holding high commands. All the older officers, who became conspicuous in the rebellion, I had also served with and known in Mexico: Lee, J.E. Johnston, A.S. Johnston, Holmes, Hebert and a number of others on the Confederate side; McCall, Mansfield, Phil. Kearney and others on the National side. The acquaintance thus formed was of immense service to me in the war of the rebellion — I mean what I learned of the characters of those to whom I was afterwards opposed. I do not pretend to say that all movements, or even many of them, were made with special reference to the characteristics of the commander against whom they were directed. But my appreciation of my enemies was certainly affected

by this knowledge. The natural disposition of most people is to clothe
a commander of a large army whom they do not know, with almost
superhuman abilities. A large part of the National army, for instance,
and most of the press of the country, clothed General Lee with just such
qualities, but I had known him personally, and knew that he was mortal;
and it was just as well that I felt this.

The treaty of peace was at last ratified, and the evacuation of Mexico
by United States troops was ordered. Early in June the troops in the City
of Mexico began to move out. Many of them, including the brigade to
which I belonged, were assembled at Jalapa, above the vomito, to await
the arrival of transports at Vera Cruz: but with all this precaution my
regiment and others were in camp on the sand beach in a July sun, for
about a week before embarking, while the fever raged with great viru-
lence in Vera Cruz, not two miles away. I can call to mind only one
person, an officer, who died of the disease. My regiment was sent to
Pascagoula, Mississippi, to spend the summer. As soon as it was settled
in camp I obtained a leave of absence for four months and proceeded
to St. Louis. On the 22d of August, 1848, I was married to Miss Julia
Dent, the lady of whom I have before spoken. We visited my parents
and relations in Ohio, and, at the end of my leave, proceeded to my
post at Sackett's Harbor, New York. In April following I was ordered to
Detroit, Michigan, where two years were spent with but few important
incidents.

The present constitution of the State of Michigan was ratified during
this time. By the terms of one of its provisions, all citizens of the United
States residing within the State at the time of the ratification became
citizens of Michigan also. During my stay in Detroit there was an
election for city officers. Mr. Zachariah Chandler was the candidate of
the Whigs for the office of Mayor, and was elected, although the city
was then reckoned democratic. All the officers stationed there at the
time who offered their votes were permitted to cast them. I did not offer
mine, however, as I did not wish to consider myself a citizen of
Michigan. This was Mr. Chandler's first entry into politics, a career he
followed ever after with great success, and in which he died enjoying
the friendship, esteem and love of his countrymen.

In the spring of 1851 the garrison at Detroit was transferred to
Sackett's Harbor, and in the following spring the entire 4th infantry
was ordered to the Pacific Coast. It was decided that Mrs. Grant should
visit my parents at first for a few months, and then remain with her
own family at their St. Louis home until an opportunity offered of
sending for her. In the month of April the regiment was assembled at
Governor's Island, New York Harbor, and on the 5th of July eight

companies sailed for Aspinwall. We numbered a little over seven hundred persons, including the families of officers and soldiers. Passage was secured for us on the old steamer Ohio, commanded at the time by Captain Schenck, of the navy. It had not been determined, until a day or two before starting, that the 4th infantry should go by the Ohio; consequently, a complement of passengers had already been secured. The addition of over seven hundred to this list crowded the steamer most uncomfortably, especially for the tropics in July.

In eight days Aspinwall was reached. At that time the streets of the town were eight or ten inches under water, and foot passengers passed from place to place on raised foot-walks. July is at the height of the wet season, on the Isthmus. At intervals the rain would pour down in streams, followed in not many minutes by a blazing, tropical summer's sun. These alternate changes, from rain to sunshine, were continuous in the afternoons. I wondered how any person could live many months in Aspinwall, and wondered still more why anyone tried.

In the summer of 1852 the Panama railroad was completed only to the point where it now crosses the Chagres River. From there passengers were carried by boats to Gorgona, at which place they took mules for Panama, some twenty-five miles further. Those who traveled over the Isthmus in those days will remember that boats on the Chagres River were propelled by natives not inconveniently burdened with clothing. These boats carried thirty to forty passengers each. The crews consisted of six men to a boat, armed with long poles. There were planks wide enough for a man to walk on conveniently, running along the sides of each boat from end to end. The men would start from the bow, place one end of their poles against the river bottom, brace their shoulders against the other end, and then walk to the stern as rapidly as they could. In this way from a mile to a mile and a half an hour could be made, against the current of the river.

I, as regimental quartermaster, had charge of the public property and had also to look after the transportation. A contract had been entered into with the steamship company in New York for the transportation of the regiment to California, including the Isthmus transit. A certain amount of baggage was allowed per man, and saddle animals were to be furnished to commissioned officers and to all disabled persons. The regiment, with the exception of one company left as guards to the public property — camp and garrison equipage principally — and the soldiers with families, took boats, propelled as above described, for Gorgona. From this place they marched to Panama, and were soon comfortably on the steamer anchored in the bay, some three or four miles from the town. I, with one company of troops and all the soldiers with families, all the tents, mess chests and camp kettles, was sent to Cruces, a town a few miles higher up the Chagres River than Gorgona. There I found an impecunious American who had taken the contract to furnish transportation for the regiment at a stipulated price per hundred pounds for the freight and so much for each saddle animal. But when we reached Cruces there was not a mule, either for pack or saddle, in the place. The contractor promised that the animals should be on hand in the morning. In the morning he said that they were on the way from some imaginary place, and would arrive in the course of the day. This went on until I saw that he could not procure the animals at all at the price he had promised to furnish them for. The unusual number of passengers that had come over on the steamer, and the large amount of freight to pack, had created an unprecedented demand for mules. Some of the passengers paid as high as forty dollars for the use of a mule to ride twenty-five miles, when the mule would not have sold for ten dollars in that market at other times. Meanwhile the cholera had broken out, and men were dying every hour. To diminish the food for the disease, I permitted the company detailed with me to proceed to Panama. The captain and the doctors accompanied the men, and I was left alone with the sick and the soldiers who had families. The regiment at Panama was also affected with the disease; but there were better accommodations for the well on the steamer, and a hospital, for those taken with the disease, on an old hulk anchored a mile off. There were also hospital tents on shore on the island of Flamingo, which stands in the bay.

I was about a week at Cruces before transportation began to come in. About one-third of the people with me died, either at Cruces or on the way to Panama. There was no agent of the transportation company at Cruces to consult, or to take the responsibility of procuring transportation at a price which would secure it. I therefore myself dismissed the contractor and made a new contract with a native, at more than double the original price. Thus we finally reached Panama. The steamer, however, could not proceed until the cholera abated, and the regiment was detained still longer. Altogether, on the Isthmus and on the Pacific side, we were delayed six weeks. About one-seventh of those who left New York harbor with the 4th infantry on the 5th of July, now lie buried on the Isthmus of Panama or on Flamingo island in Panama Bay.

One amusing circumstance occurred while we were lying at anchor in Panama Bay. In the regiment there was a Lieutenant Slaughter who was very liable to sea-sickness. It almost made him sick to see the wave of a tablecloth when the servants were spreading it. Soon after his graduation, Slaughter was ordered to California and took passage by a sailing vessel going around Cape Horn. The vessel was seven months making the voyage, and Slaughter was sick every moment of the time, never more so than while lying at anchor after reaching his place of destination. On landing in California he found orders which had come by the Isthmus, notifying him of a mistake in his assignment; he should have been ordered to the northern lakes. He started back by the Isthmus route and was sick all the way. But when he arrived at the East he was again ordered to California, this time definitely, and at this date was making his third trip. He was as sick as ever, and had been so for more than a month while lying at anchor in the bay. I remember him well, seated with his elbows on the table in front of him, his chin between his hands, and looking the picture of despair. At last he broke out, "I wish I had taken my father's advice; he wanted me to go into the navy; if I had done so, I should not have had to go to sea so much." Poor Slaughter! it was his last sea voyage. He was killed by Indians in Oregon.

By the last of August the cholera had so abated that it was deemed safe to start. The disease did not break out again on the way to California, and we reached San Francisco early in September.

Chapter XV

SAN FRANCISCO — EARLY CALIFORNIA EXPERIENCES — LIFE ON THE PACIFIC COAST — PROMOTED CAPTAIN — FLUSH TIMES IN CALIFORNIA

San Francisco at that day was a lively place. Gold, or placer digging as it was called, was at its height. Steamers plied daily between San Francisco and both Stockton and Sacramento. Passengers and gold from the southern mines came by the Stockton boat; from the northern mines by Sacramento. In the evening when these boats arrived, Long Wharf — there was but one wharf in San Francisco in 1852 — was alive with people crowding to meet the miners as they came down to sell their "dust" and to "have a time." Of these some were runners for hotels, boarding houses or restaurants; others belonged to a class of impecunious adventurers, of good manners and good presence, who were ever on the alert to make the acquaintance of people with some ready means, in the hope of being asked to take a meal at a restaurant. Many were young men of good family, good education and gentlemanly instincts. Their parents had been able to support them during their minority, and to give them good educations, but not to maintain them afterwards. From 1849 to 1853 there was a rush of people to the Pacific coast, of the class described. All thought that fortunes were to be picked up, without effort, in the gold fields on the Pacific. Some realized more than their most sanguine expectations; but for one such there were hundreds disappointed, many of whom now fill unknown graves; others died wrecks of their former selves, and many, without a vicious instinct, became criminals and outcasts. Many of the real scenes in early California life exceed in strangeness and interest any of the mere products of the brain of the novelist.

Those early days in California brought out character. It was a long way off then, and the journey was expensive. The fortunate could go by Cape Horn or by the Isthmus of Panama; but the mass of pioneers crossed the plains with their ox-teams. This took an entire summer. They were very lucky when they got through with a yoke of worn-out cattle. All other means were exhausted in procuring the outfit on the Missouri River. The immigrant, on arriving, found himself a stranger, in a strange land, far from friends. Time pressed, for the little means that could be realized from the sale of what was left of the outfit would not support a man long at California prices. Many became discouraged. Others would take off their coats and look for a job, no matter what it might be. These succeeded as a rule. There were many young men who had studied professions before they went to California, and who had never done a day's manual labor in their lives, who took in the situation at once and went to work to make a start at anything they could get to do. Some supplied carpenters and masons with material — carrying plank, brick, or mortar, as the case might be; others drove stages, drays, or baggage wagons, until they could do better. More became discouraged early and spent their time looking up people who would "treat," or lounging about restaurants and gambling houses where free lunches were furnished daily. They were welcomed at these places because they often brought in miners who proved good customers.

My regiment spent a few weeks at Benicia barracks, and then was ordered to Fort Vancouver, on the Columbia River, then in Oregon Territory. During the winter of 1852–3 the territory was divided, all north of the Columbia River being taken from Oregon to make Washington Territory.

Prices for all kinds of supplies were so high on the Pacific coast from 1849 until at least 1853 — that it would have been impossible for officers of the army to exist upon their pay, if it had not been that authority was given them to purchase from the commissary such supplies as he kept, at New Orleans wholesale prices. A cook could not be hired for the pay of a captain. The cook could do better. At Benicia, in 1852, flour was 25 cents per pound; potatoes were 16 cents; beets, turnips and cabbage, 6 cents; onions, 37 1/2 cents; meat and other articles in proportion. In 1853 at Vancouver vegetables were a little lower. I with three other officers concluded that we would raise a crop for ourselves, and by selling the surplus realize something handsome. I bought a pair of horses that had crossed the plains that summer and were very poor. They recuperated rapidly, however, and proved a good team to break up the ground with. I performed all the labor of breaking up the ground while the other officers planted the potatoes. Our crop was enormous. Luckily for us the Columbia River rose to a great height from the melting of the snow in the mountains in June, and overflowed and killed most of our crop. This saved digging it up, for everybody on the Pacific coast seemed to have come to the conclusion at the same time that agriculture would be profitable. In 1853 more than three-quarters of the potatoes raised were permitted to rot in the ground, or had to be thrown away. The only potatoes we sold were to our own mess.

While I was stationed on the Pacific coast we were free from Indian wars. There were quite a number of remnants of tribes in the vicinity of Portland in Oregon, and of Fort Vancouver in Washington Territory. They had generally acquired some of the vices of civilization, but none of the virtues, except in individual cases. The Hudson's Bay Company had held the Northwest with their trading posts for many years before the United States was represented on the Pacific coast. They still retained posts along the Columbia River and one at Fort Vancouver, when I was there. Their treatment of the Indians had brought out the better qualities of the savages. Farming had been undertaken by the company to supply the Indians with bread and vegetables; they raised some cattle and horses; and they had now taught the Indians to do the labor of the farm and herd. They always compensated them for their labor, and always gave them goods of uniform quality and at uniform price.

Before the advent of the American, the medium of exchange between the Indian and the white man was pelts. Afterward it was silver coin. If an Indian received in the sale of a horse a fifty dollar gold piece, not an infrequent occurrence, the first thing he did was to exchange it for

American half dollars. These he could count. He would then commence his purchases, paying for each article separately, as he got it. He would not trust anyone to add up the bill and pay it all at once. At that day fifty dollar gold pieces, not the issue of the government, were common on the Pacific coast. They were called slugs.

The Indians, along the lower Columbia as far as the Cascades and on the lower Willamette, died off very fast during the year I spent in that section; for besides acquiring the vices of the white people they had acquired also their diseases. The measles and the smallpox were both amazingly fatal. In their wild state, before the appearance of the white man among them, the principal complaints they were subject to were those produced by long involuntary fasting, violent exercise in pursuit of game, and overeating. Instinct more than reason had taught them a remedy for these ills. It was the steam bath. Something like a bake-oven was built, large enough to admit a man lying down. Bushes were stuck in the ground in two rows, about six feet long and some two or three feet apart; other bushes connected the rows at one end. The tops of the bushes were drawn together to interlace, and confined in that position; the whole was then plastered over with wet clay until every opening was filled. Just inside the open end of the oven the floor was scooped out so as to make a hole that would hold a bucket or two of water. These ovens were always built on the banks of a stream, a big spring, or pool of water. When a patient required a bath, a fire was built near the oven and a pile of stones put upon it. The cavity at the front was then filled with water. When the stones were sufficiently heated, the patient would draw himself into the oven; a blanket would be thrown over the open end, and hot stones put into the water until the patient could stand it no longer. He was then withdrawn from his steam bath and doused into the cold stream near by. This treatment may have answered with the early ailments of the Indians. With the measles or smallpox it would kill every time.

During my year on the Columbia River, the smallpox exterminated one small remnant of a band of Indians entirely, and reduced others materially. I do not think there was a case of recovery among them, until the doctor with the Hudson Bay Company took the matter in hand and established a hospital. Nearly every case he treated recovered. I never, myself, saw the treatment described in the preceding paragraph, but have heard it described by persons who have witnessed it. The decimation among the Indians I knew of personally, and the hospital, established for their benefit, was a Hudson's Bay building not a stone's throw from my own quarters.

The death of Colonel Bliss, of the Adjutant General's department, which occurred July 5th, 1853, promoted me to the captaincy of a company then stationed at Humboldt Bay, California. The notice reached me in September of the same year, and I very soon started to join my new command. There was no way of reaching Humboldt at that time except to take passage on a San Francisco sailing vessel going after lumber. Red wood, a species of cedar, which on the Pacific coast takes the place filled by white pine in the East, then abounded on the banks of Humboldt Bay. There were extensive saw-mills engaged in preparing this lumber for the San Francisco market, and sailing vessels, used in getting it to market, furnished the only means of communication between Humboldt and the balance of the world.

I was obliged to remain in San Francisco for several days before I found a vessel. This gave me a good opportunity of comparing the San Francisco of 1852 with that of 1853. As before stated, there had been but one wharf in front of the city in 1852 — Long Wharf. In 1853 the town had grown out into the bay beyond what was the end of this wharf when I first saw it. Streets and houses had been built out on piles where the year before the largest vessels visiting the port lay at anchor or tied to the wharf. There was no filling under the streets or houses. San Francisco presented the same general appearance as the year before; that is, eating, drinking and gambling houses were conspicuous for their number and publicity. They were on the first floor, with doors wide open. At all hours of the day and night in walking the streets, the eye was regaled, on every block near the water front, by the sight of players at faro. Often broken places were found in the street, large enough to let a man down into the water below. I have but little doubt that many of the people who went to the Pacific coast in the early days of the gold excitement, and have never been heard from since, or who were heard from for a time and then ceased to write, found watery graves beneath the houses or streets built over San Francisco Bay.

Besides the gambling in cards there was gambling on a larger scale in city lots. These were sold "On Change," much as stocks are now sold on Wall Street. Cash, at time of purchase, was always paid by the broker; but the purchaser had only to put up his margin. He was charged at the rate of two or three percent a month on the difference, besides commissions. The sand hills, some of them almost inaccessible to foot-passengers, were surveyed off and mapped into fifty vara lots — a vara being a Spanish yard. These were sold at first at very low prices, but were sold and resold for higher prices until they went up to many thousands of dollars. The brokers did a fine business, and so did many such purchasers as were sharp enough to quit purchasing before the final crash came.

As the city grew, the sand hills back of the town furnished material for filling up the bay under the houses and streets, and still further out. The temporary houses, first built over the water in the harbor, soon gave way to more solid structures. The main business part of the city now is on solid ground, made where vessels of the largest class lay at anchor in the early days. I was in San Francisco again in 1854. Gambling houses had disappeared from public view. The city had become staid and orderly.

Chapter XVI

RESIGNATION — PRIVATE LIFE — LIFE AT GALENA — THE COMING CRISIS

My family, all this while, was at the East. It consisted now of a wife and two children. I saw no chance of supporting them on the Pacific coast out of my pay as an army officer. I concluded, therefore, to resign, and in March applied for a leave of absence until the end of the July following, tendering my resignation to take effect at the end of that time. I left the Pacific coast very much attached to it, and with the full expectation of making it my future home. That expectation and that hope remained uppermost in my mind until the Lieutenant-Generalcy bill was introduced into Congress in the winter of 1863-4. The passage of that bill, and my promotion, blasted my last hope of ever becoming a citizen of the further West.

In the late summer of 1854 I rejoined my family, to find in it a son whom I had never seen, born while I was on the Isthmus of Panama. I was now to commence, at the age of thirty-two, a new struggle for our support. My wife had a farm near St. Louis, to which we went, but I had no means to stock it. A house had to be built also. I worked very hard, never losing a day because of bad weather, and accomplished the object in a moderate way. If nothing else could be done I would load a cord of wood on a wagon and take it to the city for sale. I managed to keep along very well until 1858, when I was attacked by fever and ague. I had suffered very severely and for a long time from this disease, while a boy in Ohio. It lasted now over a year, and, while it did not keep me in the house, it did interfere greatly with the amount of work I was able to perform. In the fall of 1858 I sold out my stock, crops and farming utensils at auction, and gave up farming.

In the winter I established a partnership with Harry Boggs, a cousin of Mrs. Grant, in the real estate agency business. I spent that winter at St. Louis myself, but did not take my family into town until the spring. Our business might have become prosperous if I had been able to wait for it to grow. As it was, there was no more than one person could attend to, and not enough to support two families. While a citizen of St. Louis and engaged in the real estate agency business, I was a candidate for the office of county engineer, an office of respectability and emolument which would have been very acceptable to me at that time. The incumbent was appointed by the county court, which consisted of five members. My opponent had the advantage of birth over me (he was a citizen by adoption) and carried off the prize. I now withdrew from the co-partnership with Boggs, and, in May, 1860, removed to Galena, Illinois, and took a clerkship in my father's store.

While a citizen of Missouri, my first opportunity for casting a vote at a Presidential election occurred. I had been in the army from before attaining my majority and had thought but little about politics, although I was a Whig by education and a great admirer of Mr. Clay. But the Whig party had ceased to exist before I had an opportunity of exercising the privilege of casting a ballot; the Know-Nothing party had taken its place, but was on the wane; and the Republican party was in a chaotic state and had not yet received a name. It had no existence in the Slave States except at points on the borders next to Free States. In St. Louis City and County, what afterwards became the Republican party was known as the Free-Soil Democracy, led by the Honorable Frank P. Blair. Most of my neighbors had known me as an officer of the army with Whig proclivities. They had been on the same side, and, on the death of their party, many had become Know-Nothings, or members of the American party. There was a lodge near my new home, and I was invited to join it. I accepted the invitation; was initiated; attended a meeting just one week later, and never went to another afterwards.

I have no apologies to make for having been one week a member of the American party; for I still think native-born citizens of the United States should have as much protection, as many privileges in their native country, as those who voluntarily select it for a home. But all secret, oath-bound political parties are dangerous to any nation, no matter how

pure or how patriotic the motives and principles which first bring them
together. No political party can or ought to exist when one of its
corner-stones is opposition to freedom of thought and to the right to
worship God "according to the dictate of one's own conscience," or
according to the creed of any religious denomination whatever. Nevertheless, if a sect sets up its laws as binding above the State laws, wherever
the two come in conflict this claim must be resisted and suppressed at
whatever cost.

Up to the Mexican war there were a few out and out abolitionists,
men who carried their hostility to slavery into all elections, from those
for a justice of the peace up to the Presidency of the United States. They
were noisy but not numerous. But the great majority of people at the
North, where slavery did not exist, were opposed to the institution, and
looked upon its existence in any part of the country as unfortunate.
They did not hold the States where slavery existed responsible for it;
and believed that protection should be given to the right of property in
slaves until some satisfactory way could be reached to be rid of the
institution. Opposition to slavery was not a creed of either political
party. In some sections more anti-slavery men belonged to the Democratic party, and in others to the Whigs. But with the inauguration of
the Mexican war, in fact with the annexation of Texas, "the inevitable
conflict" commenced.

As the time for the Presidential election of 1856 — the first at which
I had the opportunity of voting — approached, party feeling began to
run high. The Republican party was regarded in the South and the
border States not only as opposed to the extension of slavery, but as
favoring the compulsory abolition of the institution without compensation to the owners. The most horrible visions seemed to present
themselves to the minds of people who, one would suppose, ought to
have known better. Many educated and, otherwise, sensible persons
appeared to believe that emancipation meant social equality. Treason to
the Government was openly advocated and was not rebuked. It was
evident to my mind that the election of a Republican President in 1856
meant the secession of all the Slave States, and rebellion. Under these
circumstances I preferred the success of a candidate whose election
would prevent or postpone secession, to seeing the country plunged into
a war the end of which no man could foretell. With a Democrat elected
by the unanimous vote of the Slave States, there could be no pretext for
secession for four years. I very much hoped that the passions of the
people would subside in that time, and the catastrophe be averted
altogether; if it was not, I believed the country would be better prepared
to receive the shock and to resist it. I therefore voted for James Buchanan

for President. Four years later the Republican party was successful in electing its candidate to the Presidency. The civilized world has learned the consequence. Four millions of human beings held as chattels have been liberated; the ballot has been given to them; the free schools of the country have been opened to their children. The nation still lives, and the people are just as free to avoid social intimacy with the blacks as ever they were, or as they are with white people.

While living in Galena I was nominally only a clerk supporting myself and family on a stipulated salary. In reality my position was different. My father had never lived in Galena himself, but had established my two brothers there, the one next younger than myself in charge of the business, assisted by the youngest. When I went there it was my father's intention to give up all connection with the business himself, and to establish his three sons in it: but the brother who had really built up the business was sinking with consumption, and it was not thought best to make any change while he was in this condition. He lived until September, 1861, when he succumbed to that insidious disease which always flatters its victims into the belief that they are growing better up to the close of life. A more honorable man never transacted business. In September, 1861, I was engaged in an employment which required all my attention elsewhere.

During the eleven months that I lived in Galena prior to the first call for volunteers, I had been strictly attentive to my business, and had made but few acquaintances other than customers and people engaged in the same line with myself. When the election took place in November, 1860, I had not been a resident of Illinois long enough to gain citizenship and could not, therefore, vote. I was really glad of this at the time, for my pledges would have compelled me to vote for Stephen A. Douglas, who had no possible chance of election. The contest was really between Mr. Breckinridge and Mr. Lincoln; between minority rule and rule by the majority. I wanted, as between these candidates, to see Mr. Lincoln elected. Excitement ran high during the canvass, and torch-light processions enlivened the scene in the generally quiet streets of Galena many nights during the campaign. I did not parade with either party, but occasionally met with the "wide awakes" — Republicans — in their rooms, and superintended their drill. It was evident, from the time of the Chicago nomination to the close of the canvass, that the election of the Republican candidate would be the signal for some of the Southern States to secede. I still had hopes that the four years which had elapsed since the first nomination of a Presidential candidate by a party distinctly opposed to slavery extension, had given time for the extreme pro-slavery sentiment to cool down; for the Southerners to think well before they took the awful leap which they had so vehemently threatened. But I was mistaken.

The Republican candidate was elected, and solid substantial people of the Northwest, and I presume the same order of people throughout the entire North, felt very serious, but determined, after this event. It was very much discussed whether the South would carry out its threat to secede and set up a separate government, the corner-stone of which should be, protection to the "Divine" institution of slavery. For there were people who believed in the "divinity" of human slavery, as there are now people who believe Mormonism and Polygamy to be ordained by the Most High. We forgive them for entertaining such notions, but forbid their practice. It was generally believed that there would be a flurry; that some of the extreme Southern States would go so far as to pass ordinances of secession. But the common impression was that this step was so plainly suicidal for the South, that the movement would not spread over much of the territory and would not last long.

Doubtless the founders of our government, the majority of them at least, regarded the confederation of the colonies as an experiment. Each colony considered itself a separate government; that the confederation was for mutual protection against a foreign foe, and the prevention of strife and war among themselves. If there had been a desire on the part of any single State to withdraw from the compact at any time while the number of States was limited to the original thirteen, I do not suppose there would have been any to contest the right, no matter how much the determination might have been regretted. The problem changed on the ratification of the Constitution by all the colonies; it changed still more when amendments were added; and if the right of any one State to withdraw continued to exist at all after the ratification of the Constitution, it certainly ceased on the formation of new States, at least so far as the new States themselves were concerned. It was never possessed at all by Florida or the States west of the Mississippi, all of which were purchased by the treasury of the entire nation. Texas and the territory brought into the Union in consequence of annexation, were purchased with both blood and treasure; and Texas, with a domain greater than that of any European state except Russia, was permitted to retain as state property all the public lands within its borders. It would have been ingratitude and injustice of the most flagrant sort for this State to withdraw from the Union after all that had been spent and done to introduce her; yet, if separation had actually occurred, Texas must necessarily have gone with the South, both on account of her institutions and her geographical position. Secession was illogical as well as impracticable; it was revolution.

Now, the right of revolution is an inherent one. When people are oppressed by their government, it is a natural right they enjoy to relieve themselves of the oppression, if they are strong enough, either by withdrawal from it, or by overthrowing it and substituting a government more acceptable. But any people or part of a people who resort to this remedy, stake their lives, their property, and every claim for protection given by citizenship — on the issue. Victory, or the conditions imposed by the conqueror — must be the result.

In the case of the war between the States it would have been the exact truth if the South had said, — "We do not want to live with you Northern people any longer; we know our institution of slavery is obnoxious to you, and, as you are growing numerically stronger than we, it may at some time in the future be endangered. So long as you permitted us to control the government, and with the aid of a few friends at the North to enact laws constituting your section a guard against the escape of our property, we were willing to live with you. You have been submissive to our rule heretofore; but it looks now as if you did not intend to continue so, and we will remain in the Union no longer." Instead of this the seceding States cried lustily, — "Let us alone; you have no constitutional power to interfere with us." Newspapers and people at the North reiterated the cry. Individuals might ignore the constitution; but the Nation itself must not only obey it, but must enforce the strictest construction of that instrument; the construction put upon it by the Southerners themselves. The fact is the constitution did not apply to any such contingency as the one existing from 1861 to 1865. Its framers never dreamed of such a contingency occurring. If they had foreseen it, the probabilities are they would have sanctioned the right of a State or States to withdraw rather than that there should be war between brothers.

The framers were wise in their generation and wanted to do the very best possible to secure their own liberty and independence, and that also of their descendants to the latest days. It is preposterous to suppose that the people of one generation can lay down the best and only rules of government for all who are to come after them, and under unforeseen contingencies. At the time of the framing of our constitution the only physical forces that had been subdued and made to serve man and do his labor, were the currents in the streams and in the air we breathe. Rude machinery, propelled by water power, had been invented; sails to propel ships upon the waters had been set to catch the passing breeze — but the application of stream to propel vessels against both wind and current, and machinery to do all manner of work had not been thought of. The instantaneous transmission of messages around the world by means of electricity would probably at that day have been attributed to witchcraft or a league with the Devil. Immaterial circumstances had changed as greatly as material ones. We could not and ought not to be rigidly bound by the rules laid down under circumstances so different for emergencies so utterly unanticipated. The fathers themselves would have been the first to declare that their prerogatives were not irrevocable. They would surely have resisted secession could they have lived to see the shape it assumed.

I traveled through the Northwest considerably during the winter of 1860-1. We had customers in all the little towns in southwest Wisconsin, southeast Minnesota and northeast Iowa. These generally knew I had been a captain in the regular army and had served through the Mexican war. Consequently wherever I stopped at night, some of the people would come to the public-house where I was, and sit till a late hour discussing the probabilities of the future. My own views at that time were like those officially expressed by Mr. Seward at a later day, that "the war would be over in ninety days." I continued to entertain these views until after the battle of Shiloh. I believe now that there would have been no more battles at the West after the capture of Fort Donelson if all the troops in that region had been under a single commander who would have followed up that victory.

There is little doubt in my mind now that the prevailing sentiment of the South would have been opposed to secession in 1860 and 1861, if there had been a fair and calm expression of opinion, unbiased by threats, and if the ballot of one legal voter had counted for as much as that of any other. But there was no calm discussion of the question. Demagogues who were too old to enter the army if there should be a war, others who entertained so high an opinion of their own ability that they did not believe they could be spared from the direction of the affairs of state in such an event, declaimed vehemently and unceasingly against the North; against its aggressions upon the South; its interference with Southern rights, etc., etc. They denounced the Northerners as cowards, poltroons, Negro-worshippers; claimed that one Southern man was equal to five Northern men in battle; that if the South would stand up for its rights the North would back down. Mr. Jefferson Davis said in a speech, delivered at La Grange, Mississippi, before the secession of that State, that he would agree to drink all the blood spilled south of Mason and Dixon's line if there should be a war. The young men who would have the fighting to do in case of war, believed all these statements, both in regard to the aggressiveness of the North and its cowardice. They, too, cried out for a separation from such people. The great bulk of the legal voters of the South were men who owned no slaves;

their homes were generally in the hills and poor country; their facilities for educating their children, even up to the point of reading and writing, were very limited; their interest in the contest was very meager — what there was, if they had been capable of seeing it, was with the North; they too needed emancipation. Under the old regime they were looked down upon by those who controlled all the affairs in the interest of slave-owners, as poor white trash who were allowed the ballot so long as they cast it according to direction.

I am aware that this last statement may be disputed and individual testimony perhaps adduced to show that in ante-bellum days the ballot was as untrammeled in the south as in any section of the country; but in the face of any such contradiction I reassert the statement. The shot-gun was not resorted to. Masked men did not ride over the country at night intimidating voters; but there was a firm feeling that a class existed in every State with a sort of divine right to control public affairs. If they could not get this control by one means they must by another. The end justified the means. The coercion, if mild, was complete.

There were two political parties, it is true, in all the States, both strong in numbers and respectability, but both equally loyal to the institution which stood paramount in Southern eyes to all other institutions in state or nation. The slave-owners were the minority, but governed both parties. Had politics ever divided the slave-holders and the non-slave-holders, the majority would have been obliged to yield, or internecine war would have been the consequence. I do not know that the Southern people were to blame for this condition of affairs. There was a time when slavery was not profitable, and the discussion of the merits of the institution was confined almost exclusively to the territory where it existed. The States of Virginia and Kentucky came near abolishing slavery by their own acts, one State defeating the measure by a tie vote and the other only lacking one. But when the institution became profitable, all talk of its abolition ceased where it existed; and naturally, as human nature is constituted, arguments were adduced in its support. The cotton-gin probably had much to do with the justification of slavery.

The winter of 1860-1 will be remembered by middle-aged people of today as one of great excitement. South Carolina promptly seceded after the result of the Presidential election was known. Other Southern States proposed to follow. In some of them the Union sentiment was so strong that it had to be suppressed by force. Maryland, Delaware, Kentucky and Missouri, all Slave States, failed to pass ordinances of secession; but they were all represented in the so-called congress of the so-called Confederate States. The Governor and Lieutenant-Governor of Missouri, in 1861, Jackson and Reynolds, were both supporters of the rebellion and took refuge with the enemy. The governor soon died, and the lieutenant-governor assumed his office; issued proclamations as governor of the State; was recognized as such by the Confederate Government, and continued his pretensions until the collapse of the rebellion. The South claimed the sovereignty of States, but claimed the right to coerce into their confederation such States as they wanted, that is, all the States where slavery existed. They did not seem to think this course inconsistent. The fact is, the Southern slave-owners believed that, in some way, the ownership of slaves conferred a sort of patent of nobility — a right to govern independent of the interest or wishes of those who did not hold such property. They convinced themselves, first, of the divine origin of the institution and, next, that that particular institution was not safe in the hands of any body of legislators but themselves.

Meanwhile the Administration of President Buchanan looked help- lessly on and proclaimed that the general government had no power to interfere; that the Nation had no power to save its own life. Mr. Buchanan had in his cabinet two members at least, who were as earnest — to use a mild term — in the cause of secession as Mr. Davis or any Southern statesman. One of them, Floyd, the Secretary of War, scattered the army so that much of it could be captured when hostilities should commence, and distributed the cannon and small arms from Northern arsenals throughout the South so as to be on hand when treason wanted them. The navy was scattered in like manner. The President did not prevent his cabinet preparing for war upon their government, either by destroying its resources or storing them in the South until a de facto government was established with Jefferson Davis as its President, and Montgomery, Alabama, as the Capital. The secessionists had then to leave the cabinet. In their own estimation they were aliens in the country which had given them birth. Loyal men were put into their places. Treason in the executive branch of the government was estopped. But the harm had already been done. The stable door was locked after the horse had been stolen.

During all of the trying winter of 1860-1, when the Southerners were so defiant that they would not allow within their borders the expression of a sentiment hostile to their views, it was a brave man indeed who could stand up and proclaim his loyalty to the Union. On the other hand men at the North — prominent men — proclaimed that the government had no power to coerce the South into submission to the laws of the land; that if the North undertook to raise armies to go south, these armies would have to march over the dead bodies of the speakers.

A portion of the press of the North was constantly proclaiming similar views. When the time arrived for the President-elect to go to the capital of the Nation to be sworn into office, it was deemed unsafe for him to travel, not only as a President-elect, but as any private citizen should be allowed to do. Instead of going in a special car, receiving the good wishes of his constituents at all the stations along the road, he was obliged to stop on the way and to be smuggled into the capital. He disappeared from public view on his journey, and the next the country knew, his arrival was announced at the capital. There is little doubt that he would have been assassinated if he had attempted to travel openly throughout his journey.

Chapter XVII

OUTBREAK OF THE REBELLION — PRESIDING AT
A UNION MEETING — MUSTERING OFFICER OF
STATE TROOPS — LYON AT CAMP JACKSON —
SERVICES TENDERED TO THE GOVERNMENT

*T*he 4th of March, 1861, came, and Abraham Lincoln was sworn to maintain the Union against all its enemies. The secession of one State after another followed, until eleven had gone out. On the 11th of April Fort Sumter, a National fort in the harbor of Charleston, South Carolina, was fired upon by the Southerners and a few days after was captured. The Confederates proclaimed themselves aliens, and thereby debarred themselves of all right to claim protection under the Constitution of the United States. We did not admit the fact that they were aliens, but all the same, they debarred themselves of the right to expect better treatment than people of any other foreign state who make war upon an independent nation. Upon the firing on Sumter President Lincoln issued his first call for troops and soon after a proclamation convening Congress in extra session. The call was for 75,000 volunteers for ninety days' service. If the shot fired at Fort Sumter "was heard around the world," the call of the President for 75,000 men was heard throughout the Northern States. There was not a state in the North of a million of inhabitants that would not have furnished the entire number faster than arms could have been supplied to them, if it had been necessary.

As soon as the news of the call for volunteers reached Galena, posters were stuck up calling for a meeting of the citizens at the court-house in the evening. Business ceased entirely; all was excitement; for a time there were no party distinctions; all were Union men, determined to avenge the insult to the national flag. In the evening the court-house was packed. Although a comparative stranger I was called upon to preside; the sole reason, possibly, was that I had been in the army and had seen service. With much embarrassment and some prompting I made out to announce the object of the meeting. Speeches were in order, but it is doubtful whether it would have been safe just then to make other than patriotic ones. There was probably no one in the house, however, who felt like making any other. The two principal speeches were by B.B. Howard, the post-master and a Breckinridge Democrat at the November election the fall before, and John A. Rawlins, an elector on the Douglas ticket. E.B. Washburne, with whom I was not acquainted at that time, came in after the meeting had been organized, and expressed, I understood afterwards, a little surprise that Galena could not furnish a presiding officer for such an occasion without taking a stranger. He came forward and was introduced, and made a speech appealing to the patriotism of the meeting.

After the speaking was over volunteers were called for to form a company. The quota of Illinois had been fixed at six regiments; and it was supposed that one company would be as much as would be accepted from Galena. The company was raised and the officers and non-commissioned officers elected before the meeting adjourned. I declined the captaincy before the balloting, but announced that I would aid the company in every way I could and would be found in the service in some position if there should be a war. I never went into our leather store after that meeting, to put up a package or do other business.

The ladies of Galena were quite as patriotic as the men. They could not enlist, but they conceived the idea of sending their first company to the field uniformed. They came to me to get a description of the United States uniform for infantry; subscribed and bought the material; procured tailors to cut out the garments, and the ladies made them up. In a few days the company was in uniform and ready to report at the State capital for assignment. The men all turned out the morning after their enlistment, and I took charge, divided them into squads and superintended their drill. When they were ready to go to Springfield I went with them and remained there until they were assigned to a regiment.

There were so many more volunteers than had been called for that the question whom to accept was quite embarrassing to the governor, Richard Yates. The legislature was in session at the time, however, and came to his relief. A law was enacted authorizing the governor to accept the services of ten additional regiments, one from each congressional district, for one month, to be paid by the State, but pledged to go into the service of the United States if there should be a further call during their term. Even with this relief the governor was still very much embarrassed. Before the war was over he was like the President when he was taken with the varioloid: "at last he had something he could give to all who wanted it."

In time the Galena company was mustered into the United States service, forming a part of the 11th Illinois volunteer infantry. My duties, I thought, had ended at Springfield, and I was prepared to start home by the evening train, leaving at nine o'clock. Up to that time I do not think I had been introduced to Governor Yates, or had ever spoken to him. I knew him by sight, however, because he was living at the same hotel and I often saw him at table. The evening I was to quit the capital I left the supper room before the governor and was standing at the front door when he came out. He spoke to me, calling me by my old army title "Captain," and said he understood that I was about leaving the city. I answered that I was. He said he would be glad if I would remain overnight and call at the Executive office the next morning. I complied with his request, and was asked to go into the Adjutant-General's office and render such assistance as I could, the governor saying that my army experience would be of great service there. I accepted the proposition.

My old army experience I found indeed of very great service. I was no clerk, nor had I any capacity to become one. The only place I ever found in my life to put a paper so as to find it again was either a side coat-pocket or the hands of a clerk or secretary more careful than myself. But I had been quartermaster, commissary and adjutant in the field. The army forms were familiar to me and I could direct how they should be made out. There was a clerk in the office of the Adjutant-General who supplied my deficiencies. The ease with which the State of Illinois settled its accounts with the government at the close of the war is evidence of the efficiency of Mr. Loomis as an accountant on a large scale. He remained in the office until that time.

As I have stated, the legislature authorized the governor to accept the services of ten additional regiments. I had charge of mustering these regiments into the State service. They were assembled at the most

convenient railroad centers in their respective congressional districts. I
detailed officers to muster in a portion of them, but mustered three in
the southern part of the State myself. One of these was to assemble at
Belleville, some eighteen miles southeast of St. Louis. When I got there
I found that only one or two companies had arrived. There was no
probability of the regiment coming together under five days. This gave
me a few idle days which I concluded to spend in St. Louis.

There was a considerable force of State militia at Camp Jackson, on
the outskirts of St. Louis, at the time. There is but little doubt that it
was the design of Governor Claiborn Jackson to have these troops ready
to seize the United States arsenal and the city of St. Louis. Why they
did not do so I do not know. There was but a small garrison, two
companies I think, under Captain N. Lyon at the arsenal, and but for
the timely services of the Hon. F.P. Blair, I have little doubt that St.
Louis would have gone into rebel hands, and with it the arsenal with
all its arms and ammunition.

Blair was a leader among the Union men of St. Louis in 1861. There
was no State government in Missouri at the time that would sanction
the raising of troops or commissioned officers to protect United States
property, but Blair had probably procured some form of authority from
the President to raise troops in Missouri and to muster them into the
service of the United States. At all events, he did raise a regiment and
took command himself as Colonel. With this force he reported to
Captain Lyon and placed himself and regiment under his orders. It was
whispered that Lyon thus reinforced intended to break up Camp Jackson and capture the militia. I went down to the arsenal in the morning
to see the troops start out. I had known Lyon for two years at West Point
and in the old army afterwards. Blair I knew very well by sight. I had
heard him speak in the canvass of 1858, possibly several times, but I
had never spoken to him. As the troops marched out of the enclosure
around the arsenal, Blair was on his horse outside forming them into
line preparatory to their march. I introduced myself to him and had a
few moments' conversation and expressed my sympathy with his purpose. This was my first personal acquaintance with the Honorable —
afterwards Major-General F.P. Blair. Camp Jackson surrendered without
a fight and the garrison was marched down to the arsenal as prisoners
of war.

Up to this time the enemies of the government in St. Louis had been
bold and defiant, while Union men were quiet but determined. The
enemies had their head-quarters in a central and public position on Pine
Street, near Fifth — from which the rebel flag was flaunted boldly. The
Union men had a place of meeting somewhere in the city, I did not

know where, and I doubt whether they dared to enrage the enemies of the government by placing the national flag outside their head-quarters. As soon as the news of the capture of Camp Jackson reached the city the condition of affairs was changed. Union men became rampant, aggressive, and, if you will, intolerant. They proclaimed their sentiments boldly, and were impatient at anything like disrespect for the Union. The secessionists became quiet but were filled with suppressed rage. They had been playing the bully. The Union men ordered the rebel flag taken down from the building on Pine Street. The command was given in tones of authority and it was taken down, never to be raised again in St. Louis.

I witnessed the scene. I had heard of the surrender of the camp and that the garrison was on its way to the arsenal. I had seen the troops start out in the morning and had wished them success. I now determined to go to the arsenal and await their arrival and congratulate them. I stepped on a car standing at the corner of 4th and Pine streets, and saw a crowd of people standing quietly in front of the head-quarters, who were there for the purpose of hauling down the flag. There were squads of other people at intervals down the street. They too were quiet but filled with suppressed rage, and muttered their resentment at the insult to, what they called, "their" flag. Before the car I was in had started, a dapper little fellow — he would be called a dude at this day — stepped in. He was in a great state of excitement and used adjectives freely to express his contempt for the Union and for those who had just perpetrated such an outrage upon the rights of a free people. There was only one other passenger in the car besides myself when this young man entered. He evidently expected to find nothing but sympathy when he got away from the "mud sills" engaged in compelling a "free people" to pull down a flag they adored. He turned to me saying: "Things have come to a ——— pretty pass when a free people can't choose their own flag. Where I came from if a man dares to say a word in favor of the Union we hang him to a limb of the first tree we come to." I replied that "after all we were not so intolerant in St. Louis as we might be; I had not seen a single rebel hung yet, nor heard of one; there were plenty of them who ought to be, however." The young man subsided. He was so crestfallen that I believe if I had ordered him to leave the car he would have gone quietly out, saying to himself: "More Yankee oppression."

By nightfall the late defenders of Camp Jackson were all within the walls of the St. Louis arsenal, prisoners of war. The next day I left St. Louis for Mattoon, Illinois, where I was to muster in the regiment from that congressional district. This was the 21st Illinois infantry, the regiment of which I subsequently became colonel. I mustered one regiment afterwards, when my services for the State were about closed.

Brigadier-General John Pope was stationed at Springfield, as United States mustering officer, all the time I was in the State service. He was a native of Illinois and well acquainted with most of the prominent men in the State. I was a carpetbagger and knew but few of them. While I was on duty at Springfield the senators, representatives in Congress, ax-governors and the State legislators were nearly all at the State capital. The only acquaintance I made among them was with the governor, whom I was serving, and, by chance, with Senator S.A. Douglas. The only members of Congress I knew were Washburne and Philip Foulk. With the former, though he represented my district and we were citizens of the same town, I only became acquainted at the meeting when the first company of Galena volunteers was raised. Foulk I had known in St. Louis when I was a citizen of that city. I had been three years at West Point with Pope and had served with him a short time during the Mexican war, under General Taylor. I saw a good deal of him during my service with the State. On one occasion he said to me that I ought to go into the United States service. I told him I intended to do so if there was a war. He spoke of his acquaintance with the public men of the State, and said he could get them to recommend me for a position and that he would do all he could for me. I declined to receive endorsement for permission to fight for my country.

Going home for a day or two soon after this conversation with General Pope, I wrote from Galena the following letter to the Adjutant-General of the Army.

GALENA, ILLINOIS,
May 24, 1861.

COL. L. THOMAS
Adjt. Gen. U.S.A.,
Washington, D.C.

SIR: —

Having served for fifteen years in the regular army, including four years at West Point, and feeling it the duty of everyone who has been educated at the Government expense to offer their services for the support of that Government, I have the honor, very respectfully, to tender my services, until the close of the war, in such capacity as may be offered. I would say, in view of my present age and length of service, I feel myself competent to command a regiment, if the President, in his judgment, should see fit to entrust one to me.

Since the first call of the President I have been serving on the staff of the Governor of this State, rendering such aid as I could in the organization of our State militia, and am still engaged in that capacity. A letter addressed to me at Springfield, Illinois, will reach me.

I am very respectfully,

Your obt. svt.,
U.S. GRANT

This letter failed to elicit an answer from the Adjutant-General of the Army. I presume it was hardly read by him, and certainly it could not have been submitted to higher authority. Subsequent to the war General Badeau having heard of this letter applied to the War Department for a copy of it. The letter could not be found and no one recollected ever having seen it. I took no copy when it was written. Long after the application of General Badeau, General Townsend, who had become Adjutant-General of the Army, while packing up papers preparatory to the removal of his office, found this letter in some out-of-the-way place. It had not been destroyed, but it had not been regularly filed away.

I felt some hesitation in suggesting rank as high as the colonelcy of a regiment, feeling somewhat doubtful whether I would be equal to the position. But I had seen nearly every colonel who had been mustered in from the State of Illinois, and some from Indiana, and felt that if they could command a regiment properly, and with credit, I could also.

Having but little to do after the muster of the last of the regiments authorized by the State legislature, I asked and obtained of the governor leave of absence for a week to visit my parents in Covington, Kentucky, immediately opposite Cincinnati. General McClellan had been made a major-general and had his headquarters at Cincinnati. In reality I wanted to see him. I had known him slightly at West Point, where we served one year together, and in the Mexican war. I was in hopes that when he saw me he would offer me a position on his staff. I called on two successive days at his office but failed to see him on either occasion, and returned to Springfield.

Chapter XVIII

APPOINTED COLONEL OF THE 21ST ILLINOIS —
PERSONNEL OF THE REGIMENT — GENERAL
LOGAN — MARCH TO MISSOURI — MOVEMENT
AGAINST HARRIS AT FLORIDA, MO. — GENERAL
POPE IN COMMAND — STATIONED AT MEXICO,
MO

*W*hile I was absent from the State capital on this occasion the President's second call for troops was issued. This time it was for 300,000 men, for three years or the war. This brought into the United States service all the regiments then in the State service. These had elected their officers from highest to lowest and were accepted with their organizations as they were, except in two instances. A Chicago regiment, the 19th infantry, had elected a very young man to the colonelcy. When it came to taking the field the regiment asked to have another appointed colonel and the one they had previously chosen made lieutenant-colonel. The 21st regiment of infantry, mustered in by me at Mattoon, refused to go into the service with the colonel of their selection in any position. While I was still absent Governor Yates appointed me colonel of this latter regiment. A few days after I was in charge of it and in camp on the fair grounds near Springfield.

My regiment was composed in large part of young men of as good social position as any in their section of the State. It embraced the sons of farmers, lawyers, physicians, politicians, merchants, bankers and ministers, and some men of maturer years who had filled such positions themselves. There were also men in it who could be led astray; and the colonel, elected by the votes of the regiment, had proved to be fully capable of developing all there was in his men of recklessness. It was said that he even went so far at times as to take the guard from their posts and go with them to the village near by and make a night of it. When there came a prospect of battle the regiment wanted to have someone else to lead them. I found it very hard work for a few days to bring all the men into anything like subordination; but the great majority favored discipline, and by the application of a little regular army punishment all were reduced to as good discipline as one could ask.

The ten regiments which had volunteered in the State service for thirty days, it will be remembered, had done so with a pledge to go into the National service if called upon within that time. When they volunteered the government had only called for ninety days' enlistments. Men were called now for three years or the war. They felt that this change of period released them from the obligation of re-volunteering. When I was appointed colonel, the 21st regiment was still in the State service. About the time they were to be mustered into the United States service, such of them as would go, two members of Congress from the State, McClernand and Logan, appeared at the capital and I was introduced to them. I had never seen either of them before, but I had read a great deal about them, and particularly about Logan, in the newspapers. Both were democratic members of Congress, and Logan had been elected from the southern district of the State, where he had a majority of eighteen thousand over his Republican competitor. His district had been settled originally by people from the Southern States, and at the breaking out of secession they sympathized with the South. At the first outbreak of war some of them joined the Southern army; many others were preparing to do so; others rode over the country at night denouncing the Union, and made it as necessary to guard railroad bridges over which National troops had to pass in southern Illinois, as it was in Kentucky or any of the border slave states. Logan's popularity in this district was unbounded. He knew almost enough of the people in it by their Christian names, to form an ordinary congressional district. As he went in politics, so his district was sure to go. The Republican papers had been demanding that he should announce where he stood on the questions which at that time engrossed the whole of public thought. Some were very bitter in their denunciations of his silence. Logan was not a man to be coerced into an utterance by threats. He did, however, come out in a speech before the adjournment of the special session of Congress which was convened by the President soon after his inauguration, and announced his undying loyalty and devotion to the Union. But I had not happened to see that speech, so that when I first met Logan my impressions were those formed from reading denunciations of him. McClernand, on the other hand, had early taken strong grounds for the maintenance of the Union and had been praised accordingly by the Republican papers. The gentlemen who presented these two members of Congress asked me if I would have any objections to their addressing my regiment. I hesitated a little before answering. It was but a few days before the time set for mustering into the United States service such of the men as were willing to volunteer for three years or the war. I had some doubt as to the effect a speech from Logan might have; but as he was with McClernand, whose sentiments on the all-absorbing questions of the day were well known, I gave my consent. McClernand spoke first; and Logan followed in a speech which he has hardly equaled since for force and eloquence. It breathed a loyalty and devotion to the Union which inspired my men to such a point that they would have volunteered to remain in the army as long as an enemy of the country continued to bear arms against it. They entered the United States service almost to a man.

General Logan went to his part of the State and gave his attention to raising troops. The very men who at first made it necessary to guard the roads in southern Illinois became the defenders of the Union. Logan entered the service himself as colonel of a regiment and rapidly rose to the rank of major-general. His district, which had promised at first to give much trouble to the government, filled every call made upon it for troops, without resorting to the draft. There was no call made when there were not more volunteers than were asked for. That congressional district stands credited at the War Department today with furnishing more men for the army than it was called on to supply.

I remained in Springfield with my regiment until the 3d of July, when I was ordered to Quincy, Illinois. By that time the regiment was in a good state of discipline and the officers and men were well up in the company drill. There was direct railroad communication between Springfield and Quincy, but I thought it would be good preparation for the troops to march there. We had no transportation for our camp and garrison equipage, so wagons were hired for the occasion and on the 3d of July we started. There was no hurry, but fair marches were made every day until the Illinois River was crossed. There I was overtaken by a dispatch saying that the destination of the regiment had been changed to Ironton, Missouri, and ordering me to halt where I was and await the arrival of a steamer which had been dispatched up the Illinois River to take the regiment to St. Louis. The boat, when it did come, grounded on a sand-bar a few miles below where we were in camp. We remained there several days waiting to have the boat get off the bar, but before this occurred news came that an Illinois regiment was surrounded by rebels at a point on the Hannibal and St. Joe Railroad some miles west of Palmyra, in Missouri, and I was ordered to proceed with all dispatch to their relief. We took the cars and reached Quincy in a few hours.

When I left Galena for the last time to take command of the 21st regiment I took with me my oldest son, Frederick D. Grant, then a lad of eleven years of age. On receiving the order to take rail for Quincy I wrote to Mrs. Grant, to relieve what I supposed would be her great anxiety for one so young going into danger, that I would send Fred home from Quincy by river. I received a prompt letter in reply decidedly disapproving my proposition, and urging that the lad should be allowed to accompany me. It came too late. Fred was already on his way up the Mississippi bound for Dubuque, Iowa, from which place there was a railroad to Galena.

My sensations as we approached what I supposed might be "a field of battle" were anything but agreeable. I had been in all the engagements in Mexico that it was possible for one person to be in; but not in command. If someone else had been colonel and I had been lieutenant-colonel I do not think I would have felt any trepidation. Before we were prepared to cross the Mississippi River at Quincy my anxiety was relieved; for the men of the besieged regiment came straggling into town. I am inclined to think both sides got frightened and ran away.

I took my regiment to Palmyra and remained there for a few days, until relieved by the 19th Illinois infantry. From Palmyra I proceeded to Salt River, the railroad bridge over which had been destroyed by the enemy. Colonel John M. Palmer at that time commanded the 13th Illinois, which was acting as a guard to workmen who were engaged in rebuilding this bridge. Palmer was my senior and commanded the two regiments as long as we remained together. The bridge was finished in about two weeks, and I received orders to move against Colonel Thomas Harris, who was said to be encamped at the little town of Florida, some twenty-five miles south of where we then were.

At the time of which I now write we had no transportation and the country about Salt River was sparsely settled, so that it took some days to collect teams and drivers enough to move the camp and garrison equipage of a regiment nearly a thousand strong, together with a week's supply of provision and some ammunition. While preparations for the move were going on I felt quite comfortable; but when we got on the road and found every house deserted I was anything but easy. In the twenty-five miles we had to march we did not see a person, old or young, male or female, except two horsemen who were on a road that crossed ours. As soon as they saw us they decamped as fast as their horses could carry them. I kept my men in the ranks and forbade their entering any of the deserted houses or taking anything from them. We halted at night on the road and proceeded the next morning at an early hour. Harris had been encamped in a creek bottom for the sake of being near water.

The hills on either side of the creek extend to a considerable height, possibly more than a hundred feet. As we approached the brow of the hill from which it was expected we could see Harris' camp, and possibly find his men ready formed to meet us, my heart kept getting higher and higher until it felt to me as though it was in my throat. I would have given anything then to have been back in Illinois, but I had not the moral courage to halt and consider what to do; I kept right on. When we reached a point from which the valley below was in full view I halted. The place where Harris had been encamped a few days before was still there and the marks of a recent encampment were plainly visible, but the troops were gone. My heart resumed its place. It occurred to me at once that Harris had been as much afraid of me as I had been of him. This was a view of the question I had never taken before; but it was one I never forgot afterwards. From that event to the close of the war, I never experienced trepidation upon confronting an enemy, though I always felt more or less anxiety. I never forgot that he had as much reason to fear my forces as I had his. The lesson was valuable.

Inquiries at the village of Florida divulged the fact that Colonel Harris, learning of my intended movement, while my transportation was being collected took time by the forelock and left Florida before I had started from Salt River. He had increased the distance between us by forty miles. The next day I started back to my old camp at Salt River bridge. The citizens living on the line of our march had returned to their houses after we passed, and finding everything in good order, nothing carried away, they were at their front doors ready to greet us now. They had evidently been led to believe that the National troops carried death and devastation with them wherever they went.

In a short time after our return to Salt River bridge I was ordered with my regiment to the town of Mexico. General Pope was then commanding the district embracing all of the State of Missouri between the Mississippi and Missouri rivers, with his headquarters in the village of Mexico. I was assigned to the command of a sub-district embracing the troops in the immediate neighborhood, some three regiments of infantry and a section of artillery. There was one regiment encamped by the side of mine. I assumed command of the whole and the first night sent the commander of the other regiment the parole and countersign. Not wishing to be outdone in courtesy, he immediately sent me the countersign for his regiment for the night. When he was informed that the countersign sent to him was for use with his regiment as well as mine, it was difficult to make him understand that this was not an unwarranted interference of one colonel over another. No doubt he attributed it for the time to the presumption of a graduate of West Point over a volunteer pure and simple. But the question was soon settled and we had no further trouble.

My arrival in Mexico had been preceded by that of two or three regiments in which proper discipline had not been maintained, and the men had been in the habit of visiting houses without invitation and helping themselves to food and drink, or demanding them from the occupants. They carried their muskets while out of camp and made every man they found take the oath of allegiance to the government. I at once published orders prohibiting the soldiers from going into private houses unless invited by the inhabitants, and from appropriating private property to their own or to government uses. The people were no longer molested or made afraid. I received the most marked courtesy from the citizens of Mexico as long as I remained there.

Up to this time my regiment had not been carried in the school of the soldier beyond the company drill, except that it had received some training on the march from Springfield to the Illinois River. There was now a good opportunity of exercising it in the battalion drill. While I was at West Point the tactics used in the army had been Scott's and the musket the flint lock. I had never looked at a copy of tactics from the time of my graduation. My standing in that branch of studies had been near the foot of the class. In the Mexican war in the summer of 1846, I had been appointed regimental quartermaster and commissary and had not been at a battalion drill since. The arms had been changed since then and Hardee's tactics had been adopted. I got a copy of tactics and studied one lesson, intending to confine the exercise of the first day to the commands I had thus learned. By pursuing this course from day to day I thought I would soon get through the volume.

We were encamped just outside of town on the common, among scattering suburban houses with enclosed gardens, and when I got my regiment in line and rode to the front I soon saw that if I attempted to follow the lesson I had studied I would have to clear away some of the houses and garden fences to make room. I perceived at once, however, that Hardee's tactics — a mere translation from the French with Hardee's name attached — was nothing more than common sense and the progress of the age applied to Scott's system. The commands were abbreviated and the movement expedited. Under the old tactics almost every change in the order of march was preceded by a "halt," then came the change, and then the "forward march." With the new tactics all these changes could be made while in motion. I found no trouble in giving commands that would take my regiment where I wanted it to go and carry it around all obstacles. I do not believe that the officers of the regiment ever discovered that I had never studied the tactics that I used.

Chapter XIX

COMMISSIONED BRIGADIER-GENERAL —
COMMAND AT IRONTON, MO. — JEFFERSON
CITY — CAPE GIRARDEAU — GENERAL
PRENTISS — SEIZURE OF PADUCAH —
HEADQUARTERS AT CAIRO

I had not been in Mexico many weeks when, reading a St. Louis paper, I found the President had asked the Illinois delegation in Congress to recommend some citizens of the State for the position of brigadier-general, and that they had unanimously recommended me as first on a list of seven. I was very much surprised because, as I have said, my acquaintance with the Congressmen was very limited and I did not know of anything I had done to inspire such confidence. The papers of the next day announced that my name, with three others, had been sent to the Senate, and a few days after our confirmation was announced.

When appointed brigadier-general I at once thought it proper that one of my aides should come from the regiment I had been commanding, and so selected Lieutenant C.B. Lagow. While living in St. Louis, I had had a desk in the law office of McClellan, Moody and Hillyer. Difference in views between the members of the firm on the questions of the day, and general hard times in the border cities, had broken up this firm. Hillyer was quite a young man, then in his twenties, and very brilliant. I asked him to accept a place on my staff. I also wanted to take one man from my new home, Galena. The canvass in the Presidential campaign the fall before had brought out a young lawyer by the name of John A. Rawlins, who proved himself one of the ablest speakers in the State. He was also a candidate for elector on the Douglas ticket. When Sumter was fired upon and the integrity of the Union threatened, there was no man more ready to serve his country than he. I wrote at once asking him to accept the position of assistant adjutant-general with the rank of captain, on my staff. He was about entering the service as major of a new regiment then organizing in the northwestern part of the State; but he threw this up and accepted my offer.

Neither Hillyer nor Lagow proved to have any particular taste or special qualifications for the duties of the soldier, and the former resigned during the Vicksburg campaign; the latter I relieved after the battle of Chattanooga. Rawlins remained with me as long as he lived, and rose to the rank of brigadier general and chief-of-staff to the General of the Army — an office created for him — before the war closed. He was an able man, possessed of great firmness, and could say "no" so emphatically to a request which he thought should not be granted that the person he was addressing would understand at once that there was no use of pressing the matter. General Rawlins was a very useful officer in other ways than this. I became very much attached to him.

Shortly after my promotion I was ordered to Ironton, Missouri, to command a district in that part of the State, and took the 21st Illinois, my old regiment, with me. Several other regiments were ordered to the same destination about the same time. Ironton is on the Iron Mountain railroad, about seventy miles south of St. Louis, and situated among hills rising almost to the dignity of mountains. When I reached there, about the 8th of August, Colonel B. Gratz Brown — afterwards Governor of Missouri and in 1872 Vice-Presidential candidate — was in command. Some of his troops were ninety days' men and their time had expired some time before. The men had no clothing but what they had volunteered in, and much of this was so worn that it would hardly stay on. General Hardee — the author of the tactics I did not study — was at Greenville some twenty-five miles further south, it was said, with five thousand Confederate troops. Under these circumstances Colonel Brown's command was very much demoralized. A squadron of cavalry could have ridden into the valley and captured the entire force. Brown himself was gladder to see me on that occasion than he ever has been since. I relieved him and sent all his men home within a day or two, to be mustered out of service.

Within ten days after reading Ironton I was prepared to take the offensive against the enemy at Greenville. I sent a column east out of the valley we were in, with orders to swing around to the south and west and come into the Greenville road ten miles south of Ironton. Another column marched on the direct road and went into camp at the point designated for the two columns to meet. I was to ride out the next morning and take personal command of the movement. My experience against Harris, in northern Missouri, had inspired me with confidence. But when the evening train came in, it brought General B.M. Prentiss with orders to take command of the district. His orders did not relieve me, but I knew that by law I was senior, and at that time even the President did not have the authority to assign a junior to command a senior of the same grade. I therefore gave General Prentiss the situation of the troops and the general condition of affairs, and started for St. Louis the same day. The movement against the rebels at Greenville went no further.

From St. Louis I was ordered to Jefferson City, the capital of the State, to take command. General Sterling Price, of the Confederate army, was thought to be threatening the capital, Lexington, Chillicothe and other comparatively large towns in the central part of Missouri. I found a good many troops in Jefferson City, but in the greatest confusion, and no one person knew where they all were. Colonel Mulligan, a gallant man, was in command, but he had not been educated as yet to his new profession and did not know how to maintain discipline. I found that volunteers had obtained permission from the department commander, or claimed they had, to raise, some of them, regiments; some battalions; some companies — the officers to be commissioned according to the number of men they brought into the service. There were recruiting stations all over town, with notices, rudely lettered on boards over the doors, announcing the arm of service and length of time for which recruits at that station would be received. The law required all volunteers to serve for three years or the war. But in Jefferson City in August, 1861, they were recruited for different periods and on different conditions; some were enlisted for six months, some for a year, some without any condition as to where they were to serve, others were not to be sent out of the State. The recruits were principally men from regiments stationed there and already in the service, bound for three years if the war lasted that long.

The city was filled with Union fugitives who had been driven by guerilla bands to take refuge with the National troops. They were in a deplorable condition and must have starved but for the support the government gave them. They had generally made their escape with a team or two, sometimes a yoke of oxen with a mule or a horse in the lead. A little bedding besides their clothing and some food had been thrown into the wagon. All else of their worldly goods were abandoned and appropriated by their former neighbors; for the Union man in Missouri who staid at home during the rebellion, if he was not immediately under the protection of the National troops, was at perpetual war with his neighbors. I stopped the recruiting service, and disposed the troops about the outskirts of the city so as to guard all approaches. Order was soon restored.

I had been at Jefferson City but a few days when I was directed from department headquarters to fit out an expedition to Lexington, Booneville and Chillicothe, in order to take from the banks in those cities all the funds they had and send them to St. Louis. The western army had not yet been supplied with transportation. It became necessary therefore to press into the service teams belonging to sympathizers with the rebellion or to hire those of Union men. This afforded an opportunity of giving employment to such of the refugees within our lines as had teams suitable for our purposes. They accepted the service with alacrity. As fast as troops could be got off they were moved west some twenty miles or more. In seven or eight days from my assuming command at Jefferson City, I had all the troops, except a small garrison, at an advanced position and expected to join them myself the next day.

But my campaigns had not yet begun, for while seated at my office door, with nothing further to do until it was time to start for the front, I saw an officer of rank approaching, who proved to be Colonel Jefferson C. Davis. I had never met him before, but he introduced himself by handing me an order for him to proceed to Jefferson City and relieve me of the command. The orders directed that I should report at department headquarters at St. Louis without delay, to receive important special instructions. It was about an hour before the only regular train of the day would start. I therefore turned over to Colonel Davis my orders, and hurriedly stated to him the progress that had been made to carry out the department instructions already described. I had at that time but one staff officer, doing myself all the detail work usually performed by an adjutant-general. In an hour after being relieved from the command I was on my way to St. Louis, leaving my single staff officer* to follow the next day with our horses and baggage.

The "important special instructions" which I received the next day, assigned me to the command of the district of southeast Missouri, embracing all the territory south of St. Louis, in Missouri, as well as all southern Illinois. At first I was to take personal command of a combined expedition that had been ordered for the capture of Colonel Jeff. Thompson, a sort of independent or partisan commander who was disputing with us the possession of southeast Missouri. Troops had been ordered to move from Ironton to Cape Girardeau, sixty or seventy miles to the southeast, on the Mississippi River; while the forces at Cape Girardeau had been ordered to move to Jacksonville, ten miles out towards Ironton; and troops at Cairo and Bird's Point, at the junction of the Ohio and Mississippi rivers, were to hold themselves in readiness

---

* C.B. Lagow, the others not yet having joined me.

to go down the Mississippi to Belmont, eighteen miles below, to be moved west from there when an officer should come to command them. I was the officer who had been selected for this purpose. Cairo was to become my headquarters when the expedition terminated.

In pursuance of my orders I established my temporary headquarters at Cape Girardeau and sent instructions to the commanding officer at Jackson, to inform me of the approach of General Prentiss from Ironton. Hired wagons were kept moving night and day to take additional rations to Jackson, to supply the troops when they started from there. Neither General Prentiss nor Colonel Marsh, who commanded at Jackson, knew their destination. I drew up all the instructions for the contemplated move, and kept them in my pocket until I should hear of the junction of our troops at Jackson. Two or three days after my arrival at Cape Girardeau, word came that General Prentiss was approaching that place (Jackson). I started at once to meet him there and to give him his orders. As I turned the first corner of a street after starting, I saw a column of cavalry passing the next street in front of me. I turned and rode around the block the other way, so as to meet the head of the column. I found there General Prentiss himself, with a large escort. He had halted his troops at Jackson for the night, and had come on himself to Cape Girardeau, leaving orders for his command to follow him in the morning. I gave the General his orders — which stopped him at Jackson — but he was very much aggrieved at being placed under another brigadier-general, particularly as he believed himself to be the senior. He had been a brigadier, in command at Cairo, while I was mustering officer at Springfield without any rank. But we were nominated at the same time for the United States service, and both our commissions bore date May 17th, 1861. By virtue of my former army rank I was, by law, the senior. General Prentiss failed to get orders to his troops to remain at Jackson, and the next morning early they were reported as approaching Cape Girardeau. I then ordered the General very peremptorily to countermarch his command and take it back to Jackson. He obeyed the order, but bade his command adieu when he got them to Jackson, and went to St. Louis and reported himself. This broke up the expedition. But little harm was done, as Jeff. Thompson moved light and had no fixed place for even nominal headquarters. He was as much at home in Arkansas as he was in Missouri and would keep out of the way of a superior force. Prentiss was sent to another part of the State.

General Prentiss made a great mistake on the above occasion, one that he would not have committed later in the war. When I came to know him better, I regretted it much. In consequence of this occurrence he was off duty in the field when the principal campaign at the West was going on, and his juniors received promotion while he was where none could be obtained. He would have been next to myself in rank in the district of southeast Missouri, by virtue of his services in the Mexican war. He was a brave and very earnest soldier. No man in the service was more sincere in his devotion to the cause for which we were battling; none more ready to make sacrifices or risk life in it.

On the 4th of September I removed my headquarters to Cairo and found Colonel Richard Oglesby in command of the post. We had never met, at least not to my knowledge. After my promotion I had ordered my brigadier-general's uniform from New York, but it had not yet arrived, so that I was in citizen's dress. The Colonel had his office full of people, mostly from the neighboring States of Missouri and Kentucky, making complaints or asking favors. He evidently did not catch my name when I was presented, for on my taking a piece of paper from the table where he was seated and writing the order assuming command of the district of southeast Missouri, Colonel Richard J. Oglesby to command the post at Bird's Point, and handing it to him, he put on an expression of surprise that looked a little as if he would like to have someone identify me. But he surrendered the office without question.

The day after I assumed command at Cairo a man came to me who said he was a scout of General Fremont. He reported that he had just come from Columbus, a point on the Mississippi twenty miles below on the Kentucky side, and that troops had started from there, or were about to start, to seize Paducah, at the mouth of the Tennessee. There was no time for delay; I reported by telegraph to the department commander the information I had received, and added that I was taking steps to get off that night to be in advance of the enemy in securing that important point. There was a large number of steamers lying at Cairo and a good many boatmen were staying in the town. It was the work of only a few hours to get the boats manned, with coal aboard and steam up. Troops were also designated to go aboard. The distance from Cairo to Paducah is about forty-five miles. I did not wish to get there before daylight of the 6th, and directed therefore that the boats should lie at anchor out in the stream until the time to start. Not having received an answer to my first dispatch, I again telegraphed to department headquarters that I should start for Paducah that night unless I received further orders. Hearing nothing, we started before midnight and arrived early the following morning, anticipating the enemy by probably not over six or eight hours. It proved very fortunate that the expedition against Jeff. Thompson had been broken up. Had it not been, the enemy would have seized Paducah and fortified it, to our very great annoyance.

When the National troops entered the town the citizens were taken by surprise. I never after saw such consternation depicted on the faces of the people. Men, women and children came out of their doors looking pale and frightened at the presence of the invader. They were expecting rebel troops that day. In fact, nearly four thousand men from Columbus were at that time within ten or fifteen miles of Paducah on their way to occupy the place. I had but two regiments and one battery with me, but the enemy did not know this and returned to Columbus. I stationed my troops at the best points to guard the roads leading into the city, left gunboats to guard the riverfronts and by noon was ready to start on my return to Cairo. Before leaving, however, I addressed a short printed proclamation to the citizens of Paducah assuring them of our peaceful intentions, that we had come among them to protect them against the enemies of our country, and that all who chose could continue their usual avocations with assurance of the protection of the government. This was evidently a relief to them; but the majority would have much preferred the presence of the other army. I reinforced Paducah rapidly from the troops at Cape Girardeau; and a day or two later General C.F. Smith, a most accomplished soldier, reported at Cairo and was assigned to the command of the post at the mouth of the Tennessee. In a short time it was well fortified and a detachment was sent to occupy Smithland, at the mouth of the Cumberland.

The State government of Kentucky at that time was rebel in sentiment, but wanted to preserve an armed neutrality between the North and the South, and the governor really seemed to think the State had a perfect right to maintain a neutral position. The rebels already occupied two towns in the State, Columbus and Hickman, on the Mississippi; and at the very moment the National troops were entering Paducah from the Ohio front, General Lloyd Tilghman – a Confederate – with his staff and a small detachment of men, were getting out in the other direction, while, as I have already said, nearly four thousand Confederate troops were on Kentucky soil on their way to take possession of the town. But, in the estimation of the governor and of those who thought with him, this did not justify the National authorities in invading the soil of Kentucky. I informed the legislature of the State of what I was doing, and my action was approved by the majority of that body. On my return to Cairo I found authority from department headquarters for me to take Paducah "if I felt strong enough," but very soon after I was reprimanded from the same quarters for my correspondence with the legislature and warned against a repetition of the offence.

Soon after I took command at Cairo, General Fremont entered into arrangements for the exchange of the prisoners captured at Camp

Jackson in the month of May. I received orders to pass them through my lines to Columbus as they presented themselves with proper credentials. Quite a number of these prisoners I had been personally acquainted with before the war. Such of them as I had so known were received at my headquarters as old acquaintances, and ordinary routine business was not disturbed by their presence. On one occasion when several were present in my office my intention to visit Cape Girardeau the next day, to inspect the troops at that point, was mentioned. Something transpired which postponed my trip; but a steamer employed by the government was passing a point some twenty or more miles above Cairo, the next day, when a section of rebel artillery with proper escort brought her to. A major, one of those who had been at my headquarters the day before, came at once aboard and after some search made a direct demand for my delivery. It was hard to persuade him that I was not there. This officer was Major Barrett, of St. Louis. I had been acquainted with his family before the war.

Chapter XX

GENERAL FREMONT IN COMMAND — MOVEMENT AGAINST BELMONT — BATTLE OF BELMONT — A NARROW ESCAPE — AFTER THE BATTLE

*F*rom the occupation of Paducah up to the early part of November nothing important occurred with the troops under my command. I was reinforced from time to time and the men were drilled and disciplined preparatory for the service which was sure to come. By the 1st of November I had not fewer than 20,000 men, most of them under good drill and ready to meet any equal body of men who, like themselves, had not yet been in an engagement. They were growing impatient at lying idle so long, almost in hearing of the guns of the enemy they had volunteered to fight against. I asked on one or two occasions to be allowed to move against Columbus. It could have been taken soon after the occupation of Paducah; but before November it was so strongly fortified that it would have required a large force and a long siege to capture it.

In the latter part of October General Fremont took the field in person and moved from Jefferson City against General Sterling Price, who was then in the State of Missouri with a considerable command. About the first of November I was directed from department headquarters to make a demonstration on both sides of the Mississippi River with the view of detaining the rebels at Columbus within their lines. Before my troops could be got off, I was notified from the same quarter that there were some 3,000 of the enemy on the St. Francis River about fifty miles west, or southwest, from Cairo, and was ordered to send another force against them. I dispatched Colonel Oglesby at once with troops sufficient to compete with the reported number of the enemy. On the 5th word came from the same source that the rebels were about to detach a large force from Columbus to be moved by boats down the Mississippi and up the White River, in Arkansas, in order to reinforce Price, and I was directed to prevent this movement if possible. I accordingly sent a regiment from Bird's Point under Colonel W.H.L. Wallace to overtake and reinforce Oglesby, with orders to march to New Madrid, a point some distance below Columbus, on the Missouri side. At the same time I directed General C.F. Smith to move all the troops he could spare from Paducah directly against Columbus, halting them, however, a few miles from the town to await further orders from me. Then I gathered up all the troops at Cairo and Fort Holt, except suitable guards, and moved them down the river on steamers convoyed by two gunboats, accompanying them myself. My force consisted of a little over 3,000 men and embraced five regiments of infantry, two guns and two companies of cavalry. We dropped down the river on the 6th to within about six miles of Columbus, debarked a few men on the Kentucky side and established pickets to connect with the troops from Paducah.

I had no orders which contemplated an attack by the National troops, nor did I intend anything of the kind when I started out from Cairo; but after we started I saw that the officers and men were elated at the prospect of at last having the opportunity of doing what they had volunteered to do — fight the enemies of their country. I did not see how I could maintain discipline, or retain the confidence of my command, if we should return to Cairo without an effort to do something. Columbus, besides being strongly fortified, contained a garrison much more numerous than the force I had with me. It would not do, therefore, to attack that point. About two o'clock on the morning of the 7th, I learned that the enemy was crossing troops from Columbus to the west bank to be dispatched, presumably, after Oglesby. I knew there was a small camp of Confederates at Belmont, immediately opposite Columbus, and I speedily resolved to push down the river, land on the Missouri side, capture Belmont, break up the camp and return. Accordingly, the pickets above Columbus were drawn in at once, and about daylight the boats moved out from shore. In an hour we were debarking on the west bank of the Mississippi, just out of range of the batteries at Columbus.

The ground on the west shore of the river, opposite Columbus, is low and in places marshy and cut up with sloughs. The soil is rich and the timber large and heavy. There were some small clearings between Belmont and the point where we landed, but most of the country was covered with the native forests. We landed in front of a cornfield. When the debarkation commenced, I took a regiment down the river to post it as a guard against surprise. At that time I had no staff officer who could be trusted with that duty. In the woods, at a short distance below the clearing, I found a depression, dry at the time, but which at high water became a slough or bayou. I placed the men in the hollow, gave them their instructions and ordered them to remain there until they were properly relieved. These troops, with the gunboats, were to protect our transports.

Up to this time the enemy had evidently failed to divine our intentions. From Columbus they could, of course, see our gunboats and transports loaded with troops. But the force from Paducah was threatening them from the land side, and it was hardly to be expected that if Columbus was our object we would separate our troops by a wide river. They doubtless thought we meant to draw a large force from the east bank, then embark ourselves, land on the east bank and make a sudden assault on Columbus before their divided command could be united.

About eight o'clock we started from the point of debarkation, marching by the flank. After moving in this way for a mile or a mile and a half, I halted where there was marshy ground covered with a heavy growth of timber in our front, and deployed a large part of my force as skirmishers. By this time the enemy discovered that we were moving upon Belmont and sent out troops to meet us. Soon after we had started in line, his skirmishers were encountered and fighting commenced. This continued, growing fiercer and fiercer, for about four hours, the enemy being forced back gradually until he was driven into his camp. Early in this engagement my horse was shot under me, but I got another from one of my staff and kept well up with the advance until the river was reached.

The officers and men engaged at Belmont were then under fire for the first time. Veterans could not have behaved better than they did up to the moment of reaching the rebel camp. At this point they became demoralized from their victory and failed to reap its full reward. The enemy had been followed so closely that when he reached the clear ground on which his camp was pitched he beat a hasty retreat over the riverbank, which protected him from our shots and from view. This precipitate retreat at the last moment enabled the National forces to pick their way without hindrance through the abatis — the only artificial defense the enemy had. The moment the camp was reached our men laid down their arms and commenced rummaging the tents to pick up trophies. Some of the higher officers were little better than the privates. They galloped about from one cluster of men to another and at every halt delivered a short eulogy upon the Union cause and the achievements of the command.

All this time the troops we had been engaged with for four hours, lay crouched under cover of the riverbank, ready to come up and surrender if summoned to do so; but finding that they were not pursued, they worked their way up the river and came up on the bank between us and our transports. I saw at the same time two steamers coming from the Columbus side towards the west shore, above us, black — or grey — with soldiers from boiler-deck to roof. Some of my men were engaged in firing from captured guns at empty steamers down the river, out of range, cheering at every shot. I tried to get them to turn their guns upon the loaded steamers above and not so far away. My efforts were in vain. At last I directed my staff officers to set fire to the camps. This drew the fire of the enemy's guns located on the heights of Columbus. They had abstained from firing before, probably because they were afraid of hitting their own men; or they may have supposed, until the camp was on fire, that it was still in the possession of their friends. About this time, too, the men we had driven over the bank were seen in line up the river between us and our transports. The alarm "surrounded" was given. The guns of the enemy and the report of being surrounded, brought officers and men completely under control. At first some of the officers seemed to think that to be surrounded was to be placed in a hopeless position, where there was nothing to do but surrender. But when I announced that we had cut our way in and could cut our way out just as well, it seemed a new revelation to officers and soldiers. They formed line rapidly and we started back to our boats, with the men deployed as skirmishers as they had been on entering camp. The enemy was soon encountered, but his resistance this time was feeble. Again the Confederates sought shelter under the riverbanks. We could not stop, however, to pick them up, because the troops we had seen crossing the river had debarked by this time and were nearer our transports than we were. It would be prudent to get them behind us; but we were not again molested on our way to the boats.

From the beginning of the fighting our wounded had been carried to the houses at the rear, near the place of debarkation. I now set the troops to bringing their wounded to the boats. After this had gone on for some little time I rode down the road, without even a staff officer, to visit the guard I had stationed over the approach to our transports. I knew the enemy had crossed over from Columbus in considerable numbers and might be expected to attack us as we were embarking. This guard would be encountered first and, as they were in a natural entrenchment, would be able to hold the enemy for a considerable time. My surprise was great to find there was not a single man in the trench. Riding back to the boat I found the officer who had commanded the guard and learned that he had withdrawn his force when the main body fell back. At first I ordered the guard to return, but finding that it would take some time to get the men together and march them back to their position, I countermanded the order. Then fearing that the enemy we had seen crossing the river below might be coming upon us unawares, I rode out in the field to our front, still entirely alone, to observe whether the enemy was passing. The field was grown up with corn so tall and thick as to cut off the view of even a person on horseback, except directly along the rows. Even in that direction, owing to the overhanging blades of corn, the view was not extensive. I had not gone more than a few hundred yards when I saw a body of troops marching past me not fifty yards away. I looked at them for a moment and then turned my horse towards the river and started back, first in a walk, and when I thought myself concealed from the view of the enemy, as fast as my horse could carry me. When at the riverbank I still had to ride a few hundred yards to the point where the nearest transport lay.

The cornfield in front of our transports terminated at the edge of a dense forest. Before I got back the enemy had entered this forest and had opened a brisk fire upon the boats. Our men, with the exception of details that had gone to the front after the wounded, were now either aboard the transports or very near them. Those who were not aboard soon got there, and the boats pushed off. I was the only man of the National army between the rebels and our transports. The captain of a boat that had just pushed out but had not started, recognized me and ordered the engineer not to start the engine; he then had a plank run out for me. My horse seemed to take in the situation. There was no path down the bank and everyone acquainted with the Mississippi River knows that its banks, in a natural state, do not vary at any great angle from the perpendicular. My horse put his fore feet over the bank without hesitation or urging, and with his hind feet well under him, slid down the bank and trotted aboard the boat, twelve or fifteen feet away, over a single gang plank. I dismounted and went at once to the upper deck.

The Mississippi River was low on the 7th of November, 1861, so that the banks were higher than the heads of men standing on the upper decks of the steamers. The rebels were some distance back from the river, so that their fire was high and did us but little harm. Our smoke-stack was riddled with bullets, but there were only three men wounded on the boats, two of whom were soldiers. When I first went on deck I entered the captain's room adjoining the pilot-house, and threw myself on a sofa. I did not keep that position a moment, but rose to go out on the deck to observe what was going on. I had scarcely left when a musket ball entered the room, struck the head of the sofa, passed through it and lodged in the foot.

When the enemy opened fire on the transports our gunboats returned it with vigor. They were well out in the stream and some distance down, so that they had to give but very little elevation to their guns to clear the banks of the river. Their position very nearly enfiladed the line of the enemy while he was marching through the cornfield. The execution was very great, as we could see at the time and as I afterwards learned more positively. We were very soon out of range and went peacefully on our way to Cairo, every man feeling that Belmont was a great victory and that he had contributed his share to it.

Our loss at Belmont was 485 in killed, wounded and missing. About 125 of our wounded fell into the hands of the enemy. We returned with 175 prisoners and two guns, and spiked four other pieces. The loss of the enemy, as officially reported, was 642 men, killed, wounded and missing. We had engaged about 2,500 men, exclusive of the guard left with the transports. The enemy had about 7,000; but this includes the troops brought over from Columbus who were not engaged in the first defense of Belmont.

The two objects for which the battle of Belmont was fought were fully accomplished. The enemy gave up all idea of detaching troops from Columbus. His losses were very heavy for that period of the war. Columbus was beset by people looking for their wounded or dead kin, to take them home for medical treatment or burial. I learned later, when I had moved further south, that Belmont had caused more mourning than almost any other battle up to that time. The National troops acquired a confidence in themselves at Belmont that did not desert them through the war.

The day after the battle I met some officers from General Polk's command, arranged for permission to bury our dead at Belmont and also commenced negotiations for the exchange of prisoners. When our men went to bury their dead, before they were allowed to land they were conducted below the point where the enemy had engaged our transports. Some of the officers expressed a desire to see the field; but the request was refused with the statement that we had no dead there.

While on the truce-boat I mentioned to an officer, whom I had known both at West Point and in the Mexican war, that I was in the cornfield near their troops when they passed; that I had been on horseback and had worn a soldier's overcoat at the time. This officer was on General Polk's staff. He said both he and the general had seen me and that Polk had said to his men, "There is a Yankee; you may try your marksmanship on him if you wish," but nobody fired at me.

Belmont was severely criticized in the North as a wholly unnecessary battle, barren of results, or the possibility of them from the beginning. If it had not been fought, Colonel Oglesby would probably have been captured or destroyed with his three thousand men. Then I should have been culpable indeed.

Chapter XXI

GENERAL HALLECK IN COMMAND — COMMANDING THE DISTRICT OF CAIRO — MOVEMENT ON FORT HENRY — CAPTURE OF FORT HENRY

*W*hile at Cairo I had frequent opportunities of meeting the rebel officers of the Columbus garrison. They seemed to be very fond of coming up on steamers under flags of truce. On two or three occasions I went down in like manner. When one of their boats was seen coming up carrying a white flag, a gun would be fired from the lower battery at

Fort Holt, throwing a shot across the bow as a signal to come no farther. I would then take a steamer and, with my staff and occasionally a few other officers, go down to receive the party. There were several officers among them whom I had known before, both at West Point and in Mexico. Seeing these officers who had been educated for the profession of arms, both at school and in actual war, which is a far more efficient training, impressed me with the great advantage the South possessed over the North at the beginning of the rebellion. They had from thirty to forty percent of the educated soldiers of the Nation. They had no standing army and, consequently, these trained soldiers had to find employment with the troops from their own States. In this way what there was of military education and training was distributed throughout their whole army. The whole loaf was leavened.

The North had a great number of educated and trained soldiers, but the bulk of them were still in the army and were retained, generally with their old commands and rank, until the war had lasted many months. In the Army of the Potomac there was what was known as the "regular brigade," in which, from the commanding officer down to the youngest second lieutenant, everyone was educated to his profession. So, too, with many of the batteries; all the officers, generally four in number to each, were men educated for their profession. Some of these went into battle at the beginning under division commanders who were entirely without military training. This state of affairs gave me an idea which I expressed while at Cairo; that the government ought to disband the regular army, with the exception of the staff corps, and notify the disbanded officers that they would receive no compensation while the war lasted except as volunteers. The register should be kept up, but the names of all officers who were not in the volunteer service at the close, should be stricken from it.

On the 9th of November, two days after the battle of Belmont, Major-General H.W. Halleck superseded General Fremont in command of the Department of the Missouri. The limits of his command took in Arkansas and west Kentucky east to the Cumberland River. From the battle of Belmont until early in February, 1862, the troops under my command did little except prepare for the long struggle which proved to be before them.

The enemy at this time occupied a line running from the Mississippi River at Columbus to Bowling Green and Mill Springs, Kentucky. Each of these positions was strongly fortified, as were also points on the Tennessee and Cumberland rivers near the Tennessee state line. The works on the Tennessee were called Fort Heiman and Fort Henry, and that on the Cumberland was Fort Donelson. At these points the two rivers approached within eleven miles of each other. The lines of rifle pits at each place extended back from the water at least two miles, so that the garrisons were in reality only seven miles apart. These positions were of immense importance to the enemy; and of course correspondingly important for us to possess ourselves of. With Fort Henry in our hands we had a navigable stream open to us up to Muscle Shoals, in Alabama. The Memphis and Charleston Railroad strikes the Tennessee at Eastport, Mississippi, and follows close to the banks of the river up to the shoals. This road, of vast importance to the enemy, would cease to be of use to them for through traffic the moment Fort Henry became ours. Fort Donelson was the gate to Nashville — a place of great military and political importance — and to a rich country extending far east in Kentucky. These two points in our possession the enemy would necessarily be thrown back to the Memphis and Charleston road, or to the boundary of the cotton states, and, as before stated, that road would be lost to them for through communication.

The designation of my command had been changed after Halleck's arrival, from the District of Southeast Missouri to the District of Cairo, and the small district commanded by General C.F. Smith, embracing the mouths of the Tennessee and Cumberland rivers, had been added to my jurisdiction. Early in January, 1862, I was directed by General McClellan, through my department commander, to make a reconnaissance in favor of Brigadier-General Don Carlos Buell, who commanded the Department of the Ohio, with headquarters at Louisville, and who was confronting General S.B. Buckner with a larger Confederate force at Bowling Green. It was supposed that Buell was about to make some move against the enemy, and my demonstration was intended to prevent the sending of troops from Columbus, Fort Henry or Donelson to Buckner. I at once ordered General Smith to send a force up the west bank of the Tennessee to threaten forts Heiman and Henry; McClernand at the same time with a force of 6,000 men was sent out into west Kentucky, threatening Columbus with one column and the Tennessee River with another. I went with McClernand's command. The weather was very bad; snow and rain fell; the roads, never good in that section, were intolerable. We were out more than a week splashing through the mud, snow and rain, the men suffering very much. The object of the expedition was accomplished. The enemy did not send reinforcements to Bowling Green, and General George H. Thomas fought and won the battle of Mill Springs before we returned.

As a result of this expedition General Smith reported that he thought it practicable to capture Fort Heiman. This fort stood on high ground, completely commanding Fort Henry on the opposite side of the river, and its possession by us, with the aid of our gunboats, would insure the capture of Fort Henry. This report of Smith's confirmed views I had previously held, that the true line of operations for us was up the Tennessee and Cumberland rivers. With us there, the enemy would be compelled to fall back on the east and west entirely out of the State of Kentucky. On the 6th of January, before receiving orders for this expedition, I had asked permission of the general commanding the department to go to see him at St. Louis. My object was to lay this plan of campaign before him. Now that my views had been confirmed by so able a general as Smith, I renewed my request to go to St. Louis on what I deemed important military business. The leave was granted, but not graciously. I had known General Halleck but very slightly in the old army, not having met him either at West Point or during the Mexican war. I was received with so little cordiality that I perhaps stated the object of my visit with less clearness than I might have done, and I had not uttered many sentences before I was cut short as if my plan was preposterous. I returned to Cairo very much crestfallen.

Flag-officer Foote commanded the little fleet of gunboats then in the neighborhood of Cairo and, though in another branch of the service, was subject to the command of General Halleck. He and I consulted freely upon military matters and he agreed with me perfectly as to the feasibility of the campaign up the Tennessee. Notwithstanding the rebuff I had received from my immediate chief, I therefore, on the 28th of January, renewed the suggestion by telegraph that "if permitted, I could take and hold Fort Henry on the Tennessee." This time I was backed by Flag-officer Foote, who sent a similar dispatch. On the 29th I wrote fully in support of the proposition. On the 1st of February I received full instructions from department headquarters to move upon Fort Henry. On the 2d the expedition started.

In February, 1862, there were quite a good many steamers laid up at Cairo for want of employment, the Mississippi River being closed against navigation below that point. There were also many men in the town whose occupation had been following the river in various capacities, from captain down to deck hand But there were not enough of either boats or men to move at one time the 17,000 men I proposed to take with me up the Tennessee. I loaded the boats with more than half the force, however, and sent General McClernand in command. I followed with one of the later boats and found McClernand had stopped, very properly, nine miles below Fort Henry. Seven gunboats under Flag-officer Foote had accompanied the advance. The transports we had with us had to return to Paducah to bring up a division from there, with General C.F. Smith in command.

Before sending the boats back I wanted to get the troops as near to the enemy as I could without coming within range of their guns. There was a stream emptying into the Tennessee on the east side, apparently at about long range distance below the fort. On account of the narrow water-shed separating the Tennessee and Cumberland rivers at that point, the stream must be insignificant at ordinary stages, but when we were there, in February, it was a torrent. It would facilitate the investment of Fort Henry materially if the troops could be landed south of that stream. To test whether this could be done I boarded the gunboat Essex and requested Captain Wm. Porter commanding it, to approach the fort to draw its fire. After we had gone some distance past the mouth of the stream we drew the fire of the fort, which fell much short of us. In consequence I had made up my mind to return and bring the troops to the upper side of the creek, when the enemy opened upon us with a rifled gun that sent shot far beyond us and beyond the stream. One shot passed very near where Captain Porter and I were standing, struck the deck near the stern, penetrated and passed through the cabin and so out into the river. We immediately turned back, and the troops were debarked below the mouth of the creek.

When the landing was completed I returned with the transports to Paducah to hasten up the balance of the troops. I got back on the 5th with the advance the remainder following as rapidly as the steamers could carry them. At ten o'clock at night, on the 5th, the whole command was not yet up. Being anxious to commence operations as soon as possible before the enemy could reinforce heavily, I issued my orders for an advance at 11 A.M. on the 6th. I felt sure that all the troops would be up by that time.

Fort Henry occupies a bend in the river which gave the guns in the water battery a direct fire down the stream. The camp outside the fort was entrenched, with rifle pits and outworks two miles back on the road to Donelson and Dover. The garrison of the fort and camp was about 2,800, with strong reinforcements from Donelson halted some miles out. There were seventeen heavy guns in the fort. The river was very high, the banks being overflowed except where the bluffs come to the water's edge. A portion of the ground on which Fort Henry stood was two feet deep in water. Below, the water extended into the woods several hundred yards back from the bank on the east side. On the west bank Fort Heiman stood on high ground, completely commanding Fort Henry. The distance from Fort Henry to Donelson is but eleven miles. The two positions were so important to the enemy, *as he saw his interest,* that it was natural to suppose that reinforcements would come from every quarter from which they could be got. Prompt action on our part was imperative.

The plan was for the troops and gunboats to start at the same moment. The troops were to invest the garrison and the gunboats to attack the fort at close quarters. General Smith was to land a brigade of his division on the west bank during the night of the 5th and get it in rear of Heiman.

At the hour designated the troops and gunboats started. General Smith found Fort Heiman had been evacuated before his men arrived. The gunboats soon engaged the water batteries at very close quarters, but the troops which were to invest Fort Henry were delayed for want of roads, as well as by the dense forest and the high water in what would in dry weather have been unimportant beds of streams. This delay made no difference in the result. On our first appearance Tilghman had sent his entire command, with the exception of about one hundred men left to man the guns in the fort, to the outworks on the road to Dover and Donelson, so as to have them out of range of the guns of our navy; and before any attack on the 6th he had ordered them to retreat on Donelson. He stated in his subsequent report that the defense was intended solely to give his troops time to make their escape.

Tilghman was captured with his staff and ninety men, as well as the armament of the fort, the ammunition and whatever stores were there. Our cavalry pursued the retreating column towards Donelson and picked up two guns and a few stragglers; but the enemy had so much the start, that the pursuing force did not get in sight of any except the stragglers.

All the gunboats engaged were hit many times. The damage, however, beyond what could be repaired by a small expenditure of money, was slight, except to the Essex. A shell penetrated the boiler of that vessel and exploded it, killing and wounding forty-eight men, nineteen of whom were soldiers who had been detailed to act with the navy. On several occasions during the war such details were made when the complement of men with the navy was insufficient for the duty before them. After the fall of Fort Henry Captain Phelps, commanding the iron-clad Carondelet, at my request ascended the Tennessee River and thoroughly destroyed the bridge of the Memphis and Ohio Railroad.

Chapter XXII

INVESTMENT OF FORT DONELSON — THE
NAVAL OPERATIONS — ATTACK OF THE ENEMY
— ASSAULTING THE WORKS — SURRENDER OF
THE FORT

*I*nformed the department commander of our success at Fort Henry
and that on the 8th I would take Fort Donelson. But the rain continued
to fall so heavily that the roads became impassable for artillery and
wagon trains. Then, too, it would not have been prudent to proceed
without the gunboats. At least it would have been leaving behind a
valuable part of our available force.

On the 7th, the day after the fall of Fort Henry, I took my staff and
the cavalry — a part of one regiment — and made a reconnaissance to
within about a mile of the outer line of works at Donelson. I had known
General Pillow in Mexico, and judged that with any force, no matter
how small, I could march up to within gunshot of any entrenchments
he was given to hold. I said this to the officers of my staff at the time.
I knew that Floyd was in command, but he was no soldier, and I judged
that he would yield to Pillow's pretensions. I met, as I expected, no
opposition in making the reconnaissance and, besides learning the
topography of the country on the way and around Fort Donelson, found
that there were two roads available for marching; one leading to the
village of Dover, the other to Donelson.

Fort Donelson is two miles north, or down the river, from Dover.
The fort, as it stood in 1861, embraced about one hundred acres of land.
On the east it fronted the Cumberland; to the north it faced Hickman's
creek, a small stream which at that time was deep and wide because of
the back-water from the river; on the south was another small stream,
or rather a ravine, opening into the Cumberland. This also was filled
with back-water from the river. The fort stood on high ground, some of
it as much as a hundred feet above the Cumberland. Strong protection
to the heavy guns in the water batteries had been obtained by cutting

away places for them in the bluff. To the west there was a line of rifle pits some two miles back from the river at the farthest point. This line ran generally along the crest of high ground, but in one place crossed a ravine which opens into the river between the village and the fort. The ground inside and outside of this entrenched line was very broken and generally wooded. The trees outside of the rifle-pits had been cut down for a considerable way out, and had been felled so that their tops lay outwards from the entrenchments. The limbs had been trimmed and pointed, and thus formed an abatis in front of the greater part of the line. Outside of this entrenched line, and extending about half the entire length of it, is a ravine running north and south and opening into Hickman creek at a point north of the fort. The entire side of this ravine next to the works was one long abatis.

General Halleck commenced his efforts in all quarters to get reinforcements to forward to me immediately on my departure from Cairo. General Hunter sent men freely from Kansas, and a large division under General Nelson, from Buell's army, was also dispatched. Orders went out from the War Department to consolidate fragments of companies that were being recruited in the Western States so as to make full companies, and to consolidate companies into regiments. General Halleck did not approve or disapprove of my going to Fort Donelson. He said nothing whatever to me on the subject. He informed Buell on the 7th that I would march against Fort Donelson the next day; but on the 10th he directed me to fortify Fort Henry strongly, particularly to the land side, saying that he forwarded me entrenching tools for that purpose. I received this dispatch in front of Fort Donelson.

I was very impatient to get to Fort Donelson because I knew the importance of the place to the enemy and supposed he would reinforce it rapidly. I felt that 15,000 men on the 8th would be more effective than 50,000 a month later. I asked Flag-officer Foote, therefore, to order his gunboats still about Cairo to proceed up the Cumberland River and not to wait for those gone to Eastport and Florence; but the others got back in time and we started on the 12th. I had moved McClernand out a few miles the night before so as to leave the road as free as possible.

Just as we were about to start the first reinforcement reached me on transports. It was a brigade composed of six full regiments commanded by Colonel Thayer, of Nebraska. As the gunboats were going around to Donelson by the Tennessee, Ohio and Cumberland rivers, I directed Thayer to turn about and go under their convoy.

I started from Fort Henry with 15,000 men, including eight batteries and part of a regiment of cavalry, and, meeting with no obstruction to detain us, the advance arrived in front of the enemy by noon. That afternoon and the next day were spent in taking up ground to make the investment as complete as possible. General Smith had been directed to leave a portion of his division behind to guard forts Henry and Heiman. He left General Lew. Wallace with 2,500 men. With the remainder of his division he occupied our left, extending to Hickman creek. McClernand was on the right and covered the roads running south and southwest from Dover. His right extended to the back-water up the ravine opening into the Cumberland south of the village. The troops were not entrenched, but the nature of the ground was such that they were just as well protected from the fire of the enemy as if rifle-pits had been thrown up. Our line was generally along the crest of ridges. The artillery was protected by being sunk in the ground. The men who were not serving the guns were perfectly covered from fire on taking position a little back from the crest. The greatest suffering was from want of shelter. It was midwinter and during the siege we had rain and snow, thawing and freezing alternately. It would not do to allow campfires except far down the hill out of sight of the enemy, and it would not do to allow many of the troops to remain there at the same time. In the march over from Fort Henry numbers of the men had thrown away their blankets and overcoats. There was therefore much discomfort and absolute suffering.

During the 12th and 13th, and until the arrival of Wallace and Thayer on the 14th, the National forces, composed of but 15,000 men, without entrenchments, confronted an entrenched army of 21,000, without conflict further than what was brought on by ourselves. Only one gunboat had arrived. There was a little skirmishing each day, brought on by the movement of our troops in securing commanding positions; but there was no actual fighting during this time except once, on the 13th, in front of McClernand's command. That general had undertaken to capture a battery of the enemy which was annoying his men. Without orders or authority he sent three regiments to make the assault. The battery was in the main line of the enemy, which was defended by his whole army present. Of course the assault was a failure, and of course the loss on our side was great for the number of men engaged. In this assault Colonel William Morrison fell badly wounded. Up to this time the surgeons with the army had no difficulty in finding room in the houses near our line for all the sick and wounded; but now hospitals were overcrowded. Owing, however, to the energy and skill of the surgeons the suffering was not so great as it might have been. The hospital arrangements at Fort Donelson were as complete as it was possible to make them, considering the inclemency of the weather and the lack of tents, in a sparsely settled country where the houses were generally of but one or two rooms.

On the return of Captain Walke to Fort Henry on the 10th, I had requested him to take the vessels that had accompanied him on his expedition up the Tennessee, and get possession of the Cumberland as far up towards Donelson as possible. He started without delay, taking, however, only his own gunboat, the Carondelet, towed by the steamer Alps. Captain Walke arrived a few miles below Donelson on the 12th, a little after noon. About the time the advance of troops reached a point within gunshot of the fort on the land side, he engaged the water batteries at long range. On the 13th I informed him of my arrival the day before and of the establishment of most of our batteries, requesting him at the same time to attack again that day so that I might take advantage of any diversion. The attack was made and many shots fell within the fort, creating some consternation, as we now know. The investment on the land side was made as complete as the number of troops engaged would admit of.

During the night of the 13th Flag-officer Foote arrived with the ironclads St. Louis, Louisville and Pittsburg and the wooden gunboats Tyler and Conestoga, convoying Thayer's brigade. On the morning of the 14th Thayer was landed. Wallace, whom I had ordered over from Fort Henry, also arrived about the same time. Up to this time he had been commanding a brigade belonging to the division of General C.F. Smith. These troops were now restored to the division they belonged to, and General Lew. Wallace was assigned to the command of a division composed of the brigade of Colonel Thayer and other reinforcements that arrived the same day. This new division was assigned to the center, giving the two flanking divisions an opportunity to close up and form a stronger line.

The plan was for the troops to hold the enemy within his lines, while the gunboats should attack the water batteries at close quarters and silence his guns if possible. Some of the gunboats were to run the batteries, get above the fort and above the village of Dover. I had ordered a reconnaissance made with the view of getting troops to the river above Dover in case they should be needed there. That position attained by the gunboats it would have been but a question of time — and a very short time, too — when the garrison would have been compelled to surrender.

By three in the afternoon of the 14th Flag-officer Foote was ready, and advanced upon the water batteries with his entire fleet. After coming in range of the batteries of the enemy the advance was slow, but a constant fire was delivered from every gun that could be brought to bear upon the fort. I occupied a position on shore from which I could see the advancing navy. The leading boat got within a very short distance of the water battery, not further off I think than two hundred yards, and I soon saw one and then another of them dropping down the river, visibly disabled. Then the whole fleet followed and the engagement closed for the day. The gunboat which Flag-officer Foote was on, besides having been hit about sixty times, several of the shots passing through near the waterline, had a shot enter the pilot-house which killed the pilot, carried away the wheel and wounded the flag-officer himself. The tiller-ropes of another vessel were carried away and she, too, dropped helplessly back. Two others had their pilot-houses so injured that they scarcely formed a protection to the men at the wheel.

The enemy had evidently been much demoralized by the assault, but they were jubilant when they saw the disabled vessels dropping down the river entirely out of the control of the men on board. Of course I only witnessed the falling back of our gunboats and felt sad enough at the time over the repulse. Subsequent reports, now published, show that the enemy telegraphed a great victory to Richmond. The sun went down on the night of the 14th of February, 1862, leaving the army confronting Fort Donelson anything but comforted over the prospects. The weather had turned intensely cold; the men were without tents and could not keep up fires where most of them had to stay, and, as previously stated, many had thrown away their overcoats and blankets. Two of the strongest of our gunboats had been disabled, presumably beyond the possibility of rendering any present assistance. I retired this night not knowing but that I would have to entrench my position, and bring up tents for the men or build huts under the cover of the hills.

On the morning of the 15th, before it was yet broad day, a messenger from Flag-officer Foote handed me a note, expressing a desire to see me on the flag-ship and saying that he had been injured the day before so much that he could not come himself to me. I at once made my preparations for starting. I directed my adjutant-general to notify each of the division commanders of my absence and instruct them to do nothing to bring on an engagement until they received further orders, but to hold their positions. From the heavy rains that had fallen for days and weeks preceding and from the constant use of the roads between the troops and the landing four to seven miles below, these roads had become cut up so as to be hardly passable. The intense cold of the night of the 14th-15th had frozen the ground solid. This made travel on horseback even slower than through the mud; but I went as fast as the roads would allow.

When I reached the fleet I found the flag-ship was anchored out in the stream. A small boat, however, awaited my arrival and I was soon on board with the flag-officer. He explained to me in short the condition in which he was left by the engagement of the evening before, and suggested that I should entrench while he returned to Mound City with his disabled boats, expressing at the time the belief that he could have the necessary repairs made and be back in ten days. I saw the absolute necessity of his gunboats going into hospital and did not know but I should be forced to the alternative of going through a siege. But the enemy relieved me from this necessity.

When I left the National line to visit Flag-officer Foote I had no idea that there would be any engagement on land unless I brought it on myself. The conditions for battle were much more favorable to us than they had been for the first two days of the investment. From the 12th to the 14th we had but 15,000 men of all arms and no gunboats. Now we had been reinforced by a fleet of six naval vessels, a large division of troops under General L. Wallace and 2,500 men brought over from Fort Henry belonging to the division of C.F. Smith. The enemy, however, had taken the initiative. Just as I landed I met Captain Hillyer of my staff, white with fear, not for his personal safety, but for the safety of the National troops. He said the enemy had come out of his lines in full force and attacked and scattered McClernand's division, which was in full retreat. The roads, as I have said, were unfit for making fast time, but I got to my command as soon as possible. The attack had been made on the National right. I was some four or five miles north of our left. The line was about three miles long. In reaching the point where the disaster had occurred I had to pass the divisions of Smith and Wallace. I saw no sign of excitement on the portion of the line held by Smith; Wallace was nearer the scene of conflict and had taken part in it. He had, at an opportune time, sent Thayer's brigade to the support of McClernand and thereby contributed to hold the enemy within his lines.

I saw everything favorable for us along the line of our left and center. When I came to the right appearances were different. The enemy had come out in full force to cut his way out and make his escape. McClernand's division had to bear the brunt of the attack from this combined force. His men had stood up gallantly until the ammunition in their cartridge-boxes gave out. There was abundance of ammunition near by lying on the ground in boxes, but at that stage of the war it was not all of our commanders of regiments, brigades, or even divisions, who had been educated up to the point of seeing that their men were constantly supplied with ammunition during an engagement. When the men found themselves without ammunition they could not stand up against troops who seemed to have plenty of it. The division broke and a portion fled, but most of the men, as they were not pursued, only fell back out of range of the fire of the enemy. It must have been about this time that Thayer pushed his brigade in between the enemy and those of our troops that were without ammunition. At all events the enemy fell back within his entrenchments and was there when I got on the field.

I saw the men standing in knots talking in the most excited manner. No officer seemed to be giving any directions. The soldiers had their muskets, but no ammunition, while there were tons of it close at hand. I heard some of the men say that the enemy had come out with knapsacks, and haversacks filled with rations. They seemed to think this indicated a determination on his part to stay out and fight just as long as the provisions held out. I turned to Colonel J.D. Webster, of my staff, who was with me, and said: "Some of our men are pretty badly demoralized, but the enemy must be more so, for he has attempted to force his way out, but has fallen back: the one who attacks first now will be victorious and the enemy will have to be in a hurry if he gets ahead of me." I determined to make the assault at once on our left. It was clear to my mind that the enemy had started to march out with his entire force, except a few pickets, and if our attack could be made on the left before the enemy could redistribute his forces along the line, we would find but little opposition except from the intervening abatis. I directed Colonel Webster to ride with me and call out to the men as we passed: "Fill your cartridge-boxes, quick, and get into line; the enemy is trying to escape and he must not be permitted to do so." This acted like a charm. The men only wanted someone to give them a command. We rode rapidly to Smith's quarters, when I explained the situation to him and directed him to charge the enemy's works in his front with his whole division, saying at the same time that he would find nothing but a very thin line to contend with. The general was off in an incredibly short time, going in advance himself to keep his men from firing while they were working their way through the abatis intervening between them and the enemy. The outer line of rifle-pits was passed, and the night of the 15th General Smith, with much of his division, bivouacked within the lines of the enemy. There was now no doubt but that the Confederates must surrender or be captured the next day.

There seems from subsequent accounts to have been much consternation, particularly among the officers of high rank, in Dover during the night of the 15th. General Floyd, the commanding officer, who was a man of talent enough for any civil position, was no soldier and, possibly, did not possess the elements of one. He was further unfitted for command, for the reason that his conscience must have troubled him and made him afraid. As Secretary of War he had taken a solemn oath to maintain the Constitution of the United States and to uphold the same against all its enemies. He had betrayed that trust. As Secretary of War he was reported through the northern press to have scattered the little army the country had so that the most of it could be picked up in detail when secession occurred. About a year before leaving the Cabinet he had removed arms from northern to southern arsenals. He continued in the Cabinet of President Buchanan until about the 1st of January, 1861, while he was working vigilantly for the establishment of a confederacy made out of United States territory. Well may he have been afraid to fall into the hands of National troops. He would no doubt have been tried for misappropriating public property, if not for treason, had he been captured. General Pillow, next in command, was conceited, and prided himself much on his services in the Mexican war. He telegraphed to General Johnston, at Nashville, after our men were within the rebel rifle-pits, and almost on the eve of his making his escape, that the Southern troops had had great success all day. Johnston forwarded the dispatch to Richmond. While the authorities at the capital were reading it Floyd and Pillow were fugitives.

A council of war was held by the enemy at which all agreed that it would be impossible to hold out longer. General Buckner, who was third in rank in the garrison but much the most capable soldier, seems to have regarded it a duty to hold the fort until the general commanding the department, A.S. Johnston, should get back to his headquarters at Nashville. Buckner's report shows, however, that he considered Donelson lost and that any attempt to hold the place longer would be at the sacrifice of the command. Being assured that Johnston was already in Nashville, Buckner too agreed that surrender was the proper thing. Floyd turned over the command to Pillow, who declined it. It then devolved upon Buckner, who accepted the responsibility of the position. Floyd and Pillow took possession of all the river transports at Dover and before morning both were on their way to Nashville, with the brigade formerly commanded by Floyd and some other troops, in all about 3,000. Some marched up the east bank of the Cumberland; others went on the steamers. During the night Forrest also, with his cavalry and some other troops about a thousand in all, made their way out, passing between our right and the river. They had to ford or swim over the back-water in the little creek just south of Dover.

Before daylight General Smith brought to me the following letter from General Buckner:

HEADQUARTERS, FORT DONELSON,
February 16, 1862.

SIR: —

In consideration of all the circumstances governing the present situation of affairs at this station, I propose to the Commanding Officer of the Federal forces the appointment of Commissioners to agree upon terms of capitulation of the forces and fort under my command, and in that view suggest an armistice until 12 o'clock today.

I am, sir, very respectfully,

Your ob't se'v't,
S.B. BUCKNER, Brig. Gen. C.S.A.

To Brigadier-General U.S. Grant,
Com'ding U.S. Forces, Near Fort Donelson

To this I responded as follows:

HEADQUARTERS ARMY IN THE FIELD,
Camp near Donelson, February 16, 1862
General S.B. BUCKNER, Confederate Army

SIR: —

Yours of this date, proposing armistice and appointment of Commissioners to settle terms of capitulation, is just received. No terms except an unconditional and immediate surrender can be accepted. I propose to move immediately upon your works.

I am, sir, very respectfully,

Your ob't se'v't,
U.S. GRANT, Brig. Gen.

To this I received the following reply:

HEADQUARTERS, DOVER, TENNESSEE,
February 16, 1862

To Brig. Gen'l U.S. GRANT, U.S. Army

SIR: —

The distribution of the forces under my command, incident to an unexpected change of commanders, and the overwhelming force under your command, compel me, notwithstanding the brilliant success of the Confederate arms yesterday, to accept the ungenerous and unchivalrous terms which you propose.

I am, sir,

Your very ob't se'v't,
S.B. BUCKNER, Brig. Gen. C.S.A.

General Buckner, as soon as he had dispatched the first of the above letters, sent word to his different commanders on the line of rifle-pits, notifying them that he had made a proposition looking to the surrender of the garrison, and directing them to notify National troops in their front so that all fighting might be prevented. White flags were stuck at intervals along the line of rifle-pits, but none over the fort. As soon as the last letter from Buckner was received I mounted my horse and rode to Dover. General Wallace, I found, had preceded me an hour or more. I presume that, seeing white flags exposed in his front, he rode up to see what they meant and, not being fired upon or halted, he kept on until he found himself at the headquarters of General Buckner.

I had been at West Point three years with Buckner and afterwards served with him in the army, so that we were quite well acquainted. In the course of our conversation, which was very friendly, he said to me that if he had been in command I would not have got up to Donelson as easily as I did. I told him that if he had been in command I should not have tried in the way I did: I had invested their lines with a smaller force than they had to defend them, and at the same time had sent a brigade full 5,000 strong, around by water; I had relied very much upon their commander to allow me to come safely up to the outside of their works. I asked General Buckner about what force he had to surrender. He replied that he could not tell with any degree of accuracy; that all the sick and weak had been sent to Nashville while we were about Fort Henry; that Floyd and Pillow had left during the night, taking many men with them; and that Forrest, and probably others, had also escaped during the preceding night: the number of casualties he could not tell; but he said I would not find fewer than 12,000, nor more than 15,000.

He asked permission to send parties outside of the lines to bury his dead, who had fallen on the 15th when they tried to get out. I gave directions that his permit to pass our limits should be recognized. I have no reason to believe that this privilege was abused, but it familiarized our guards so much with the sight of Confederates passing to and fro that I have no doubt many got beyond our pickets unobserved and went on. The most of the men who went in that way no doubt thought they had had war enough, and left with the intention of remaining out of the army. Some came to me and asked permission to go, saying that they were tired of the war and would not be caught in the ranks again, and I bade them go.

The actual number of Confederates at Fort Donelson can never be given with entire accuracy. The largest number admitted by any writer on the Southern side, is by Colonel Preston Johnston. He gives the number at 17,000. But this must be an underestimate. The commissary general of prisoners reported having issued rations to 14,623 Fort Donelson prisoners at Cairo, as they passed that point. General Pillow reported the killed and wounded at 2,000; but he had less opportunity of knowing the actual numbers than the officers of McClernand's division, for most of the killed and wounded fell outside their works, in front of that division, and were buried or cared for by Buckner after the surrender and when Pillow was a fugitive. It is known that Floyd and Pillow escaped during the night of the 15th, taking with them not less than 3,000 men. Forrest escaped with about 1,000 and others were leaving singly and in squads all night. It is probable that the Confederate force at Donelson, on the 15th of February, 1862, was 21,000 in round numbers.

On the day Fort Donelson fell I had 27,000 men to confront the Confederate lines and guard the road four or five miles to the left, over which all our supplies had to be drawn on wagons. During the 16th, after the surrender, additional reinforcements arrived.

During the siege General Sherman had been sent to Smithland, at the mouth of the Cumberland River, to forward reinforcements and supplies to me. At that time he was my senior in rank and there was no authority of law to assign a junior to command a senior of the same grade. But every boat that came up with supplies or reinforcements brought a note of encouragement from Sherman, asking me to call upon him for any assistance he could render and saying that if he could be of service at the front I might send for him and he would waive rank.

Chapter XXIII

PROMOTED MAJOR-GENERAL OF VOLUNTEERS
— UNOCCUPIED TERRITORY — ADVANCE UPON
NASHVILLE — SITUATION OF THE TROOPS —
CONFEDERATE RETREAT — RELIEVED OF THE
COMMAND — RESTORED TO THE COMMAND —
GENERAL SMITH

*T*he news of the fall of Fort Donelson caused great delight all over the North. At the South, particularly in Richmond, the effect was correspondingly depressing. I was promptly promoted to the grade of Major-General of Volunteers, and confirmed by the Senate. All three of my division commanders were promoted to the same grade and the colonels who commanded brigades were made brigadier-generals in the volunteer service. My chief, who was in St. Louis, telegraphed his congratulations to General Hunter in Kansas for the services he had rendered in securing the fall of Fort Donelson by sending reinforcements so rapidly. To Washington he telegraphed that the victory was due to General C.F. Smith; "promote him," he said, "and the whole country will applaud." On the 19th there was published at St. Louis a formal order thanking Flag-officer Foote and myself, and the forces under our command, for the victories on the Tennessee and the Cumberland. I received no other recognition whatever from General Halleck. But General Cullum, his chief of staff, who was at Cairo, wrote me a warm congratulatory letter on his own behalf. I approved of General Smith's promotion highly, as I did all the promotions that were made.

My opinion was and still is that immediately after the fall of Fort Donelson the way was opened to the National forces all over the Southwest without much resistance. If one general who would have taken the responsibility had been in command of all the troops west of the Alleghenies, he could have marched to Chattanooga, Corinth, Memphis and Vicksburg with the troops we then had, and as volunteering was going on rapidly over the North there would soon have been force enough at all these centers to operate offensively against any body of the enemy that might be found near them. Rapid movements and the acquisition of rebellious territory would have promoted volunteering, so that reinforcements could have been had as fast as transportation could have been obtained to carry them to their destination. On the other hand there were tens of thousands of strong able-bodied young men still at their homes in the Southwestern States, who had not gone into the Confederate army in February, 1862, and who had no particular desire to go. If our lines had been extended to protect their homes, many of them never would have gone. Providence ruled differently. Time was given the enemy to collect armies and fortify his new positions; and twice afterwards he came near forcing his northwestern front up to the Ohio River.

I promptly informed the department commander of our success at Fort Donelson and that the way was open now to Clarksville and Nashville; and that unless I received orders to the contrary I should take Clarksville on the 21st and Nashville about the 1st of March. Both these places are on the Cumberland River above Fort Donelson. As I heard nothing from headquarters on the subject, General C.F. Smith was sent to Clarksville at the time designated and found the place evacuated. The capture of forts Henry and Donelson had broken the line the enemy had taken from Columbus to Bowling Green, and it was known that he was falling back from the eastern point of this line and that Buell was following, or at least advancing. I should have sent troops to Nashville at the time I sent to Clarksville, but my transportation was limited and there were many prisoners to be forwarded north.

None of the reinforcements from Buell's army arrived until the 24th of February. Then General Nelson came up, with orders to report to me with two brigades, he having sent one brigade to Cairo. I knew General Buell was advancing on Nashville from the north, and I was advised by scouts that the rebels were leaving that place, and trying to get out all the supplies they could. Nashville was, at that time, one of the best provisioned posts in the South. I had no use for reinforcements now, and thinking Buell would like to have his troops again, I ordered Nelson to proceed to Nashville without debarking at Fort Donelson. I sent a gunboat also as a convoy. The Cumberland River was very high at the time; the railroad bridge at Nashville had been burned, and all river craft had been destroyed, or would be before the enemy left. Nashville is on the west bank of the Cumberland, and Buell was approaching from the east. I thought the steamers carrying Nelson's division would be useful in ferrying the balance of Buell's forces across. I ordered Nelson to put himself in communication with Buell as soon as possible, and if he found him more than two days off from Nashville to return below the city and await orders. Buell, however, had already arrived in person at Edgefield, opposite Nashville, and Mitchell's division of his command reached there the same day. Nelson immediately took possession of the city.

After Nelson had gone and before I had learned of Buell's arrival, I sent word to department headquarters that I should go to Nashville myself on the 28th if I received no orders to the contrary. Hearing nothing, I went as I had informed my superior officer I would do. On arriving at Clarksville I saw a fleet of steamers at the shore — the same that had taken Nelson's division — and troops going aboard. I landed and called on the commanding officer, General C.F. Smith. As soon as he saw me he showed an order he had just received from Buell in these words:

NASHVILLE, February 25, 1862.

GENERAL C.F. SMITH,
Commanding U.S. Forces, Clarksville

GENERAL: —
The landing of a portion of our troops, contrary to my intentions, on the south side of the river has compelled me to hold this side at every hazard. If the enemy should assume the offensive, and I am assured by reliable persons that in view of my position such is his intention, my force present is altogether inadequate, consisting of only 15,000 men. I have to request you, therefore, to come forward with all the available force under your command. So important do I consider the occasion that I think it necessary to give this communication all the force of orders, and I send four boats, the Diana, Woodford, John Rain, and Autocrat, to bring you up. In five or six days my force will probably be sufficient to relieve you.

Very respectfully, your ob't srv't,
D.C. BUELL, Brigadier-General Comd'g.
P.S. — The steamers will leave here at 12 o'clock tonight.

General Smith said this order was nonsense. But I told him it was better to obey it. The General replied, "of course I must obey," and said his men were embarking as fast as they could. I went on up to Nashville and inspected the position taken by Nelson's troops. I did not see Buell during the day, and wrote him a note saying that I had been in Nashville since early morning and had hoped to meet him. On my return to the boat we met. His troops were still east of the river, and the steamers that had carried Nelson's division up were mostly at Clarksville to bring Smith's division. I said to General Buell my information was that the enemy was retreating as fast as possible. General Buell said there was fighting going on then only ten or twelve miles away. I said: "Quite probably; Nashville contained valuable stores of arms, ammunition and provisions, and the enemy is probably trying to carry away all he can. The fighting is doubtless with the rear-guard who are trying to protect the trains they are getting away with." Buell spoke very positively of the danger Nashville was in of an attack from the enemy. I said, in the absence of positive information, I believed my information was correct. He responded that he "knew." "Well," I said, "I do not know; but as I came by Clarksville General Smith's troops were embarking to join you."

Smith's troops were returned the same day. The enemy were trying to get away from Nashville and not to return to it.

At this time General Albert Sidney Johnston commanded all the Confederate troops west of the Allegheny Mountains, with the exception of those in the extreme south. On the National side the forces confronting him were divided into, at first three, then four separate departments. Johnston had greatly the advantage in having supreme command over all troops that could possibly be brought to bear upon one point, while the forces similarly situated on the National side, divided into independent commands, could not be brought into harmonious action except by orders from Washington.

At the beginning of 1862 Johnston's troops east of the Mississippi occupied a line extending from Columbus, on his left, to Mill Springs, on his right. As we have seen, Columbus, both banks of the Tennessee River, the west bank of the Cumberland and Bowling Green, all were strongly fortified. Mill Springs was entrenched. The National troops occupied no territory south of the Ohio, except three small garrisons along its bank and a force thrown out from Louisville to confront that at Bowling Green. Johnston's strength was no doubt numerically inferior to that of the National troops; but this was compensated for by the advantage of being sole commander of all the Confederate forces at the West, and of operating in a country where his friends would take care of his rear without any detail of soldiers. But when General George H. Thomas moved upon the enemy at Mill Springs and totally routed him, inflicting a loss of some 300 killed and wounded, and forts Henry and Heiman fell into the hands of the National forces, with their armaments and about 100 prisoners, those losses seemed to dishearten the Confederate commander so much that he immediately commenced a retreat from Bowling Green on Nashville. He reached this latter place on the 14th of February, while Donelson was still besieged. Buell followed with a portion of the Army of the Ohio, but he had to march and did not reach the east bank of the Cumberland opposite Nashville until the 24th of the month, and then with only one division of his army.

The bridge at Nashville had been destroyed and all boats removed or disabled, so that a small garrison could have held the place against any National troops that could have been brought against it within ten days after the arrival of the force from Bowling Green. Johnston seemed to lie quietly at Nashville to await the result at Fort Donelson, on which he had staked the possession of most of the territory embraced in the States of Kentucky and Tennessee. It is true, the two generals senior in rank at Fort Donelson were sending him encouraging dispatches, even claiming great Confederate victories up to the night of the 16th when they must have been preparing for their individual escape. Johnston made a fatal mistake in intrusting so important a command to Floyd, who he must have known was no soldier even if he possessed the elements of one. Pillow's presence as second was also a mistake. If these officers had been forced upon him and designated for that particular command, then he should have left Nashville with a small garrison under a trusty officer, and with the remainder of his force gone to Donelson himself. If he had been captured the result could not have been worse than it was.

Johnston's heart failed him upon the first advance of National troops. He wrote to Richmond on the 8th of February, "I think the gunboats of the enemy will probably take Fort Donelson without the necessity of employing their land force in cooperation." After the fall of that place he abandoned Nashville and Chattanooga without an effort to save either, and fell back into northern Mississippi, where, six weeks later, he was destined to end his career.

From the time of leaving Cairo I was singularly unfortunate in not receiving dispatches from General Halleck. The order of the 10th of February directing me to fortify Fort Henry strongly, particularly to the land side, and saying that entrenching tools had been sent for that purpose, reached me after Donelson was invested. I received nothing direct which indicated that the department commander knew we were in possession of Donelson. I was reporting regularly to the chief of staff, who had been sent to Cairo, soon after the troops left there, to receive all reports from the front and to telegraph the substance to the St. Louis headquarters. Cairo was at the southern end of the telegraph wire. Another line was started at once from Cairo to Paducah and Smithland, at the mouths of the Tennessee and Cumberland respectively. My dispatches were all sent to Cairo by boat, but many of those addressed to me were sent to the operator at the end of the advancing wire and he failed to forward them. This operator afterwards proved to be a rebel; he deserted his post after a short time and went south taking his dispatches with him. A telegram from General McClellan to me of February 16th, the day of the surrender, directing me to report in full the situation, was not received at my headquarters until the 3d of March.

On the 2d of March I received orders dated March 1st to move my command back to Fort Henry, leaving only a small garrison at Donelson. From Fort Henry expeditions were to be sent against Eastport, Mississippi, and Paris, Tennessee. We started from Donelson on the 4th, and the same day I was back on the Tennessee River. On March 4th I also received the following dispatch from General Halleck:

Maj.-Gen. U.S. Grant, Fort Henry:
You will place Maj.-Gen. C.F. Smith in command of expedition, and remain yourself at Fort Henry. Why do you not obey my orders to report strength and positions of your command?
H.W. Halleck, Major-General

I was surprised. This was the first intimation I had received that General Halleck had called for information as to the strength of my command. On the 6th he wrote to me again. "Your going to Nashville without authority, and when your presence with your troops was of the utmost importance, was a matter of very serious complaint at Washington, so much so that I was advised to arrest you on your return." This was the first I knew of his objecting to my going to Nashville. That place was not beyond the limits of my command, which, it had been expressly declared in orders, were "not defined." Nashville is west of the Cumberland River, and I had sent troops that had reported to me for duty to occupy the place. I turned over the command as directed and then replied to General Halleck courteously, but asked to be relieved from further duty under him.

Later I learned that General Halleck had been calling lustily for more troops, promising that he would do something important if he could only be sufficiently reinforced. McClellan asked him what force he then had. Halleck telegraphed me to supply the information so far as my command was concerned, but I received none of his dispatches. At last Halleck reported to Washington that he had repeatedly ordered me to give the strength of my force, but could get nothing out of me; that I had gone to Nashville, beyond the limits of my command, without his authority, and that my army was more demoralized by victory than the army at Bull Run had been by defeat. General McClellan, on this information, ordered that I should be relieved from duty and that an investigation should be made into any charges against me. He even authorized my arrest. Thus in less than two weeks after the victory at Donelson, the two leading generals in the army were in correspondence as to what disposition should be made of me, and in less than three weeks I was virtually in arrest and without a command.

On the 13th of March I was restored to command, and on the 17th Halleck sent me a copy of an order from the War Department which stated that accounts of my misbehavior had reached Washington and directed him to investigate and report the facts. He forwarded also a copy of a detailed dispatch from himself to Washington entirely exonerating me; but he did not inform me that it was his own reports that had created all the trouble. On the contrary, he wrote to me, "Instead of relieving you, I wish you, as soon as your new army is in the field, to assume immediate command, and lead it to new victories." In consequence I felt very grateful to him, and supposed it was his interposition that had set me right with the government. I never knew the truth until General Badeau unearthed the facts in his researches for his history of my campaigns.

General Halleck unquestionably deemed General C.F. Smith a much fitter officer for the command of all the forces in the military district than I was, and, to render him available for such command, desired his promotion to antedate mine and those of the other division commanders. It is probable that the general opinion was that Smith's long services in the army and distinguished deeds rendered him the more proper person for such command. Indeed I was rather inclined to this opinion myself at that time, and would have served as faithfully under Smith as he had done under me. But this did not justify the dispatches which General Halleck sent to Washington, or his subsequent concealment of them from me when pretending to explain the action of my superiors.

On receipt of the order restoring me to command I proceeded to Savannah on the Tennessee, to which point my troops had advanced. General Smith was delighted to see me and was unhesitating in his denunciation of the treatment I had received. He was on a sick bed at the time, from which he never came away alive. His death was a severe loss to our western army. His personal courage was unquestioned, his judgment and professional acquirements were unsurpassed, and he had the confidence of those he commanded as well as of those over him.

Chapter XXIV

THE ARMY AT PITTSBURG LANDING — INJURED
BY A FALL — THE CONFEDERATE ATTACK AT
SHILOH — THE FIRST DAY'S FIGHT AT SHILOH —
GENERAL SHERMAN — CONDITION OF THE
ARMY — CLOSE OF THE FIRST DAY'S FIGHT —
THE SECOND DAY'S FIGHT — RETREAT AND
DEFEAT OF THE CONFEDERATES

When I reassumed command on the 17th of March I found the army divided, about half being on the east bank of the Tennessee at Savannah, while one division was at Crump's landing on the west bank about four miles higher up, and the remainder at Pittsburg landing, five miles above Crump's. The enemy was in force at Corinth, the junction of the two most important railroads in the Mississippi valley — one connecting Memphis and the Mississippi River with the East, and the other leading south to all the cotton states. Still another railroad connects Corinth with Jackson, in west Tennessee. If we obtained possession of Corinth the enemy would have no railroad for the transportation of armies or supplies until that running east from Vicksburg was reached. It was the great strategic position at the West between the Tennessee and the Mississippi rivers and between Nashville and Vicksburg.

I at once put all the troops at Savannah in motion for Pittsburg landing, knowing that the enemy was fortifying at Corinth and collecting an army there under Johnston. It was my expectation to march against that army as soon as Buell, who had been ordered to reinforce me with the Army of the Ohio, should arrive; and the west bank of the river was the place to start from. Pittsburg is only about twenty miles from Corinth, and Hamburg landing, four miles further up the river, is a mile or two nearer. I had not been in command long before I selected Hamburg as the place to put the Army of the Ohio when it arrived. The roads from Pittsburg and Hamburg to Corinth converge some eight miles out. This disposition of the troops would have given additional roads to march over when the advance commenced, within supporting distance of each other.

Before I arrived at Savannah, Sherman, who had joined the Army of the Tennessee and been placed in command of a division, had made an expedition on steamers convoyed by gunboats to the neighborhood of Eastport, thirty miles south, for the purpose of destroying the railroad east of Corinth. The rains had been so heavy for some time before that the low-lands had become impassable swamps. Sherman debarked his troops and started out to accomplish the object of the expedition; but the river was rising so rapidly that the back-water up the small tributaries threatened to cut off the possibility of getting back to the boats, and the expedition had to return without reaching the railroad. The guns had to be hauled by hand through the water to get back to the boats.

On the 17th of March the army on the Tennessee River consisted of five divisions, commanded respectively by Generals C.F. Smith, McClernand, L. Wallace, Hurlbut and Sherman. General W.H.L. Wallace was temporarily in command of Smith's division, General Smith, as I have said, being confined to his bed. Reinforcements were arriving daily and as they came up they were organized, first into brigades, then into a division, and the command given to General Prentiss, who had been ordered to report to me. General Buell was on his way from Nashville with 40,000 veterans. On the 19th of March he was at Columbia, Tennessee, eighty-five miles from Pittsburg. When all reinforcements should have arrived I expected to take the initiative by marching on Corinth, and had no expectation of needing fortifications, though this subject was taken into consideration. McPherson, my only military engineer, was directed to lay out a line to entrench. He did so, but reported that it would have to be made in rear of the line of encampment as it then ran. The new line, while it would be nearer the river, was yet too far away from the Tennessee, or even from the creeks, to be easily supplied with water, and in case of attack these creeks would be in the hands of the enemy. The fact is, I regarded the campaign we were engaged in as an offensive one and had no idea that the enemy would leave strong entrenchments to take the initiative when he knew he would be attacked where he was if he remained. This view, however, did not prevent every precaution being taken and every effort made to keep advised of all movements of the enemy.

Johnston's cavalry meanwhile had been well out towards our front, and occasional encounters occurred between it and our outposts. On the 1st of April this cavalry became bold and approached our lines, showing that an advance of some kind was contemplated. On the 2d

Johnston left Corinth in force to attack my army. On the 4th his cavalry dashed down and captured a small picket guard of six or seven men, stationed some five miles out from Pittsburg on the Corinth road. Colonel Buckland sent relief to the guard at once and soon followed in person with an entire regiment, and General Sherman followed Buckland taking the remainder of a brigade. The pursuit was kept up for some three miles beyond the point where the picket guard had been captured, and after nightfall Sherman returned to camp and reported to me by letter what had occurred.

At this time a large body of the enemy was hovering to the west of us, along the line of the Mobile and Ohio railroad. My apprehension was much greater for the safety of Crump's landing than it was for Pittsburg. I had no apprehension that the enemy could really capture either place. But I feared it was possible that he might make a rapid dash upon Crump's and destroy our transports and stores, most of which were kept at that point, and then retreat before Wallace could be reinforced. Lew. Wallace's position I regarded as so well chosen that he was not removed.

At this time I generally spent the day at Pittsburg and returned to Savannah in the evening. I was intending to remove my headquarters to Pittsburg, but Buell was expected daily and would come in at Savannah. I remained at this point, therefore, a few days longer than I otherwise should have done, in order to meet him on his arrival. The skirmishing in our front, however, had been so continuous from about the 3d of April that I did not leave Pittsburg each night until an hour when I felt there would be no further danger before the morning.

On Friday the 4th, the day of Buckland's advance, I was very much injured by my horse falling with me, and on me, while I was trying to get to the front where firing had been heard. The night was one of impenetrable darkness, with rain pouring down in torrents; nothing was visible to the eye except as revealed by the frequent flashes of lightning. Under these circumstances I had to trust to the horse, without guidance, to keep the road. I had not gone far, however, when I met General W.H.L. Wallace and Colonel (afterwards General) McPherson coming from the direction of the front. They said all was quiet so far as the enemy was concerned. On the way back to the boat my horse's feet slipped from under him, and he fell with my leg under his body. The extreme softness of the ground, from the excessive rains of the few preceding days, no doubt saved me from a severe injury and protracted lameness. As it was, my ankle was very much injured, so much so that my boot had to be cut off. For two or three days after I was unable to walk except with crutches.

On the 5th General Nelson, with a division of Buell's army, arrived at Savannah and I ordered him to move up the east bank of the river, to be in a position where he could be ferried over to Crump's landing or Pittsburg as occasion required. I had learned that General Buell himself would be at Savannah the next day, and desired to meet me on his arrival. Affairs at Pittsburg landing had been such for several days that I did not want to be away during the day. I determined, therefore, to take a very early breakfast and ride out to meet Buell, and thus save time. He had arrived on the evening of the 5th, but had not advised me of the fact and I was not aware of it until some time after. While I was at breakfast, however, heavy firing was heard in the direction of Pittsburg landing, and I hastened there, sending a hurried note to Buell informing him of the reason why I could not meet him at Savannah. On the way up the river I directed the dispatch-boat to run in close to Crump's landing, so that I could communicate with General Lew. Wallace. I found him waiting on a boat apparently expecting to see me, and I directed him to get his troops in line ready to execute any orders he might receive. He replied that his troops were already under arms and prepared to move.

Up to that time I had felt by no means certain that Crump's landing might not be the point of attack. On reaching the front, however, about eight A.M., I found that the attack on Pittsburg was unmistakable, and that nothing more than a small guard, to protect our transports and stores, was needed at Crump's. Captain Baxter, a quartermaster on my staff, was accordingly directed to go back and order General Wallace to march immediately to Pittsburg by the road nearest the river. Captain Baxter made a memorandum of this order. About one P.M., not hearing from Wallace and being much in need of reinforcements, I sent two more of my staff, Colonel McPherson and Captain Rowley, to bring him up with his division. They reported finding him marching towards Purdy, Bethel, or some point west from the river, and farther from Pittsburg by several miles than when he started. The road from his first position to Pittsburg landing was direct and near the river. Between the two points a bridge had been built across Snake Creek by our troops, at which Wallace's command had assisted, expressly to enable the troops at the two places to support each other in case of need. Wallace did not arrive in time to take part in the first day's fight. General Wallace has since claimed that the order delivered to him by Captain Baxter was simply to join the right of the army, and that the road over which he marched would have taken him to the road from Pittsburg to Purdy where it crosses Owl Creek on the right of Sherman; but this is not where I had ordered him nor where I wanted him to go.

I never could see and do not now see why any order was necessary further than to direct him to come to Pittsburg landing, without specifying by what route. His was one of three veteran divisions that had been in battle, and its absence was severely felt. Later in the war General Wallace would not have made the mistake that he committed on the 6th of April, 1862. I presume his idea was that by taking the route he did he would be able to come around on the flank or rear of the enemy, and thus perform an act of heroism that would redound to the credit of his command, as well as to the benefit of his country.

Some two or three miles from Pittsburg landing was a log meeting-house called Shiloh. It stood on the ridge which divides the waters of Snake and Lick creeks, the former emptying into the Tennessee just north of Pittsburg landing, and the latter south. This point was the key to our position and was held by Sherman. His division was at that time wholly raw, no part of it ever having been in an engagement; but I thought this deficiency was more than made up by the superiority of the commander. McClernand was on Sherman's left, with troops that had been engaged at forts Henry and Donelson and were therefore veterans so far as western troops had become such at that stage of the war. Next to McClernand came Prentiss with a raw division, and on the extreme left, Stuart with one brigade of Sherman's division. Hurlbut was in rear of Prentiss, massed, and in reserve at the time of the onset. The division of General C.F. Smith was on the right, also in reserve. General Smith was still sick in bed at Savannah, but within hearing of our guns. His services would no doubt have been of inestimable value had his health permitted his presence. The command of his division devolved upon Brigadier-General W.H.L. Wallace, a most estimable and able officer; a veteran too, for he had served a year in the Mexican war and had been with his command at Henry and Donelson. Wallace was mortally wounded in the first day's engagement, and with the change of commanders thus necessarily effected in the heat of battle the efficiency of his division was much weakened.

The position of our troops made a continuous line from Lick Creek on the left to Owl Creek, a branch of Snake Creek, on the right, facing nearly south and possibly a little west. The water in all these streams was very high at the time and contributed to protect our flanks. The enemy was compelled, therefore, to attack directly in front. This he did with great vigor, inflicting heavy losses on the National side, but suffering much heavier on his own.

The Confederate assaults were made with such a disregard of losses on their own side that our line of tents soon fell into their hands. The ground on which the battle was fought was undulating, heavily timbered with scattered clearings, the woods giving some protection to the troops on both sides. There was also considerable underbrush. A number of attempts were made by the enemy to turn our right flank, where Sherman was posted, but every effort was repulsed with heavy loss. But the front attack was kept up so vigorously that, to prevent the success of these attempts to get on our flanks, the National troops were compelled, several times, to take positions to the rear nearer Pittsburg landing. When the firing ceased at night the National line was all of a mile in rear of the position it had occupied in the morning.

In one of the backward moves, on the 6th, the division commanded by General Prentiss did not fall back with the others. This left his flanks exposed and enabled the enemy to capture him with about 2,200 of his officers and men. General Badeau gives four o'clock of the 6th as about the time this capture took place. He may be right as to the time, but my recollection is that the hour was later. General Prentiss himself gave the hour as half-past five. I was with him, as I was with each of the division commanders that day, several times, and my recollection is that the last time I was with him was about half-past four, when his division was standing up firmly and the General was as cool as if expecting victory. But no matter whether it was four or later, the story that he and his command were surprised and captured in their camps is without any foundation whatever. If it had been true, as currently reported at the time and yet believed by thousands of people, that Prentiss and his division had been captured in their beds, there would not have been an all-day struggle, with the loss of thousands killed and wounded on the Confederate side.

With the single exception of a few minutes after the capture of Prentiss, a continuous and unbroken line was maintained all day from Snake Creek or its tributaries on the right to Lick Creek or the Tennessee on the left above Pittsburg.

There was no hour during the day when there was not heavy firing and generally hard fighting at some point on the line, but seldom at all points at the same time. It was a case of Southern dash against Northern pluck and endurance. Three of the five divisions engaged on Sunday were entirely raw, and many of the men had only received their arms on the way from their States to the field. Many of them had arrived but a day or two before and were hardly able to load their muskets according to the manual. Their officers were equally ignorant of their duties. Under these circumstances it is not astonishing that many of the regiments broke at the first fire. In two cases, as I now remember, colonels led their regiments from the field on first hearing the whistle of the enemy's bullets. In these cases the colonels were constitutional cowards, unfit for any military position; but not so the officers and men led out of danger by them. Better troops never went upon a battlefield than many of these, officers and men, afterwards proved themselves to be, who fled panic stricken at the first whistle of bullets and shell at Shiloh.

During the whole of Sunday I was continuously engaged in passing from one part of the field to another, giving directions to division commanders. In thus moving along the line, however, I never deemed it important to stay long with Sherman. Although his troops were then under fire for the first time, their commander, by his constant presence with them, inspired a confidence in officers and men that enabled them to render services on that bloody battlefield worthy of the best of veterans. McClernand was next to Sherman, and the hardest fighting was in front of these two divisions. McClernand told me on that day, the 6th, that he profited much by having so able a commander supporting him. A casualty to Sherman that would have taken him from the field that day would have been a sad one for the troops engaged at Shiloh. And how near we came to this! On the 6th Sherman was shot twice, once in the hand, once in the shoulder, the ball cutting his coat and making a slight wound, and a third ball passed through his hat. In addition to this he had several horses shot during the day.

The nature of this battle was such that cavalry could not be used in front; I therefore formed ours into line in rear, to stop stragglers — of whom there were many. When there would be enough of them to make a show, and after they had recovered from their fright, they would be sent to reinforce some part of the line which needed support, without regard to their companies, regiments or brigades.

On one occasion during the day I rode back as far as the river and met General Buell, who had just arrived; I do not remember the hour, but at that time there probably were as many as four or five thousand stragglers lying under cover of the river bluff, panic-stricken, most of whom would have been shot where they lay, without resistance, before they would have taken muskets and marched to the front to protect themselves. This meeting between General Buell and myself was on the dispatch-boat used to run between the landing and Savannah. It was brief, and related specially to his getting his troops over the river. As we left the boat together, Buell's attention was attracted by the men lying under cover of the riverbank. I saw him berating them and trying to shame them into joining their regiments. He even threatened them with shells from the gunboats near by. But it was all to no effect. Most of these men afterward proved themselves as gallant as any of those who saved the battle from which they had deserted. I have no doubt that this sight impressed General Buell with the idea that a line of retreat would be a good thing just then. If he had come in by the front instead of through the stragglers in the rear, he would have thought and felt differently. Could he have come through the Confederate rear, he would have witnessed there a scene similar to that at our own. The distant rear of an army engaged in battle is not the best place from which to judge correctly what is going on in front. Later in the war, while occupying the country between the Tennessee and the Mississippi, I learned that the panic in the Confederate lines had not differed much from that within our own. Some of the country people estimated the stragglers from Johnston's army as high as 20,000. Of course this was an exaggeration.

The situation at the close of Sunday was as follows: along the top of the bluff just south of the log-house which stood at Pittsburg landing, Colonel J.D. Webster, of my staff, had arranged twenty or more pieces of artillery facing south or up the river. This line of artillery was on the crest of a hill overlooking a deep ravine opening into the Tennessee. Hurlbut with his division intact was on the right of this artillery, extending west and possibly a little north. McClernand came next in the general line, looking more to the west. His division was complete in its organization and ready for any duty. Sherman came next, his right extending to Snake Creek. His command, like the other two, was complete in its organization and ready, like its chief, for any service it might be called upon to render. All three divisions were, as a matter of course, more or less shattered and depleted in numbers from the terrible battle of the day. The division of W.H.L. Wallace, as much from the disorder arising from changes of division and brigade commanders, under heavy fire, as from any other cause, had lost its organization and did not occupy a place in the line as a division. Prentiss' command was gone as a division, many of its members having been killed, wounded or captured, but it had rendered valiant services before its final dispersal, and had contributed a good share to the defense of Shiloh.

The right of my line rested near the bank of Snake Creek, a short distance above the bridge which had been built by the troops for the purpose of connecting Crump's landing and Pittsburg landing. Sherman had posted some troops in a log-house and out-buildings which overlooked both the bridge over which Wallace was expected and the creek above that point. In this last position Sherman was frequently attacked before night, but held the point until he voluntarily abandoned it to advance in order to make room for Lew. Wallace, who came up after dark.

There was, as I have said, a deep ravine in front of our left. The Tennessee River was very high and there was water to a considerable depth in the ravine. Here the enemy made a last desperate effort to turn our flank, but was repelled. The gunboats Tyler and Lexington, Gwin and Shirk commanding, with the artillery under Webster, aided the army and effectually checked their further progress. Before any of Buell's troops had reached the west bank of the Tennessee, firing had almost entirely ceased; anything like an attempt on the part of the enemy to advance had absolutely ceased. There was some artillery firing from an unseen enemy, some of his shells passing beyond us; but I do not remember that there was the whistle of a single musket-ball heard. As his troops arrived in the dusk General Buell marched several of his regiments part way down the face of the hill where they fired briskly for some minutes, but I do not think a single man engaged in this firing received an injury. The attack had spent its force.

General Lew. Wallace, with 5,000 effective men, arrived after firing had ceased for the day, and was placed on the right. Thus night came, Wallace came, and the advance of Nelson's division came; but none — unless night — in time to be of material service to the gallant men who saved Shiloh on that first day against large odds. Buell's loss on the 6th of April was two men killed and one wounded, all members of the 36th Indiana infantry. The Army of the Tennessee lost on that day at least 7,000 men. The presence of two or three regiments of Buell's army on the west bank before firing ceased had not the slightest effect in preventing the capture of Pittsburg landing.

So confident was I before firing had ceased on the 6th that the next day would bring victory to our arms if we could only take the initiative, that I visited each division commander in person before any reinforcements had reached the field. I directed them to throw out heavy lines of skirmishers in the morning as soon as they could see, and push them forward until they found the enemy, following with their entire divisions in supporting distance, and to engage the enemy as soon as found. To Sherman I told the story of the assault at Fort Donelson, and said that the same tactics would win at Shiloh. Victory was assured when Wallace arrived, even if there had been no other support. I was glad, however, to see the reinforcements of Buell and credit them with doing all there was for them to do.

During the night of the 6th the remainder of Nelson's division, Buell's army crossed the river and were ready to advance in the morning, forming the left wing. Two other divisions, Crittenden's and McCook's, came up the river from Savannah in the transports and were on the west bank early on the 7th. Buell commanded them in person. My command was thus nearly doubled in numbers and efficiency.

During the night rain fell in torrents and our troops were exposed to the storm without shelter. I made my headquarters under a tree a few hundred yards back from the riverbank. My ankle was so much swollen from the fall of my horse the Friday night preceding, and the bruise was so painful, that I could get no rest.

The drenching rain would have precluded the possibility of sleep without this additional cause. Some time after midnight, growing restive under the storm and the continuous pain, I moved back to the log-house under the bank. This had been taken as a hospital, and all night wounded men were being brought in, their wounds dressed, a leg or an arm amputated as the case might require, and everything being done to save life or alleviate suffering. The sight was more unendurable than encountering the enemy's fire, and I returned to my tree in the rain.

The advance on the morning of the 7th developed the enemy in the camps occupied by our troops before the battle began, more than a mile back from the most advanced position of the Confederates on the day before. It is known now that they had not yet learned of the arrival of Buell's command. Possibly they fell back so far to get the shelter of our tents during the rain, and also to get away from the shells that were dropped upon them by the gunboats every fifteen minutes during the night.

The position of the Union troops on the morning of the 7th was as follows: General Lew. Wallace on the right; Sherman on his left; then McClernand and then Hurlbut. Nelson, of Buell's army, was on our extreme left, next to the river.

Crittenden was next in line after Nelson and on his right, McCook followed and formed the extreme right of Buell's command. My old command thus formed the right wing, while the troops directly under Buell constituted the left wing of the army. These relative positions were retained during the entire day, or until the enemy was driven from the field.

In a very short time the battle became general all along the line. This day everything was favorable to the Union side. We had now become the attacking party. The enemy was driven back all day, as we had been the day before, until finally he beat a precipitate retreat. The last point held by him was near the road leading from the landing to Corinth, on the left of Sherman and right of McClernand. About three o'clock, being near that point and seeing that the enemy was giving way everywhere else, I gathered up a couple of regiments, or parts of regiments, from troops near by, formed them in line of battle and marched them forward, going in front myself to prevent premature or long-range firing. At this point there was a clearing between us and the enemy favorable for charging, although exposed. I knew the enemy were ready to break and only wanted a little encouragement from us to go quickly and join their friends who had started earlier. After marching to within musket-range I stopped and let the troops pass. The command, *charge,* was given, and was executed with loud cheers and with a run; when the last of the enemy broke.*

---

* *Note.* – Since writing this chapter I have received from Mrs. W.H.L. Wallace, widow of the gallant general who was killed in the first day's fight on the field of Shiloh, a letter from General Lew. Wallace to him dated the morning of the 5th. At the date of this letter it was well known that the Confederates had troops out along the Mobile & Ohio railroad west of Crump's landing and Pittsburg landing, and were also collecting near Shiloh. This letter shows that at that time General Lew. Wallace was making preparations for the emergency that might happen for the passing of reinforcements between Shiloh and his position, extending from Crump's landing westward, and he sends it over the road running from Adamsville to the Pittsburg landing and Purdy road. These two roads intersect nearly a mile west of the crossing of the latter over Owl Creek, where our right rested. In this letter General Lew. Wallace advises General W.H.L. Wallace that he will send "tomorrow" (and his letter also says "April 5th," which is the same day the letter was dated and which, therefore, must have been written on the 4th) some cavalry to report to him at his headquarters, and suggesting the propriety of General W. H. L. Wallace's sending a company back with them for the purpose of having the cavalry at the two landings familiarize themselves with the road so that they could "act promptly in case of emergency as guides to and from the different camps."

This modifies very materially what I have said, and what has been said by others, of the conduct of General Lew. Wallace at the battle of Shiloh. It shows that he naturally, with no more experience than he had at the time in the profession of arms, would take the particular road that he did start upon in the absence of orders to move by a different road.

The mistake he made, and which probably caused his apparent dilatoriness, was that of advancing some distance after he found that the firing, which would be at first directly to his front and then off to the left, had fallen back until it had got very much in rear of the position of his advance. This falling back had taken place before I sent General Wallace orders to move up to Pittsburg landing and, naturally, my order was to follow the road nearest the river. But my order was verbal, and to a staff officer who was to deliver it to General Wallace, so that I am not competent to say just what order the General actually received.

General Wallace's division was stationed, the First brigade at Crump's landing, the Second out two miles, and the Third two and a half miles out. Hearing the sounds of battle General Wallace early ordered his First and Third brigades to concentrate on the Second. If the position of our front had not changed, the road which Wallace took would have been somewhat shorter to our right than the River road.

U.S. GRANT.

MOUNT MACGREGOR, NEW YORK, June 21, 1885.

Chapter XXV

STRUCK BY A BULLET — PRECIPITATE RETREAT
OF THE CONFEDERATES — INTRENCHMENTS
AT SHILOH — GENERAL BUELL — GENERAL
JOHNSTON — REMARKS ON SHILOH

During this second day of the battle I had been moving from right to left and back, to see for myself the progress made. In the early part of the afternoon, while riding with Colonel McPherson and Major Hawkins, then my chief commissary, we got beyond the left of our troops. We were moving along the northern edge of a clearing, very leisurely, toward the river above the landing. There did not appear to be an enemy to our right, until suddenly a battery with musketry opened upon us from the edge of the woods on the other side of the clearing. The shells and balls whistled about our ears very fast for about a minute. I do not think it took us longer than that to get out of range and out of sight. In the sudden start we made, Major Hawkins lost his hat. He did not stop to pick it up. When we arrived at a perfectly safe position we halted to take an account of damages. McPherson's horse was panting as if ready to drop. On examination it was found that a ball had struck him forward of the flank just back of the saddle, and had gone entirely through. In a few minutes the poor beast dropped dead; he had given no sign of injury until we came to a stop. A ball had struck the metal scabbard of my sword, just below the hilt, and broken it nearly off; before the battle was over it had broken off entirely. There were three of us: one had lost a horse, killed; one a hat and one a sword-scabbard. All were thankful that it was no worse.

After the rain of the night before and the frequent and heavy rains for some days previous, the roads were almost impassable. The enemy carrying his artillery and supply trains over them in his retreat, made them still worse for troops following. I wanted to pursue, but had not the heart to order the men who had fought desperately for two days, lying in the mud and rain whenever not fighting, and I did* not feel disposed to positively order Buell, or any part of his command, to pursue. Although the senior in rank at the time I had been so only a few weeks. Buell was, and had been for some time past, a department commander, while I commanded only a district. I did not meet Buell in person until too late to get troops ready and pursue with effect; but had I seen him at the moment of the last charge I should have at least requested him to follow.

I rode forward several miles the day after the battle, and found that the enemy had dropped much, if not all, of their provisions, some ammunition and the extra wheels of their caissons, lightening their loads to enable them to get off their guns. About five miles out we found their field hospital abandoned. An immediate pursuit must have resulted in the capture of a considerable number of prisoners and probably some guns.

Shiloh was the severest battle fought at the West during the war, and but few in the East equaled it for hard, determined fighting. I saw an open field, in our possession on the second day, over which the Confederates had made repeated charges the day before, so covered with dead that it would have been possible to walk across the clearing, in any direction, stepping on dead bodies, without a foot touching the ground. On our side National and Confederate troops were mingled together in about equal proportions; but on the remainder of the field nearly all were Confederates. On one part, which had evidently not been plowed for several years, probably because the land was poor, bushes had grown

---

† *Note:* In an article on the battle of Shiloh which I wrote for the Century Magazine, I stated that General A. McD. McCook, who commanded a division of Buell's army, expressed some unwillingness to pursue the enemy on Monday, April 7th, because of the condition of his troops. General Badeau, in his history, also makes the same statement, on my authority. Out of justice to General McCook and his command, I must say that they left a point twenty-two miles east of Savannah on the morning of the 6th. From the heavy rains of a few days previous and the passage of trains and artillery, the roads were necessarily deep in mud, which made marching slow. The division had not only marched through this mud the day before, but it had been in the rain all night without rest. It was engaged in the battle of the second day and did as good service as its position allowed. In fact an opportunity occurred for it to perform a conspicuous act of gallantry which elicited the highest commendation from division commanders in the Army of the Tennessee. General Sherman both in his memoirs and report makes mention of this fact. General McCook himself belongs to a family which furnished many volunteers to the army. I refer to these circumstances with minuteness because I did General McCook injustice in my article in the Century, though not to the extent one would suppose from the public press. I am not willing to do anyone an injustice, and if convinced that I have done one, I am always willing to make the fullest admission.

up, some to the height of eight or ten feet. There was not one of these left standing unpierced by bullets. The smaller ones were all cut down.

Contrary to all my experience up to that time, and to the experience of the army I was then commanding, we were on the defensive. We were without entrenchments or defensive advantages of any sort, and more than half the army engaged the first day was without experience or even drill as soldiers. The officers with them, except the division commanders and possibly two or three of the brigade commanders, were equally inexperienced in war. The result was a Union victory that gave the men who achieved it great confidence in themselves ever after.

The enemy fought bravely, but they had started out to defeat and destroy an army and capture a position. They failed in both, with very heavy loss in killed and wounded, and must have gone back discouraged and convinced that the "Yankee" was not an enemy to be despised.

After the battle I gave verbal instructions to division commanders to let the regiments send out parties to bury their own dead, and to detail parties, under commissioned officers from each division, to bury the Confederate dead in their respective fronts and to report the numbers so buried. The latter part of these instructions was not carried out by all; but they were by those sent from Sherman's division, and by some of the parties sent out by McClernand. The heaviest loss sustained by the enemy was in front of these two divisions.

The criticism has often been made that the Union troops should have been entrenched at Shiloh. Up to that time the pick and spade had been but little resorted to at the West. I had, however, taken this subject under consideration soon after re-assuming command in the field, and, as already stated, my only military engineer reported unfavorably. Besides this, the troops with me, officers and men, needed discipline and drill more than they did experience with the pick, shovel and axe. Reinforcements were arriving almost daily, composed of troops that had been hastily thrown together into companies and regiments — fragments of incomplete organizations, the men and officers strangers to each other. Under all these circumstances I concluded that drill and discipline were worth more to our men than fortifications.

General Buell was a brave, intelligent officer, with as much professional pride and ambition of a commendable sort as I ever knew. I had been two years at West Point with him, and had served with him afterwards, in garrison and in the Mexican war, several years more. He was not given in early life or in mature years to forming intimate acquaintances. He was studious by habit, and commanded the confidence and respect of all who knew him. He was a strict disciplinarian, and perhaps did not distinguish sufficiently between the volunteer who "enlisted for the war" and the soldier who serves in time of peace. One system embraced men who risked life for a principle, and often men of social standing, competence, or wealth and independence of character. The other includes, as a rule, only men who could not do as well in any other occupation. General Buell became an object of harsh criticism later, some going so far as to challenge his loyalty. No one who knew him ever believed him capable of a dishonorable act, and nothing could be more dishonorable than to accept high rank and command in war and then betray the trust. When I came into command of the army in 1864, I requested the Secretary of War to restore General Buell to duty.

After the war, during the summer of 1865, I traveled considerably through the North, and was everywhere met by large numbers of people. Everyone had his opinion about the manner in which the war had been conducted: who among the generals had failed, how, and why. Correspondents of the press were ever on hand to hear every word dropped, and were not always disposed to report correctly what did not confirm their preconceived notions, either about the conduct of the war or the individuals concerned in it. The opportunity frequently occurred for me to defend General Buell against what I believed to be most unjust charges. On one occasion a correspondent put in my mouth the very charge I had so often refuted — of disloyalty. This brought from General Buell a very severe retort, which I saw in the New York World some time before I received the letter itself. I could very well understand his grievance at seeing untrue and disgraceful charges apparently sustained by an officer who, at the time, was at the head of the army. I replied to him, but not through the press. I kept no copy of my letter, nor did I ever see it in print; neither did I receive an answer.

General Albert Sidney Johnston, who commanded the Confederate forces at the beginning of the battle, was disabled by a wound on the afternoon of the first day. This wound, as I understood afterwards, was not necessarily fatal, or even dangerous. But he was a man who would not abandon what he deemed an important trust in the face of danger and consequently continued in the saddle, commanding, until so exhausted by the loss of blood that he had to be taken from his horse, and soon after died. The news was not long in reaching our side and I suppose was quite an encouragement to the National soldiers.

I had known Johnston slightly in the Mexican war and later as an officer in the regular army. He was a man of high character and ability. His contemporaries at West Point, and officers generally who came to know him personally later and who remained on our side, expected him to prove the most formidable man to meet that the Confederacy would produce.

I once wrote that nothing occurred in his brief command of an army to prove or disprove the high estimate that had been placed upon his military ability; but after studying the orders and dispatches of Johnston I am compelled to materially modify my views of that officer's qualifications as a soldier. My judgment now is that he was vacillating and undecided in his actions.

All the disasters in Kentucky and Tennessee were so discouraging to the authorities in Richmond that Jefferson Davis wrote an unofficial letter to Johnston expressing his own anxiety and that of the public, and saying that he had made such defense as was dictated by long friendship, but that in the absence of a report he needed facts. The letter was not a reprimand in direct terms, but it was evidently as much felt as though it had been one. General Johnston raised another army as rapidly as he could, and fortified or strongly entrenched at Corinth. He knew the National troops were preparing to attack him in his chosen position. But he had evidently become so disturbed at the results of his operations that he resolved to strike out in an offensive campaign which would restore all that was lost, and if successful accomplish still more. We have the authority of his son and biographer for saying that his plan was to attack the forces at Shiloh and crush them; then to cross the Tennessee and destroy the army of Buell, and push the war across the Ohio River. The design was a bold one; but we have the same authority for saying that in the execution Johnston showed vacillation and indecision. He left Corinth on the 2d of April and was not ready to attack until the 6th. The distance his army had to march was less than twenty miles. Beauregard, his second in command, was opposed to the attack for two reasons: first, he thought, if let alone the National troops would attack the Confederates in their entrenchments; second, we were in ground of our own choosing and would necessarily be entrenched. Johnston not only listened to the objection of Beauregard to an attack, but held a council of war on the subject on the morning of the 5th. On the evening of the same day he was in consultation with some of his generals on the same subject, and still again on the morning of the 6th. During this last consultation, and before a decision had been reached, the battle began by the National troops opening fire on the enemy. This seemed to settle the question as to whether there was to be any battle of Shiloh. It also seems to me to settle the question as to whether there was a surprise.

I do not question the personal courage of General Johnston, or his ability. But he did not win the distinction predicted for him by many of his friends. He did prove that as a general he was overestimated.

General Beauregard was next in rank to Johnston and succeeded to the command, which he retained to the close of the battle and during the subsequent retreat on Corinth, as well as in the siege of that place. His tactics have been severely criticized by Confederate writers, but I do not believe his fallen chief could have done any better under the circumstances. Some of these critics claim that Shiloh was won when Johnston fell, and that if he had not fallen the army under me would have been annihilated or captured. *Ifs* defeated the Confederates at Shiloh. There is little doubt that we would have been disgracefully beaten *if* all the shells and bullets fired by us had passed harmlessly over the enemy and *if* all of theirs had taken effect. Commanding generals are liable to be killed during engagements; and the fact that when he was shot Johnston was leading a brigade to induce it to make a charge which had been repeatedly ordered, is evidence that there was neither the universal demoralization on our side nor the unbounded confidence on theirs which has been claimed. There was, in fact, no hour during the day when I doubted the eventual defeat of the enemy, although I was disappointed that reinforcements so near at hand did not arrive at an earlier hour.

The description of the battle of Shiloh given by Colonel Wm. Preston Johnston is very graphic and well told. The reader will imagine that he can see each blow struck, a demoralized and broken mob of Union soldiers, each blow sending the enemy more demoralized than ever towards the Tennessee River, which was a little more than two miles away at the beginning of the onset. If the reader does not stop to inquire why, with such Confederate success for more than twelve hours of hard fighting, the National troops were not all killed, captured or driven into the river, he will regard the pen picture as perfect. But I witnessed the fight from the National side from eight o'clock in the morning until night closed the contest. I see but little in the description that I can recognize. The Confederate troops fought well and deserve commendation enough for their bravery and endurance on the 6th of April, without detracting from their antagonists or claiming anything more than their just dues.

The reports of the enemy show that their condition at the end of the first day was deplorable; their losses in killed and wounded had been very heavy, and their stragglers had been quite as numerous as on the National side, with the difference that those of the enemy left the field entirely and were not brought back to their respective commands for many days. On the Union side but few of the stragglers fell back further than the landing on the river, and many of these were in line for duty on the second day. The admissions of the highest Confederate officers engaged at Shiloh make the claim of a victory for them absurd. The victory was not to either party until the battle was over. It was then a Union victory, in which the Armies of the Tennessee and the Ohio both participated. But the Army of the Tennessee fought the entire rebel army on the 6th and held it at bay until near night; and night alone closed the conflict and not the three regiments of Nelson's division.

The Confederates fought with courage at Shiloh, but the particular skill claimed I could not and still cannot see; though there is nothing to criticize except the claims put forward for it since. But the Confederate claimants for superiority in strategy, superiority in generalship and superiority in dash and prowess are not so unjust to the Union troops engaged at Shiloh as are many Northern writers. The troops on both sides were American, and united they need not fear any foreign foe. It is possible that the Southern man started in with a little more dash than his Northern brother; but he was correspondingly less enduring.

The endeavor of the enemy on the first day was simply to hurl their men against ours — first at one point, then at another, sometimes at several points at once. This they did with daring and energy, until at night the rebel troops were worn out. Our effort during the same time was to be prepared to resist assaults wherever made. The object of the Confederates on the second day was to get away with as much of their army and material as possible. Ours then was to drive them from our front, and to capture or destroy as great a part as possible of their men and material. We were successful in driving them back, but not so successful in captures as if farther pursuit could have been made. As it was, we captured or recaptured on the second day about as much artillery as we lost on the first; and, leaving out the one great capture of Prentiss, we took more prisoners on Monday than the enemy gained from us on Sunday. On the 6th Sherman lost seven pieces of artillery, McClernand six, Prentiss eight, and Hurlbut two batteries. On the 7th Sherman captured seven guns, McClernand three and the Army of the Ohio twenty.

At Shiloh the effective strength of the Union forces on the morning of the 6th was 33,000 men. Lew. Wallace brought 5,000 more after nightfall. Beauregard reported the enemy's strength at 40,955. According to the custom of enumeration in the South, this number probably excluded every man enlisted as musician or detailed as guard or nurse, and all commissioned officers — everybody who did not carry a musket or serve a cannon. With us everybody in the field receiving pay from the government is counted. Excluding the troops who fled, panic-stricken, before they had fired a shot, there was not a time during the 6th when we had more than 25,000 men in line. On the 7th Buell brought 20,000 more. Of his remaining two divisions, Thomas's did not reach the field during the engagement; Wood's arrived before firing had ceased, but not in time to be of much service.

Our loss in the two days' fight was 1,754 killed, 8,408 wounded and 2,885 missing. Of these, 2,103 were in the Army of the Ohio. Beauregard reported a total loss of 10,699, of whom 1,728 were killed, 8,012 wounded and 957 missing. This estimate must be incorrect. We buried, by actual count, more of the enemy's dead in front of the divisions of McClernand and Sherman alone than here reported, and 4,000 was the estimate of the burial parties of the whole field. Beauregard reports the Confederate force on the 6th at over 40,000, and their total loss during the two days at 10,699; and at the same time declares that he could put only 20,000 men in battle on the morning of the 7th.

The navy gave a hearty support to the army at Shiloh, as indeed it always did both before and subsequently when I was in command. The nature of the ground was such, however, that on this occasion it could do nothing in aid of the troops until sundown on the first day. The country was broken and heavily timbered, cutting off all view of the battle from the river, so that friends would be as much in danger from fire from the gunboats as the foe. But about sundown, when the National troops were back in their last position, the right of the enemy was near the river and exposed to the fire of the two gun-boats, which was delivered with vigor and effect. After nightfall, when firing had entirely ceased on land, the commander of the fleet informed himself, approximately, of the position of our troops and suggested the idea of dropping a shell within the lines of the enemy every fifteen minutes during the night. This was done with effect, as is proved by the Confederate reports.

Up to the battle of Shiloh I, as well as thousands of other citizens, believed that the rebellion against the Government would collapse suddenly and soon, if a decisive victory could be gained over any of its armies. Donelson and Henry were such victories. An army of more than 21,000 men was captured or destroyed. Bowling Green, Columbus and Hickman, Kentucky, fell in consequence, and Clarksville and Nashville, Tennessee, the last two with an immense amount of stores, also fell into our hands. The Tennessee and Cumberland rivers, from their mouths to the head of navigation, were secured. But when Confederate armies were collected which not only attempted to hold a line farther south, from Memphis to Chattanooga, Knoxville and on to the Atlantic, but assumed the offensive and made such a gallant effort to regain what had been lost, then, indeed, I gave up all idea of saving the Union except by complete conquest. Up to that time it had been the policy of our army, certainly of that portion commanded by me, to protect the property of the citizens whose territory was invaded, without regard to their sentiments, whether Union or Secession. After this, however, I regarded it as humane to both sides to protect the persons of those found at their homes, but to consume everything that could be used to support or supply armies. Protection was still continued over such supplies as were within lines held by us and which we expected to continue to hold; but such supplies within the reach of Confederate armies I regarded as much contraband as arms or ordnance stores. Their destruction was accomplished without bloodshed and tended to the same result as the destruction of armies. I continued this policy to the close of the war. Promiscuous pillaging, however, was discouraged and punished. Instructions were always given to take provisions and forage under the direction of commissioned officers who should give receipts to owners, if at home, and turn the property over to officers of the quartermaster or commissary departments to be issued as if furnished from our Northern depots. But much was destroyed without receipts to owners, when it could not be brought within our lines and would otherwise have gone to the support of secession and rebellion.

This policy I believe exercised a material influence in hastening the end.

The battle of Shiloh, or Pittsburg landing, has been perhaps less understood, or, to state the case more accurately, more persistently misunderstood, than any other engagement between National and Confederate troops during the entire rebellion. Correct reports of the battle have been published, notably by Sherman, Badeau and, in a speech before a meeting of veterans, by General Prentiss; but all of these appeared long subsequent to the close of the rebellion and after public opinion had been most erroneously formed.

I myself made no report to General Halleck, further than was contained in a letter, written immediately after the battle informing him that an engagement had been fought and announcing the result. A few days afterwards General Halleck moved his headquarters to Pittsburg landing and assumed command of the troops in the field. Although next to him in rank, and nominally in command of my old district and army, I was ignored as much as if I had been at the most distant point of territory within my jurisdiction; and although I was in command of all the troops engaged at Shiloh I was not permitted to see one of the reports of General Buell or his subordinates in that battle, until they were published by the War Department long after the event. For this reason I never made a full official report of this engagement.

Chapter XXVI

HALLECK ASSUMES COMMAND IN THE FIELD —
THE ADVANCE UPON CORINTH — OCCUPATION
OF CORINTH — THE ARMY SEPARATED

General Halleck arrived at Pittsburg landing on the 11th of April and immediately assumed command in the field. On the 21st General Pope arrived with an army 30,000 strong, fresh from the capture of Island Number Ten in the Mississippi River. He went into camp at Hamburg landing five miles above Pittsburg. Halleck had now three armies: the Army of the Ohio, Buell commanding; the Army of the Mississippi, Pope commanding; and the Army of the Tennessee. His orders divided the combined force into the right wing, reserve, center and left wing. Major-General George H. Thomas, who had been in Buell's army, was transferred with his division to the Army of the Tennessee and given command of the right wing, composed of all of that army except McClernand's and Lew. Wallace's divisions. McClernand was assigned to the command of the reserve, composed of his own and Lew. Wallace's divisions. Buell commanded the center, the Army of the Ohio; and Pope the left wing, the Army of the Mississippi. I was named second in command of the whole, and was also supposed to be in command of the right wing and reserve.

Orders were given to all the commanders engaged at Shiloh to send in their reports without delay to department headquarters. Those from officers of the Army of the Tennessee were sent through me; but from the Army of the Ohio they were sent by General Buell without passing through my hands. General Halleck ordered me, verbally, to send in my report, but I positively declined on the ground that he had received the reports of a part of the army engaged at Shiloh without their coming through me. He admitted that my refusal was justifiable under the circumstances, but explained that he had wanted to get the reports off before moving the command, and as fast as a report had come to him he had forwarded it to Washington.

Preparations were at once made upon the arrival of the new commander for an advance on Corinth. Owl Creek, on our right, was bridged, and expeditions were sent to the northwest and west to ascertain if our position was being threatened from those quarters; the roads towards Corinth were corduroyed and new ones made; lateral roads were also constructed, so that in case of necessity troops marching by different routes could reinforce each other. All commanders were cautioned against bringing on an engagement and informed in so many words that it would be better to retreat than to fight. By the 30th of April all preparations were complete; the country west to the Mobile and Ohio railroad had been reconnoitered, as well as the road to Corinth as far as Monterey twelve miles from Pittsburg. Everywhere small bodies of the enemy had been encountered, but they were observers and not in force to fight battles.

Corinth, Mississippi, lies in a southwesterly direction from Pittsburg landing and about nineteen miles away as the bird would fly, but probably twenty-two by the nearest wagon-road. It is about four miles south of the line dividing the States of Tennessee and Mississippi, and at the junction of the Mississippi and Chattanooga railroad with the Mobile and Ohio road which runs from Columbus to Mobile. From Pittsburg to Corinth the land is rolling, but at no point reaching an elevation that makes high hills to pass over. In 1862 the greater part of the country was covered with forest with intervening clearings and houses. Underbrush was dense in the low grounds along the creeks and ravines, but generally not so thick on the high land as to prevent men passing through with ease. There are two small creeks running from north of the town and connecting some four miles south, where they form Bridge Creek which empties into the Tuscumbia River. Corinth is on the ridge between these streams and is a naturally strong defensive position. The creeks are insignificant in volume of water, but the stream to the east widens out in front of the town into a swamp impassable in the presence of an enemy. On the crest of the west bank of this stream the enemy was strongly entrenched.

Corinth was a valuable strategic point for the enemy to hold, and consequently a valuable one for us to possess ourselves of. We ought to have seized it immediately after the fall of Donelson and Nashville, when it could have been taken without a battle, but failing then it should have been taken, without delay on the concentration of troops at Pittsburg landing after the battle of Shiloh. In fact the arrival of Pope should not have been awaited. There was no time from the battle of Shiloh up to the evacuation of Corinth when the enemy would not have left if pushed. The demoralization among the Confederates from their defeats at Henry and Donelson; their long marches from Bowling Green, Columbus, and Nashville, and their failure at Shiloh; in fact from having been driven out of Kentucky and Tennessee, was so great that a stand for the time would have been impossible. Beauregard made strenuous efforts to reinforce himself and partially succeeded. He appealed to the people of the Southwest for new regiments, and received a few. A.S. Johnston had made efforts to reinforce in the same quarter, before the battle of Shiloh, but in a different way. He had Negroes sent out to him to take the place of teamsters, company cooks and laborers in every capacity, so as to put all his white men into the ranks. The people, while willing to send their sons to the field, were not willing to part with their Negroes. It is only fair to state that they probably wanted their blacks to raise supplies for the army and for the families left at home.

Beauregard, however, was reinforced by Van Dorn immediately after Shiloh with 17,000 men. Interior points, less exposed, were also depleted to add to the strength at Corinth. With these reinforcements and the new regiments, Beauregard had, during the month of May, 1862, a large force on paper, but probably not much over 50,000 effective men. We estimated his strength at 70,000. Our own was, in round numbers, 120,000. The defensible nature of the ground at Corinth, and the fortifications, made 50,000 then enough to maintain their position against double that number for an indefinite time but for the demoralization spoken of.

On the 30th of April the grand army commenced its advance from Shiloh upon Corinth. The movement was a siege from the start to the close. The National troops were always behind entrenchments, except of course the small reconnoitering parties sent to the front to clear the way for an advance. Even the commanders of these parties were cautioned, "not to bring on an engagement." "It is better to retreat than to fight." The enemy were constantly watching our advance, but as they were simply observers there were but few engagements that even threatened to become battles. All the engagements fought ought to have served to encourage the enemy. Roads were again made in our front, and again corduroyed; a line was entrenched, and the troops were advanced to the new position. Cross roads were constructed to these new positions to enable the troops to concentrate in case of attack. The National armies were thoroughly entrenched all the way from the Tennessee River to Corinth.

For myself I was little more than an observer. Orders were sent direct to the right wing or reserve, ignoring me, and advances were made from one line of entrenchments to another without notifying me. My position was so embarrassing in fact that I made several applications during the siege to be relieved.

General Halleck kept his headquarters generally, if not all the time, with the right wing. Pope being on the extreme left did not see so much of his chief, and consequently got loose as it were at times. On the 3d of May he was at Seven Mile Creek with the main body of his command, but threw forward a division to Farmington, within four miles of Corinth. His troops had quite a little engagement at Farmington on that day, but carried the place with considerable loss to the enemy. There would then have been no difficulty in advancing the center and right so as to form a new line well up to the enemy, but Pope was ordered back to conform with the general line. On the 8th of May he moved again, taking his whole force to Farmington, and pushed out two divisions close to the rebel line. Again he was ordered back. By the 4th of May the center and right wing reached Monterey, twelve miles out. Their advance was slow from there, for they entrenched with every forward movement. The left wing moved up again on the 25th of May and entrenched itself close to the enemy. The creek with the marsh before described, separated the two lines. Skirmishers thirty feet apart could have maintained either line at this point.

Our center and right were, at this time, extended so that the right of the right wing was probably five miles from Corinth and four from the works in their front. The creek, which was a formidable obstacle for either side to pass on our left, became a very slight obstacle on our right. Here the enemy occupied two positions. One of them, as much as two miles out from his main line, was on a commanding elevation and defended by an entrenched battery with infantry supports. A heavy wood intervened between this work and the National forces. In rear to the south there was a clearing extending a mile or more, and south of this clearing a log-house which had been loopholed and was occupied by infantry. Sherman's division carried these two positions with some loss to himself, but with probably greater to the enemy, on the 28th of May, and on that day the investment of Corinth was complete, or as complete as it was ever made. Thomas' right now rested west of the Mobile and Ohio railroad. Pope's left commanded the Memphis and Charleston railroad east of Corinth.

Some days before I had suggested to the commanding general that I thought if he would move the Army of the Mississippi at night, by the rear of the center and right, ready to advance at daylight, Pope would find no natural obstacle in his front and, I believed, no serious artificial one. The ground, or works, occupied by our left could be held by a thin picket line, owing to the stream and swamp in front. To the right the troops would have a dry ridge to march over. I was silenced so quickly that I felt that possibly I had suggested an unmilitary movement.

Later, probably on the 28th of May, General Logan, whose command was then on the Mobile and Ohio railroad, said to me that the enemy had been evacuating for several days and that if allowed he could go into Corinth with his brigade. Trains of cars were heard coming in and going out of Corinth constantly. Some of the men who had been engaged in various capacities on railroads before the war claimed that they could tell, by putting their ears to the rail, not only which way the trains were moving but which trains were loaded and which were empty. They said loaded trains had been going out for several days and empty ones coming in. Subsequent events proved the correctness of their judgment. Beauregard published his orders for the evacuation of Corinth on the 26th of May and fixed the 29th for the departure of his troops, and on the 30th of May General Halleck had his whole army drawn up prepared for battle and announced in orders that there was every indication that our left was to be attacked that morning. Corinth had already been evacuated and the National troops marched on and took possession without opposition. Everything had been destroyed or carried away. The Confederate commander had instructed his soldiers to cheer on the arrival of every train to create the impression among the Yankees that reinforcements were arriving. There was not a sick or wounded man left by the Confederates, nor stores of any kind. Some ammunition had been blown up — not removed — but the trophies of war were a few Quaker guns, logs of about the diameter of ordinary cannon, mounted on wheels of wagons and pointed in the most threatening manner towards us.

The possession of Corinth by the National troops was of strategic importance, but the victory was barren in every other particular. It was nearly bloodless. It is a question whether the *morale* of the Confederate troops engaged at Corinth was not improved by the immunity with which they were permitted to remove all public property and then withdraw themselves. On our side I know officers and men of the Army of the Tennessee — and I presume the same is true of those of the other commands — were disappointed at the result. They could not see how the mere occupation of places was to close the war while large and effective rebel armies existed. They believed that a well-directed attack would at least have partially destroyed the army defending Corinth. For myself I am satisfied that Corinth could have been captured in a two days' campaign commenced promptly on the arrival of reinforcements after the battle of Shiloh.

General Halleck at once commenced erecting fortifications around Corinth on a scale to indicate that this one point must be held if it took the whole National army to do it. All commanding points two or three miles to the south, southeast and southwest were strongly fortified. It was expected in case of necessity to connect these forts by rifle-pits. They were laid out on a scale that would have required 100,000 men to fully man them. It was probably thought that a final battle of the war would be fought at that point. These fortifications were never used. Immediately after the occupation of Corinth by the National troops, General Pope was sent in pursuit of the retreating garrison and General Buell soon followed. Buell was the senior of the two generals and commanded the entire column. The pursuit was kept up for some thirty miles, but did not result in the capture of any material of war or prisoners, unless a few stragglers who had fallen behind and were willing captives. On the 10th of June the pursuing column was all back at Corinth. The Army of the Tennessee was not engaged in any of these movements.

The Confederates were now driven out of West Tennessee, and on the 6th of June, after a well-contested naval battle, the National forces took possession of Memphis and held the Mississippi river from its source to that point. The railroad from Columbus to Corinth was at once put in good condition and held by us. We had garrisons at Donelson, Clarksville and Nashville, on the Cumberland River, and held the Tennessee River from its mouth to Eastport. New Orleans and Baton Rouge had fallen into the possession of the National forces, so that now the Confederates at the west were narrowed down for all communication with Richmond to the single line of road running east from Vicksburg. To dispossess them of this, therefore, became a matter of the first importance. The possession of the Mississippi by us from Memphis to Baton Rouge was also a most important object. It would be equal to the amputation of a limb in its weakening effects upon the enemy.

After the capture of Corinth a movable force of 80,000 men, besides enough to hold all the territory acquired, could have been set in motion for the accomplishment of any great campaign for the suppression of the rebellion. In addition to this fresh troops were being raised to swell the effective force. But the work of depletion commenced. Buell with the Army of the Ohio was sent east, following the line of the Memphis and Charleston railroad. This he was ordered to repair as he advanced — only to have it destroyed by small guerilla bands or other troops as soon as he was out of the way. If he had been sent directly to Chattanooga as rapidly as he could march, leaving two or three divisions along the line of the railroad from Nashville forward, he could have arrived with but little fighting, and would have saved much of the loss of life which was afterwards incurred in gaining Chattanooga. Bragg would then not have had time to raise an army to contest the possession of middle and east Tennessee and Kentucky; the battles of Stone River and Chickamauga would not necessarily have been fought; Burnside would not have been besieged in Knoxville without the power of helping himself or escaping; the battle of Chattanooga would not have been fought. These are the negative advantages, if the term negative is applicable, which would probably have resulted from prompt movements after Corinth fell into the possession of the National forces. The positive results might have been: a bloodless advance to Atlanta, to Vicksburg, or to any other desired point south of Corinth in the interior of Mississippi.

Chapter XXVII

HEADQUARTERS MOVED TO MEMPHIS — ON
THE ROAD TO MEMPHIS — ESCAPING JACKSON
— COMPLAINTS AND REQUESTS — HALLECK
APPOINTED COMMANDER-IN-CHIEF — RETURN
TO CORINTH — MOVEMENTS OF BRAGG —
SURRENDER OF CLARKSVILLE — THE ADVANCE
UPON CHATTANOOGA — SHERIDAN COLONEL
OF A MICHIGAN REGIMENT

My position at Corinth, with a nominal command and yet no command, became so unbearable that I asked permission of Halleck to remove my headquarters to Memphis. I had repeatedly asked, between the fall of Donelson and the evacuation of Corinth, to be relieved from duty under Halleck; but all my applications were refused until the occupation of the town. I then obtained permission to leave the department, but General Sherman happened to call on me as I was about starting and urged me so strongly not to think of going, that I concluded to remain. My application to be permitted to remove my headquarters to Memphis was, however, approved, and on the 21st of June I started for that point with my staff and a cavalry escort of only a part of one company. There was a detachment of two or three companies going some twenty-five miles west to be stationed as a guard to the railroad. I went under cover of this escort to the end of their march, and the next morning proceeded to La Grange with no convoy but the few cavalry men I had with me.

From La Grange to Memphis the distance is forty-seven miles. There were no troops stationed between these two points, except a small force guarding a working party which was engaged in repairing the railroad. Not knowing where this party would be found I halted at La Grange. General Hurlbut was in command there at the time and had his headquarters tents pitched on the lawn of a very commodious country house. The proprietor was at home and, learning of my arrival, he invited General Hurlbut and me to dine with him. I accepted the invitation and spent a very pleasant afternoon with my host, who was a thorough Southern gentleman fully convinced of the justice of secession. After dinner, seated in the capacious porch, he entertained me with a recital of the services he was rendering the cause. He was too old to be in the ranks himself — he must have been quite seventy then — but his means enabled him to be useful in other ways. In ordinary times the homestead where he was now living produced the bread and meat to supply the slaves on his main plantation, in the low-lands of Mississippi. Now he raised food and forage on both places, and thought he would have that year a surplus sufficient to feed three hundred families of poor men who had gone into the war and left their families dependent upon the "patriotism" of those better off. The crops around me looked fine, and I had at the moment an idea that about the time they were ready to be gathered the "Yankee" troops would be in the neighborhood and harvest them for the benefit of those engaged in the suppression of the rebellion instead of its support. I felt, however, the greatest respect for the candor of my host and for his zeal in a cause he thoroughly believed in, though our views were as wide apart as it is possible to conceive.

The 23d of June, 1862, on the road from La Grange to Memphis was very warm, even for that latitude and season. With my staff and small escort I started at an early hour, and before noon we arrived within twenty miles of Memphis. At this point I saw a very comfortable-looking white-haired gentleman seated at the front of his house, a little distance from the road. I let my staff and escort ride ahead while I halted and, for an excuse, asked for a glass of water. I was invited at once to dismount and come in. I found my host very genial and communicative, and staid longer than I had intended, until the lady of the house announced dinner and asked me to join them. The host, however, was not pressing, so that I declined the invitation and, mounting my horse, rode on.

About a mile west from where I had been stopping a road comes up from the southeast, joining that from La Grange to Memphis. A mile west of this junction I found my staff and escort halted and enjoying the shade of forest trees on the lawn of a house located several hundred feet back from the road, their horses hitched to the fence along the line of the road. I, too, stopped and we remained there until the cool of the afternoon, and then rode into Memphis.

The gentleman with whom I had stopped twenty miles from Memphis was a Mr. De Loche, a man loyal to the Union. He had not pressed me to tarry longer with him because in the early part of my visit a neighbor, a Dr. Smith, had called and, on being presented to me, backed off the porch as if something had hit him. Mr. De Loche knew that the rebel General Jackson was in that neighborhood with a detachment of cavalry. His neighbor was as earnest in the southern cause as was Mr. De Loche in that of the Union. The exact location of Jackson was entirely unknown to Mr. De Loche; but he was sure that his neighbor would know it and would give information of my presence, and this made my stay unpleasant to him after the call of Dr. Smith.

I have stated that a detachment of troops was engaged in guarding workmen who were repairing the railroad east of Memphis. On the day I entered Memphis, Jackson captured a small herd of beef cattle which had been sent east for the troops so engaged. The drovers were not enlisted men and he released them. A day or two after one of these drovers came to my headquarters and, relating the circumstances of his capture, said Jackson was very much disappointed that he had not captured me; that he was six or seven miles south of the Memphis and Charleston railroad when he learned that I was stopping at the house of Mr. De Loche, and had ridden with his command to the junction of the road he was on with that from La Grange and Memphis, where he learned that I had passed three-quarters of an hour before. He thought it would be useless to pursue with jaded horses a well-mounted party with so much of a start. Had he gone three-quarters of a mile farther he would have found me with my party quietly resting under the shade of trees and without even arms in our hands with which to defend ourselves.

General Jackson of course did not communicate his disappointment at not capturing me to a prisoner, a young drover; but from the talk among the soldiers the facts related were learned. A day or two later Mr. De Loche called on me in Memphis to apologize for his apparent incivility in not insisting on my staying for dinner. He said that his wife accused him of marked discourtesy, but that, after the call of his neighbor, he had felt restless until I got away. I never met General Jackson before the war, nor during it, but have met him since at his very comfortable summer home at Manitou Springs, Colorado. I reminded him of the above incident, and this drew from him the response that he was thankful now he had not captured me. I certainly was very thankful too.

My occupation of Memphis as district headquarters did not last long. The period, however, was marked by a few incidents which were novel to me. Up to that time I had not occupied anyplace in the South where the citizens were at home in any great numbers. Dover was within the fortifications at Fort Donelson, and, as far as I remember, every citizen was gone. There were no people living at Pittsburg landing, and but very few at Corinth. Memphis, however, was a populous city, and there were many of the citizens remaining there who were not only thoroughly impressed with the justice of their cause, but who thought that even the "Yankee soldiery" must entertain the same views if they could only be induced to make an honest confession. It took hours of my time every day to listen to complaints and requests. The latter were generally reasonable, and it so they were granted; but the complaints were not always, or even often, well founded. Two instances will mark the general character. First: the officer who commanded at Memphis immediately after the city fell into the hands of the National troops had ordered one of the churches of the city to be opened to the soldiers. Army chaplains were authorized to occupy the pulpit. Second: at the beginning of the war the Confederate Congress had passed a law confiscating all property of "alien enemies" at the South, including the debts of Southerners to Northern men. In consequence of this law, when Memphis was occupied the provost-marshal had forcibly collected all the evidences he could obtain of such debts.

Almost the first complaints made to me were these two outrages. The gentleman who made the complaints informed me first of his own high standing as a lawyer, a citizen and a Christian. He was a deacon in the church which had been defiled by the occupation of Union troops, and by a Union chaplain filling the pulpit. He did not use the word "defile," but he expressed the idea very clearly. He asked that the church be restored to the former congregation. I told him that no order had been issued prohibiting the congregation attending the church. He said of course the congregation could not hear a Northern clergyman who differed so radically with them on questions of government. I told him the troops would continue to occupy that church for the present, and that they would not be called upon to hear disloyal sentiments proclaimed from the pulpit. This closed the argument on the first point.

Then came the second. The complainant said that he wanted the papers restored to him which had been surrendered to the provost-marshal under protest; he was a lawyer, and before the establishment of the "Confederate States Government" had been the attorney for a number of large business houses at the North; that "his government" had confiscated all debts due "alien enemies," and appointed commissioners, or officers, to collect such debts and pay them over to the "government": but in his case, owing to his high standing, he had been permitted to hold these claims for collection, the responsible officials knowing that he would account to the "government" for every dollar received. He said that his "government," when it came in possession of all its territory, would hold him personally responsible for the claims he had surrendered to the provost-marshal. His impudence was so sublime that I was rather amused than indignant. I told him, however, that if he would remain in Memphis I did not believe the Confederate government would ever molest him. He left, no doubt, as much amazed at my assurance as I was at the brazenness of his request.

On the 11th of July General Halleck received telegraphic orders appointing him to the command of all the armies, with headquarters in Washington. His instructions pressed him to proceed to his new field of duty with as little delay as was consistent with the safety and interests of his previous command. I was next in rank, and he telegraphed me the same day to report at department headquarters at Corinth. I was not informed by the dispatch that my chief had been ordered to a different field and did not know whether to move my headquarters or not. I telegraphed asking if I was to take my staff with me, and received word in reply: "This place will be your headquarters. You can judge for yourself." I left Memphis for my new field without delay, and reached Corinth on the 15th of the month. General Halleck remained until the 17th of July; but he was very uncommunicative, and gave me no information as to what I had been called to Corinth for.

When General Halleck left to assume the duties of general-in-chief I remained in command of the district of West Tennessee. Practically I became a department commander, because no one was assigned to that position over me and I made my reports direct to the general-in-chief; but I was not assigned to the position of department commander until the 25th of October. General Halleck while commanding the Department of the Mississippi had had control as far east as a line drawn from

Chattanooga north. My district only embraced West Tennessee and Kentucky west of the Cumberland River. Buell, with the Army of the Ohio, had, as previously stated, been ordered east towards Chattanooga, with instructions to repair the Memphis and Charleston railroad as he advanced. Troops had been sent north by Halleck along the line of the Mobile and Ohio railroad to put it in repair as far as Columbus. Other troops were stationed on the railroad from Jackson, Tennessee, to Grand Junction, and still others on the road west to Memphis.

The remainder of the magnificent army of 120,000 men which entered Corinth on the 30th of May had now become so scattered that I was put entirely on the defensive in a territory whose population was hostile to the Union. One of the first things I had to do was to construct fortifications at Corinth better suited to the garrison that could be spared to man them. The structures that had been built during the months of May and June were left as monuments to the skill of the engineer, and others were constructed in a few days, plainer in design but suited to the command available to defend them.

I disposed the troops belonging to the district in conformity with the situation as rapidly as possible. The forces at Donelson, Clarksville and Nashville, with those at Corinth and along the railroad eastward, I regarded as sufficient for protection against any attack from the west. The Mobile and Ohio railroad was guarded from Rienzi, south of Corinth, to Columbus; and the Mississippi Central railroad from Jackson, Tennessee, to Bolivar. Grand Junction and La Grange on the Memphis railroad were abandoned.

South of the Army of the Tennessee, and confronting it, was Van Dorn, with a sufficient force to organize a movable army of thirty-five to forty thousand men, after being reinforced by Price from Missouri. This movable force could be thrown against either Corinth, Bolivar or Memphis; and the best that could be done in such event would be to weaken the points not threatened in order to reinforce the one that was. Nothing could be gained on the National side by attacking elsewhere, because the territory already occupied was as much as the force present could guard. The most anxious period of the war, to me, was during the time the Army of the Tennessee was guarding the territory acquired by the fall of Corinth and Memphis and before I was sufficiently reinforced to take the offensive. The enemy also had cavalry operating in our rear, making it necessary to guard every point of the railroad back to Columbus, on the security of which we were dependent for all our supplies. Headquarters were connected by telegraph with all points of the command except Memphis and the Mississippi below Columbus. With these points communication was had by the railroad to Columbus, then down the river by boat. To reinforce Memphis would take three or four days, and to get an order there for troops to move elsewhere would have taken at least two days. Memphis therefore was practically isolated from the balance of the command. But it was in Sherman's hands. Then too the troops were well entrenched and the gunboats made a valuable auxiliary.

During the two months after the departure of General Halleck there was much fighting between small bodies of the contending armies, but these encounters were dwarfed by the magnitude of the main battles so as to be now almost forgotten except by those engaged in them. Some of them, however, estimated by the losses on both sides in killed and wounded, were equal in hard fighting to most of the battles of the Mexican war which attracted so much of the attention of the public when they occurred. About the 23d of July Colonel Ross, commanding at Bolivar, was threatened by a large force of the enemy so that he had to be reinforced from Jackson and Corinth. On the 27th there was skirmishing on the Hatchie River, eight miles from Bolivar. On the 30th I learned from Colonel P.H. Sheridan, who had been far to the south, that Bragg in person was at Rome, Georgia, with his troops moving by rail (by way of Mobile) to Chattanooga and his wagon train marching overland to join him at Rome. Price was at this time at Holly Springs, Mississippi, with a large force, and occupied Grand Junction as an outpost. I proposed to the general-in-chief to be permitted to drive him away, but was informed that, while I had to judge for myself, the best use to make of my troops *was not to scatter them,* but hold them ready to reinforce Buell.

The movement of Bragg himself with his wagon trains to Chattanooga across country, while his troops were transported over a long round-about road to the same destination, without need of guards except when in my immediate front, demonstrates the advantage which troops enjoy while acting in a country where the people are friendly. Buell was marching through a hostile region and had to have his communications thoroughly guarded back to a base of supplies. More men were required the farther the National troops penetrated into the enemy's country. I, with an army sufficiently powerful to have destroyed Bragg, was purely on the defensive and accomplishing no more than to hold a force far inferior to my own.

On the 2d of August I was ordered from Washington to live upon the country, on the resources of citizens hostile to the government, so far as practicable. I was also directed to "handle rebels within our lines without gloves," to imprison them, or to expel them from their homes and from our lines. I do not recollect having arrested and confined a citizen (not a soldier) during the entire rebellion. I am aware that a great many were sent to northern prisons, particularly to Joliet, Illinois, by some of my subordinates with the statement that it was my order. I had all such released the moment I learned of their arrest; and finally sent a staff officer north to release every prisoner who was said to be confined by my order. There were many citizens at home who deserved punishment because they were soldiers when an opportunity was afforded to inflict an injury to the National cause. This class was not of the kind that were apt to get arrested, and I deemed it better that a few guilty men should escape than that a great many innocent ones should suffer.

On the 14th of August I was ordered to send two more divisions to Buell. They were sent the same day by way of Decatur. On the 22d Colonel Rodney Mason surrendered Clarksville with six companies of his regiment.

Colonel Mason was one of the officers who had led their regiments off the field at almost the first fire of the rebels at Shiloh. He was by nature and education a gentleman, and was terribly mortified at his action when the battle was over. He came to me with tears in his eyes and begged to be allowed to have another trial. I felt great sympathy for him and sent him, with his regiment, to garrison Clarksville and Donelson. He selected Clarksville for his headquarters, no doubt because he regarded it as the post of danger, it being nearer the enemy. But when he was summoned to surrender by a band of guerillas, his constitutional weakness overcame him. He inquired the number of men the enemy had, and receiving a response indicating a force greater than his own he said if he could be satisfied of that fact he would surrender. Arrangements were made for him to count the guerillas, and having satisfied himself that the enemy had the greater force he surrendered and informed his subordinate at Donelson of the fact, advising him to do the same. The guerillas paroled their prisoners and moved upon Donelson, but the officer in command at that point marched out to meet them and drove them away.

Among other embarrassments, at the time of which I now write, was the fact that the government wanted to get out all the cotton possible from the South and directed me to give every facility toward that end. Pay in gold was authorized, and stations on the Mississippi River and on the railroad in our possession had to be designated where cotton would be received. This opened to the enemy not only the means of converting cotton into money, which had a value all over the world and which they so much needed, but it afforded them means of obtaining accurate and intelligent information in regard to our position and strength. It was also demoralizing to the troops. Citizens obtaining permits from the treasury department had to be protected within our lines and given facilities to get out cotton by which they realized enormous profits. Men who had enlisted to fight the battles of their country did not like to be engaged in protecting a traffic which went to the support of an enemy they had to fight, and the profits of which went to men who shared none of their dangers.

On the 30th of August Colonel M.D. Leggett, near Bolivar, with the 20th and 29th Ohio volunteer infantry, was attacked by a force supposed to be about 4,000 strong. The enemy was driven away with a loss of more than one hundred men. On the 1st of September the bridge guard at Medon was attacked by guerillas. The guard held the position until reinforced, when the enemy were routed leaving about fifty of their number on the field dead or wounded, our loss being only two killed and fifteen wounded. On the same day Colonel Dennis, with a force of less than 500 infantry and two pieces of artillery, met the cavalry of the enemy in strong force, a few miles west of Medon, and drove them away with great loss. Our troops buried 179 of the enemy's dead, left upon the field. Afterwards it was found that all the houses in the vicinity of the battlefield were turned into hospitals for the wounded. Our loss, as reported at the time, was forty-five killed and wounded. On the 2d of September I was ordered to send more reinforcements to Buell. Jackson and Bolivar were yet threatened, but I sent the reinforcements. On the 4th I received direct orders to send Granger's division also to Louisville, Kentucky.

General Buell had left Corinth about the 10th of June to march upon Chattanooga; Bragg, who had superseded Beauregard in command, sent one division from Tupelo on the 27th of June for the same place. This gave Buell about seventeen days' start. If he had not been required to repair the railroad as he advanced, the march could have been made in eighteen days at the outside, and Chattanooga must have been reached by the National forces before the rebels could have possibly got there. The road between Nashville and Chattanooga could easily have been put in repair by other troops, so that communication with the North would have been opened in a short time after the occupation of the place by the National troops. If Buell had been permitted to move in the first instance, with the whole of the Army of the Ohio and that portion of the Army of the Mississippi afterwards sent to him, he could have thrown four divisions from his own command along the line of road to repair and guard it.

Granger's division was promptly sent on the 4th of September. I was at the station at Corinth when the troops reached that point, and found General P.H. Sheridan with them. I expressed surprise at seeing him and said that I had not expected him to go. He showed decided disappointment at the prospect of being detained. I felt a little nettled at his desire to get away and did not detain him.

Sheridan was a first lieutenant in the regiment in which I had served eleven years, the 4th infantry, and stationed on the Pacific coast when the war broke out. He was promoted to a captaincy in May, 1861, and before the close of the year managed in some way, I do not know how, to get East. He went to Missouri. Halleck had known him as a very successful young officer in managing campaigns against the Indians on the Pacific coast, and appointed him acting-quartermaster in southwest Missouri. There was no difficulty in getting supplies forward while Sheridan served in that capacity; but he got into difficulty with his immediate superiors because of his stringent rules for preventing the use of public transportation for private purposes. He asked to be relieved from further duty in the capacity in which he was engaged and his request was granted. When General Halleck took the field in April, 1862, Sheridan was assigned to duty on his staff. During the advance on Corinth a vacancy occurred in the colonelcy of the 2d Michigan cavalry. Governor Blair, of Michigan, telegraphed General Halleck asking him to suggest the name of a professional soldier for the vacancy, saying he would appoint a good man without reference to his State. Sheridan was named; and was so conspicuously efficient that when Corinth was reached he was assigned to command a cavalry brigade in the Army of the Mississippi. He was in command at Booneville on the 1st of July with two small regiments, when he was attacked by a force full three times as numerous as his own. By very skillful maneuvers and boldness of attack he completely routed the enemy. For this he was made a brigadier-general and became a conspicuous figure in the army about Corinth. On this account I was sorry to see him leaving me. His departure was probably fortunate, for he rendered distinguished services in his new field.

Granger and Sheridan reached Louisville before Buell got there, and on the night of their arrival Sheridan with his command threw up works around the railroad station for the defense of troops as they came from the front.

Chapter XXVIII

ADVANCE OF VAN DORN AND PRICE — PRICE ENTERS IUKA — BATTLE OF IUKA

*A*t this time, September 4th, I had two divisions of the Army of the Mississippi stationed at Corinth, Rienzi, Jacinto and Danville. There were at Corinth also Davies' division and two brigades of McArthur's, besides cavalry and artillery. This force constituted my left wing, of which Rosecrans was in command. General Ord commanded the center, from Bethel to Humboldt on the Mobile and Ohio railroad and from Jackson to Bolivar where the Mississippi Central is crossed by the Hatchie River. General Sherman commanded on the right at Memphis with two of his brigades back at Brownsville, at the crossing of the Hatchie River by the Memphis and Ohio railroad. This made the most convenient arrangement I could devise for concentrating all my spare forces upon any threatened point. All the troops of the command were within telegraphic communication of each other, except those under Sherman. By bringing a portion of his command to Brownsville, from which point there was a railroad and telegraph back to Memphis, communication could be had with that part of my command within a few hours by the use of couriers. In case it became necessary to reinforce Corinth, by this arrangement all the troops at Bolivar, except a small guard, could be sent by rail by the way of Jackson in less than twenty-four hours; while the troops from Brownsville could march up to Bolivar to take their place.

On the 7th of September I learned of the advance of Van Dorn and Price, apparently upon Corinth. One division was brought from Memphis to Bolivar to meet any emergency that might arise from this move of the enemy. I was much concerned because my first duty, after holding the territory acquired within my command, was to prevent further reinforcing of Bragg in Middle Tennessee. Already the Army of Northern Virginia had defeated the army under General Pope and was invading Maryland. In the center General Buell was on his way to Louisville and

Bragg marching parallel to him with a large Confederate force for the Ohio River.

I had been constantly called upon to reinforce Buell until at this time my entire force numbered less than 50,000 men, of all arms. This included everything from Cairo south within my jurisdiction. If I too should be driven back, the Ohio River would become the line dividing the belligerents west of the Alleghenies, while at the East the line was already farther north than when hostilities commenced at the opening of the war. It is true Nashville was never given up after its first capture, but it would have been isolated and the garrison there would have been obliged to beat a hasty retreat if the troops in West Tennessee had been compelled to fall back. To say at the end of the second year of the war the line dividing the contestants at the East was pushed north of Maryland, a State that had not seceded, and at the West beyond Kentucky, another State which had been always loyal, would have been discouraging indeed. As it was, many loyal people despaired in the fall of 1862 of ever saving the Union. The administration at Washington was much concerned for the safety of the cause it held so dear. But I believe there was never a day when the President did not think that, in some way or other, a cause so just as ours would come out triumphant.

Up to the 11th of September Rosecrans still had troops on the railroad east of Corinth, but they had all been ordered in. By the 12th all were in except a small force under Colonel Murphy of the 8th Wisconsin. He had been detained to guard the remainder of the stores which had not yet been brought in to Corinth.

On the 13th of September General Sterling Price entered Iuka, a town about twenty miles east of Corinth on the Memphis and Charleston railroad. Colonel Murphy with a few men was guarding the place. He made no resistance, but evacuated the town on the approach of the enemy. I was apprehensive lest the object of the rebels might be to get troops into Tennessee to reinforce Bragg, as it was afterwards ascertained to be. The authorities at Washington, including the general-in-chief of the army, were very anxious, as I have said, about affairs both in East and Middle Tennessee; and my anxiety was quite as great on their account as for any danger threatening my command. I had not force enough at Corinth to attack Price even by stripping everything; and there was danger that before troops could be got from other points he might be far on his way across the Tennessee. To prevent this all spare forces at Bolivar and Jackson were ordered to Corinth, and cars were concentrated at Jackson for their transportation. Within twenty-four hours from the transmission of the order the troops were at their destination, although there had been a delay of four hours resulting from the forward train getting off the track and stopping all the others. This gave a reinforcement of near 8,000 men, General Ord in command. General Rosecrans commanded the district of Corinth with a movable force of about 9,000 independent of the garrison deemed necessary to be left behind. It was known that General Van Dorn was about a four days' march south of us, with a large force. It might have been part of his plan to attack at Corinth, Price coming from the east while he came up from the south. My desire was to attack Price before Van Dorn could reach Corinth or go to his relief.

General Rosecrans had previously had his headquarters at Iuka, where his command was spread out along the Memphis and Charleston railroad eastward. While there he had a most excellent map prepared showing all the roads and streams in the surrounding country. He was also personally familiar with the ground, so that I deferred very much to him in my plans for the approach. We had cars enough to transport all of General Ord's command, which was to go by rail to Burnsville, a point on the road about seven miles west of Iuka. From there his troops were to march by the north side of the railroad and attack Price from the northwest, while Rosecrans was to move eastward from his position south of Corinth by way of the Jacinto road. A small force was to hold the Jacinto road where it turns to the northeast, while the main force moved on the Fulton road which comes into Iuka further east. This plan was suggested by Rosecrans.

Bear Creek, a few miles to the east of the Fulton road, is a formidable obstacle to the movement of troops in the absence of bridges, all of which, in September, 1862, had been destroyed in that vicinity. The Tennessee, to the northeast, not many miles away, was also a formidable obstacle for an army followed by a pursuing force. Ord was on the northwest, and even if a rebel movement had been possible in that direction it could have brought only temporary relief, for it would have carried Price's army to the rear of the National forces and isolated it from all support. It looked to me that, if Price would remain in Iuka until we could get there, his annihilation was inevitable.

On the morning of the 18th of September General Ord moved by rail to Burnsville, and there left the cars and moved out to perform his part of the program. He was to get as near the enemy as possible during the day and entrench himself so as to hold his position until the next morning. Rosecrans was to be up by the morning of the 19th on the two roads before described, and the attack was to be from all three quarters simultaneously. Troops enough were left at Jacinto and Rienzi to detain any cavalry that Van Dorn might send out to make a sudden dash into Corinth until I could be notified. There was a telegraph wire along the railroad, so there would be no delay in communication. I detained cars and locomotives enough at Burnsville to transport the whole of Ord's command at once, and if Van Dorn had moved against Corinth instead of Iuka I could have thrown in reinforcements to the number of 7,000 or 8,000 before he could have arrived. I remained at Burnsville with a detachment of about 900 men from Ord's command and communicated with my two wings by courier. Ord met the advance of the enemy soon after leaving Burnsville. Quite a sharp engagement ensued, but he drove the rebels back with considerable loss, including one general officer killed. He maintained his position and was ready to attack by daylight the next morning. I was very much disappointed at receiving a dispatch from Rosecrans after midnight from Jacinto, twenty-two miles from Iuka, saying that some of his command had been delayed, and that the rear of his column was not yet up as far as Jacinto. He said, however, that he would still be at Iuka by two o'clock the next day. I did not believe this possible because of the distance and the condition of the roads, which was bad; besides, troops after a forced march of twenty miles are not in a good condition for fighting the moment they get through. It might do in marching to relieve a beleaguered garrison, but not to make an assault. I immediately sent Ord a copy of Rosecrans' dispatch and ordered him to be in readiness to attack the moment he heard the sound of guns to the south or southeast. He was instructed to notify his officers to be on the alert for any indications of battle. During the 19th the wind blew in the wrong direction to transmit sound either towards the point where Ord was, or to Burnsville where I had remained.

A couple of hours before dark on the 19th Rosecrans arrived with the head of his column at garnets, the point where the Jacinto road to Iuka leaves the road going east. He here turned north without sending any troops to the Fulton road. While still moving in column up the Jacinto road he met a force of the enemy and had his advance badly beaten and driven back upon the main road. In this short engagement his loss was considerable for the number engaged, and one battery was taken from him. The wind was still blowing hard and in the wrong direction to transmit sounds towards either Ord or me. Neither he nor I nor anyone in either command heard a gun that was fired upon the battlefield. After the engagement Rosecrans sent me a dispatch announcing the result. This was brought by a courier. There was no road between Burnsville and the position then occupied by Rosecrans and the country was impassable for a man on horseback. The courier bearing the message was compelled to move west nearly to Jacinto before he found a road leading to Burnsville. This made it a late hour of the night before I learned of the battle that had taken place during the afternoon. I at once notified Ord of the fact and ordered him to attack early in the morning. The next morning Rosecrans himself renewed the attack and went into Iuka with but little resistance. Ord also went in according to orders, without hearing a gun from the south of town but supposing the troops coming from the southwest must be up by that time. Rosecrans, however, had put no troops upon the Fulton road, and the enemy had taken advantage of this neglect and retreated by that road during the night. Word was soon brought to me that our troops were in Iuka. I immediately rode into town and found that the enemy was not being pursued even by the cavalry. I ordered pursuit by the whole of Rosecrans' command and went on with him a few miles in person. He followed only a few miles after I left him and then went into camp, and the pursuit was continued no further. I was disappointed at the result of the battle of Iuka — but I had so high an opinion of General Rosecrans that I found no fault at the time.

Chapter XXIX

VAN DORN'S MOVEMENTS — BATTLE OF CORINTH — COMMAND OF THE DEPARTMENT OF THE TENNESSEE

On the 19th of September General Geo. H. Thomas was ordered east to reinforce Buell. This threw the army at my command still more on the defensive. The Memphis and Charleston railroad was abandoned, except at Corinth, and small forces were left at Chewalla and Grand Junction. Soon afterwards the latter of these two places was given up and Bolivar became our most advanced position on the Mississippi Central railroad. Our cavalry was kept well to the front and frequent expeditions were sent out to watch the movements of the enemy. We were in a country where nearly all the people, except the Negroes, were hostile to us and friendly to the cause we were trying to suppress. It was easy, therefore, for the enemy to get early information of our every move. We, on the contrary, had to go after our information in force, and then often returned without it.

On the 22d Bolivar was threatened by a large force from south of Grand Junction, supposed to be twenty regiments of infantry with cavalry and artillery. I reinforced Bolivar, and went to Jackson in person to superintend the movement of troops to whatever point the attack might be made upon. The troops from Corinth were brought up in time to repel the threatened movement without a battle. Our cavalry followed the enemy south of Davis' mills in Mississippi.

On the 30th I found that Van Dorn was apparently endeavoring to strike the Mississippi River above Memphis. At the same time other points within my command were so threatened that it was impossible to concentrate a force to drive him away. There was at this juncture a large Union force at Helena, Arkansas, which, had it been within my command, I could have ordered across the river to attack and break up the Mississippi Central railroad far to the south. This would not only have called Van Dorn back, but would have compelled the retention of a large rebel force far to the south to prevent a repetition of such raids on the enemy's line of supplies. Geographical lines between the commands during the rebellion were not always well chosen, or they were too rigidly adhered to.

Van Dorn did not attempt to get upon the line above Memphis, as had apparently been his intention. He was simply covering a deeper design; one much more important to his cause. By the 1st of October it was fully apparent that Corinth was to be attacked with great force and determination, and that Van Dorn, Lovell, Price, Villepigue and Rust had joined their strength for this purpose. There was some skirmishing outside of Corinth with the advance of the enemy on the 3d. The rebels massed in the northwest angle of the Memphis and Charleston and the Mobile and Ohio railroads, and were thus between the troops at Corinth and all possible reinforcements. Any fresh troops for us must come by a circuitous route.

On the night of the 3d, accordingly, I ordered General McPherson, who was at Jackson, to join Rosecrans at Corinth with reinforcements picked up along the line of the railroad equal to a brigade. Hurlbut had been ordered from Bolivar to march for the same destination; and as Van Dorn was coming upon Corinth from the northwest some of his men fell in with the advance of Hurlbut's and some skirmishing ensued on the evening of the 3d. On the 4th Van Dorn made a dashing attack, hoping, no doubt, to capture Rosecrans before his reinforcements could come up. In that case the enemy himself could have occupied the defenses of Corinth and held at bay all the Union troops that arrived. In fact he could have taken the offensive against the reinforcements with three or four times their number and still left a sufficient garrison in the works about Corinth to hold them. He came near success, some of his troops penetrating the National lines at least once, but the works that were built after Halleck's departure enabled Rosecrans to hold his position until the troops of both McPherson and Hurlbut approached towards the rebel front and rear. The enemy was finally driven back with great slaughter: all their charges, made with great gallantry, were re-pulsed. The loss on our side was heavy, but nothing to compare with Van Dorn's. McPherson came up with the train of cars bearing his command as close to the enemy as was prudent, debarked on the rebel flank and got in to the support of Rosecrans just after the repulse. His approach, as well as that of Hurlbut, was known to the enemy and had a moral effect. General Rosecrans, however, failed to follow up the victory, although I had given specific orders in advance of the battle for him to pursue the moment the enemy was repelled. He did not do so, and I repeated the order after the battle. In the first order he was notified that the force of 4,000 men which was going to his assistance would be in great peril if the enemy was not pursued.

General Ord had joined Hurlbut on the 4th and being senior took command of his troops. This force encountered the head of Van Dorn's retreating column just as it was crossing the Hatchie by a bridge some ten miles out from Corinth. The bottom land here was swampy and bad for the operations of troops, making a good place to get an enemy into. Ord attacked the troops that had crossed the bridge and drove them back in a panic. Many were killed, and others were drowned by being pushed off the bridge in their hurried retreat. Ord followed and met the main force. He was too weak in numbers to assault, but he held the bridge and compelled the enemy to resume his retreat by another bridge higher up the stream. Ord was wounded in this engagement and the command devolved on Hurlbut.

Rosecrans did not start in pursuit till the morning of the 5th and then took the wrong road. Moving in the enemy's country he traveled with a wagon train to carry his provisions and munitions of war. His march was therefore slower than that of the enemy, who was moving towards his supplies. Two or three hours of pursuit on the day of battle, without anything except what the men carried on their persons, would have been worth more than any pursuit commenced the next day could have possibly been. Even when he did start, if Rosecrans had followed the route taken by the enemy, he would have come upon Van Dorn in a swamp with a stream in front and Ord holding the only bridge; but he took the road leading north and towards Chewalla instead of west, and, after having marched as far as the enemy had moved to get to the Hatchie, he was as far from battle as when he started. Hurlbut had not the numbers to meet any such force as Van Dorn's if they had been in any mood for fighting, and he might have been in great peril.

I now regarded the time to accomplish anything by pursuit as past and, after Rosecrans reached Jonesboro, I ordered him to return. He kept on to Ripley, however, and was persistent in wanting to go farther. I thereupon ordered him to halt and submitted the matter to the general-in-chief, who allowed me to exercise my judgment in the matter, but inquired "why not pursue?" Upon this I ordered Rosecrans back. Had he gone much farther he would have met a greater force than Van Dorn had at Corinth and behind entrenchments or on chosen ground, and the probabilities are he would have lost his army.

The battle of Corinth was bloody, our loss being 315 killed, 1,812 wounded and 232 missing. The enemy lost many more. Rosecrans reported 1,423 dead and 2,225 prisoners. We fought behind breastworks, which accounts in some degree for the disparity. Among the killed on our side was General Hackelman. General Oglesby was badly, it was for some time supposed mortally, wounded. I received a congratulatory letter from the President, which expressed also his sorrow for the losses.

This battle was recognized by me as being a decided victory, though not so complete as I had hoped for, nor nearly so complete as I now think was within the easy grasp of the commanding officer at Corinth. Since the war it is known that the result, as it was, was a crushing blow to the enemy, and felt by him much more than it was appreciated at the North. The battle relieved me from any further anxiety for the safety of the territory within my jurisdiction, and soon after receiving rein-forcements I suggested to the general-in-chief a forward movement against Vicksburg.

On the 23d of October I learned of Pemberton's being in command at Holly Springs and much reinforced by conscripts and troops from Alabama and Texas. The same day General Rosecrans was relieved from duty with my command, and shortly after he succeeded Buell in the command of the army in Middle Tennessee. I was delighted at the promotion of General Rosecrans to a separate command, because I still believed that when independent of an immediate superior the qualities which I, at that time, credited him with possessing, would show them-selves. As a subordinate I found that I could not make him do as I wished, and had determined to relieve him from duty that very day.

At the close of the operations just described my force, in round numbers, was 48,500. Of these 4,800 were in Kentucky and Illinois, 7,000 in Memphis, 19,200 from Mound City south, and 17,500 at Corinth. General McClernand had been authorized from Washington to go north and organize troops to be used in opening the Mississippi. These new levies with other reinforcements now began to come in.

On the 25th of October I was placed in command of the Department of the Tennessee. Reinforcements continued to come from the north and by the 2d of November I was prepared to take the initiative. This was a great relief after the two and a half months of continued defense over a large district of country, and where nearly every citizen was an enemy ready to give information of our every move. I have described very imperfectly a few of the battles and skirmishes that took place during this time. To describe all would take more space than I can allot to the purpose; to make special mention of all the officers and troops who distinguished themselves, would take a volume.*

Chapter XXX

THE CAMPAIGN AGAINST VICKSBURG — EMPLOYING THE FREEDMEN — OCCUPATION OF HOLLY SPRINGS — SHERMAN ORDERED TO MEMPHIS — SHERMAN'S MOVEMENTS DOWN THE MISSISSIPPI — VAN DORN CAPTURES HOLLY SPRINGS — COLLECTING FORAGE AND FOOD

*V*icksburg was important to the enemy because it occupied the first high ground coming close to the river below Memphis. From there a railroad runs east, connecting with other roads leading to all points of

---

* *Note.* — For gallantry in the various engagements, from the time I was left in command down to 26th of October and on my recommendation, Generals McPherson and C. S. Hamilton were promoted to be Major-Generals, and Colonels C.C. Marsh, 20th Illinois, M.M. Crocker, 13th Iowa J.A. Mower, 11th Missouri, M.D. Leggett, 78th Ohio, J. D. Stevenson, 7th Missouri, and John E. Smith, 45th Illinois, to be Brigadiers.

the Southern States. A railroad also starts from the opposite side of the river, extending west as far as Shreveport, Louisiana. Vicksburg was the only channel, at the time of the events of which this chapter treats, connecting the parts of the Confederacy divided by the Mississippi. So long as it was held by the enemy, the free navigation of the river was prevented. Hence its importance. Points on the river between Vicksburg and Port Hudson were held as dependencies; but their fall was sure to follow the capture of the former place.

The campaign against Vicksburg commenced on the 2d of November as indicated in a dispatch to the general-in-chief in the following words: "I have commenced a movement on Grand Junction, with three divisions from Corinth and two from Bolivar. Will leave here [Jackson, Tennessee] tomorrow, and take command in person. If found practicable, I will go to Holly Springs, and, may be, Grenada, completing railroad and telegraph as I go."

At this time my command was holding the Mobile and Ohio railroad from about twenty-five miles south of Corinth, north to Columbus, Kentucky; the Mississippi Central from Bolivar north to its junction with the Mobile and Ohio; the Memphis and Charleston from Corinth east to Bear Creek, and the Mississippi River from Cairo to Memphis. My entire command was no more than was necessary to hold these lines, and hardly that if kept on the defensive. By moving against the enemy and into his unsubdued, or not yet captured, territory, driving their army before us, these lines would nearly hold themselves; thus affording a large force for field operations. My moving force at that time was about 30,000 men, and I estimated the enemy confronting me, under Pemberton, at about the same number. General McPherson commanded my left wing and General C.S. Hamilton the center, while Sherman was at Memphis with the right wing. Pemberton was fortified at the Tallahatchie, but occupied Holly Springs and Grand Junction on the Mississippi Central railroad. On the 8th we occupied Grand Junction and La Grange, throwing a considerable force seven or eight miles south, along the line of the railroad. The road from Bolivar forward was repaired and put in running order as the troops advanced.

Up to this time it had been regarded as an axiom in war that large bodies of troops must operate from a base of supplies which they always covered and guarded in all forward movements. There was delay therefore in repairing the road back, and in gathering and forwarding supplies to the front.

By my orders, and in accordance with previous instructions from Washington, all the forage within reach was collected under the supervision of the chief quartermaster and the provisions under the chief commissary, receipts being given when there was anyone to take them; the supplies in any event to be accounted for as government stores. The stock was bountiful, but still it gave me no idea of the possibility of supplying a moving column in an enemy's country from the country itself.

It was at this point, probably, where the first idea of a "Freedman's Bureau" took its origin. Orders of the government prohibited the expulsion of the Negroes from the protection of the army, when they came in voluntarily. Humanity forbade allowing them to starve. With such an army of them, of all ages and both sexes, as had congregated about Grand Junction, amounting to many thousands, it was impossible to advance. There was no special authority for feeding them unless they were employed as teamsters, cooks and pioneers with the army; but only able-bodied young men were suitable for such work. This labor would support but a very limited percentage of them. The plantations were all deserted; the cotton and corn were ripe: men, women and children above ten years of age could be employed in saving these crops. To do this work with contrabands, or to have it done, organization under a competent chief was necessary. On inquiring for such a man Chaplain Eaton, now and for many years the very able United States Commissioner of Education, was suggested. He proved as efficient in that field as he has since done in his present one. I gave him all the assistants and guards he called for. We together fixed the prices to be paid for the Negro labor, whether rendered to the government or to individuals. The cotton was to be picked from abandoned plantations, the laborers to receive the stipulated price (my recollection is twelve and a half cents per pound for picking and ginning) from the quartermaster, he shipping the cotton north to be sold for the benefit of the government. Citizens remaining on their plantations were allowed the privilege of having their crops saved by freedmen on the same terms.

At once the freedmen became self-sustaining. The money was not paid to them directly, but was expended judiciously and for their benefit. They gave me no trouble afterwards.

Later the freedmen were engaged in cutting wood along the Mississippi River to supply the large number of steamers on that stream. A good price was paid for chopping wood used for the supply of government steamers (steamers chartered and which the government had to supply with fuel). Those supplying their own fuel paid a much higher price. In this way a fund was created not only sufficient to feed and clothe all, old and young, male and female, but to build them comfortable cabins, hospitals for the sick, and to supply them with many comforts they had never known before.

At this stage of the campaign against Vicksburg I was very much disturbed by newspaper rumors that General McClernand was to have a separate and independent command within mine, to operate against Vicksburg by way of the Mississippi River. Two commanders on the same field are always one too many, and in this case I did not think the general selected had either the experience or the qualifications to fit him for so important a position. I feared for the safety of the troops entrusted to him, especially as he was to raise new levies, raw troops, to execute so important a trust. But on the 12th I received a dispatch from General Halleck saying that I had command of all the troops sent to my department and authorizing me to fight the enemy where I pleased. The next day my cavalry was in Holly Springs, and the enemy fell back south of the Tallahatchie.

Holly Springs I selected for my depot of supplies and munitions of war, all of which at that time came by rail from Columbus, Kentucky, except the few stores collected about La Grange and Grand Junction. This was a long line (increasing in length as we moved south) to maintain in an enemy's country. On the 15th of November, while I was still at Holly Springs, I sent word to Sherman to meet me at Columbus. We were but forty-seven miles apart, yet the most expeditious way for us to meet was for me to take the rail to Columbus and Sherman a steamer for the same place. At that meeting, besides talking over my general plans I gave him his orders to join me with two divisions and to march them down the Mississippi Central railroad if he could. Sherman, who was always prompt, was up by the 29th to Cottage Hill, ten miles north of Oxford. He brought three divisions with him, leaving a garrison of only four regiments of infantry, a couple of pieces of artillery and a small detachment of cavalry. Further reinforcements he knew were on their way from the north to Memphis. About this time General Halleck ordered troops from Helena, Arkansas (territory west of the Mississippi was not under my command then) to cut the road in Pemberton's rear. The expedition was under Generals Hovey and C.C. Washburn and was successful so far as reaching the railroad was concerned, but the damage done was very slight and was soon repaired.

The Tallahatchie, which confronted me, was very high, the railroad bridge destroyed and Pemberton strongly fortified on the south side. A crossing would have been impossible in the presence of an enemy. I sent the cavalry higher up the stream and they secured a crossing. This caused the enemy to evacuate their position, which was possibly accelerated by the expedition of Hovey and Washburn. The enemy was followed as far south as Oxford by the main body of troops, and some seventeen miles farther by McPherson's command. Here the pursuit was halted to repair the railroad from the Tallahatchie northward, in order to bring up supplies. The piles on which the railroad bridge rested had been left standing. The work of constructing a roadway for the troops was but a short matter, and, later, rails were laid for cars.

During the delay at Oxford in repairing railroads I learned that an expedition down the Mississippi now was inevitable and, desiring to have a competent commander in charge, I ordered Sherman on the 8th of December back to Memphis to take charge. The following were his orders:

> Headquarters 13th Army Corps,
> Department of the Tennessee.
> OXFORD, MISSISSIPPI,
> December 8, 1862.

MAJOR-GENERAL W.T. SHERMAN,
Commanding Right Wing:

You will proceed, with as little delay as possible, to Memphis, Tennessee, taking with you one division of your present command. On your arrival at Memphis you will assume command of all the troops there, and that portion of General Curtis's forces at present east of the Mississippi River, and organize them into brigades and divisions in your own army. As soon as possible move with them down the river to the vicinity of Vicksburg, and with the co-operation of the gunboat fleet under command of Flag-officer Porter proceed to the reduction of that place in such a manner as circumstances, and your own judgment, may dictate.

The amount of rations, forage, land transportation, etc., necessary to take, will be left entirely with yourself. The Quartermaster at St. Louis will be instructed to send you transportation for 30,000 men; should you still find yourself deficient, your quartermaster will be authorized to make up the deficiency from such transports as may come into the port of Memphis.

On arriving in Memphis, put yourself in communication with Admiral Porter, and arrange with him for his co-operation.

Inform me at the earliest practicable day of the time when you will embark, and such plans as may then be matured. I will hold the forces here in readiness to co-operate with you in such manner as the movements of the enemy may make necessary.

Leave the District of Memphis in the command of an efficient officer, and with a garrison of four regiments of infantry, the siege guns, and whatever cavalry may be there.

U.S. GRANT, Major-General

This idea had presented itself to my mind earlier, for on the 3d of December I asked Halleck if it would not be well to hold the enemy south of the Yallabusha and move a force from Helena and Memphis on Vicksburg. On the 5th again I suggested, from Oxford, to Halleck that if the Helena troops were at my command I though it would be possible to take them and the Memphis forces south of the mouth of the Yazoo River, and thus secure Vicksburg and the State of Mississippi. Halleck on the same day, the 5th of December, directed me not to attempt to hold the country south of the Tallahatchie, but to collect 25,000 troops at Memphis by the 20th for the Vicksburg expedition. I sent Sherman with two divisions at once, informed the general-in-chief of the fact, and asked whether I should command the expedition down the river myself or send Sherman. I was authorized to do as I though best for the accomplishment of the great object in view. I sent Sherman and so informed General Halleck.

As stated, my action in sending Sherman back was expedited by a desire to get him in command of the forces separated from my direct supervision. I feared that delay might bring McClernand, who was his senior and who had authority from the President and Secretary of War to exercise that particular command, — and independently. I doubted McClernand's fitness; and I had good reason to believe that in fore-stalling him I was by no means giving offence to those whose authority to command was above both him and me.

Neither my orders to General Sherman, nor the correspondence between us or between General Halleck and myself, contemplated at the time my going further south than the Yallabusha. Pemberton's force in my front was the main part of the garrison of Vicksburg, as the force with me was the defense of the territory held by us in West Tennessee and Kentucky. I hoped to hold Pemberton in my front while Sherman should get in his rear and into Vicksburg. The further north the enemy could be held the better.

It was understood, however, between General Sherman and myself that our movements were to be co-operative; if Pemberton could not be held away from Vicksburg I was to follow him; but at that time it was not expected to abandon the railroad north of the Yallabusha. With that point as a secondary base of supplies, the possibility of moving down the Yazoo until communications could be opened with the Mississippi was contemplated.

It was my intention, and so understood by Sherman and his command, that if the enemy should fall back I would follow him even to the gates of Vicksburg. I intended in such an event to hold the road to

Grenada on the Yallabusha and cut loose from there, expecting to establish a new base of supplies on the Yazoo, or at Vicksburg itself, with Grenada to fall back upon in case of failure. It should be remembered that at the time I speak of it had not been demonstrated that an army could operate in an enemy's territory depending upon the country for supplies. A halt was called at Oxford with the advance seventeen miles south of there, to bring up the road to the latter point and to bring supplies of food, forage and munitions to the front.

On the 18th of December I received orders from Washington to divide my command into four army corps, with General McClernand to command one of them and to be assigned to that part of the army which was to operate down the Mississippi. This interfered with my plans, but probably resulted in my ultimately taking the command in person. McClernand was at that time in Springfield, Illinois. The order was obeyed without any delay. Dispatches were sent to him the same day in conformity.

On the 20th General Van Dorn appeared at Holly Springs, my secondary base of supplies, captured the garrison of 1,500 men commanded by Colonel Murphy, of the 8th Wisconsin regiment, and destroyed all our munitions of war, food and forage. The capture was a disgraceful one to the officer commanding but not to the troops under him. At the same time Forrest got on our line of railroad between Jackson, Tennessee, and Columbus, Kentucky, doing much damage to it. This cut me off from all communication with the north for more than a week, and it was more than two weeks before rations or forage could be issued from stores obtained in the regular way. This demonstrated the impossibility of maintaining so long a line of road over which to draw supplies for an army moving in an enemy's country. I determined, therefore, to abandon my campaign into the interior with Columbus as a base, and returned to La Grange and Grand Junction destroying the road to my front and repairing the road to Memphis, making the Mississippi river the line over which to draw supplies. Pemberton was falling back at the same time.

The moment I received the news of Van Dorn's success I sent the cavalry at the front back to drive him from the country. He had start enough to move north destroying the railroad in many places, and to attack several small garrisons entrenched as guards to the railroad. All these he found warned of his coming and prepared to receive him. Van Dorn did not succeed in capturing a single garrison except the one at Holly Springs, which was larger than all the others attacked by him put together. Murphy was also warned of Van Dorn's approach, but made no preparations to meet him. He did not even notify his command.

Colonel Murphy was the officer who, two months before, had evacuated Iuka on the approach of the enemy. General Rosecrans denounced him for the act and desired to have him tried and punished. I sustained the colonel at the time because his command was a small one compared with that of the enemy — not one-tenth as large — and I thought he had done well to get away without falling into their hands. His leaving large stores to fall into Price's possession I looked upon as an oversight and excused it on the ground of inexperience in military matters. He should, however, have destroyed them. This last surrender demonstrated to my mind that Rosecrans' judgment of Murphy's conduct at Iuka was correct. The surrender of Holly Springs was most reprehensible and showed either the disloyalty of Colonel Murphy to the cause which he professed to serve, or gross cowardice.

After the war was over I read from the diary of a lady who accompanied General Pemberton in his retreat from the Tallahatchie, that the retreat was almost a panic. The roads were bad and it was difficult to move the artillery and trains. Why there should have been a panic I do not see. No expedition had yet started down the Mississippi River. Had I known the demoralized condition of the enemy, or the fact that central Mississippi abounded so in all army supplies, I would have been in pursuit of Pemberton while his cavalry was destroying the roads in my rear.

After sending cavalry to drive Van Dorn away, my next order was to dispatch all the wagons we had, under proper escort, to collect and bring in all supplies of forage and food from a region of fifteen miles east and west of the road from our front back to Grand Junction, leaving two months' supplies for the families of those whose stores were taken. I was amazed at the quantity of supplies the country afforded. It showed that we could have subsisted off the country for two months instead of two weeks without going beyond the limits designated. This taught me a lesson which was taken advantage of later in the campaign when our army lived twenty days with the issue of only five days' rations by the commissary. Our loss of supplies was great at Holly Springs, but it was more than compensated for by those taken from the country and by the lesson taught.

The news of the capture of Holly Springs and the destruction of our supplies caused much rejoicing among the people remaining in Oxford. They came with broad smiles on their faces, indicating intense joy, to ask what I was going to do now without anything for my soldiers to eat. I told them that I was not disturbed; that I had already sent troops and wagons to collect all the food and forage they could find for fifteen miles on each side of the road. Countenances soon changed, and so did the inquiry. The next was, "What are *we* to do?" My response was that we had endeavored to feed ourselves from our own northern resources while visiting them; but their friends in grey had been uncivil enough to destroy what we had brought along, and it could not be expected that men, with arms in their hands, would starve in the midst of plenty. I advised them to emigrate east, or west, fifteen miles and assist in eating up what we left.

Chapter XXXI

HEADQUARTERS MOVED TO HOLLY SPRINGS — GENERAL M'CLERNAND IN COMMAND — ASSUMING COMMAND AT YOUNG'S POINT — OPERATIONS ABOVE VICKSBURG — FORTIFICATIONS ABOUT VICKSBURG — THE CANAL — LAKE PROVIDENCE — OPERATIONS AT YAZOO PASS

*T*his interruption in my communications north — I was really cut off from communication with a great part of my own command during this time — resulted in Sherman's moving from Memphis before McClernand could arrive, for my dispatch of the 18th did not reach McClernand. Pemberton got back to Vicksburg before Sherman got there. The rebel positions were on a bluff on the Yazoo River, some miles above its mouth. The waters were high so that the bottoms were generally overflowed, leaving only narrow causeways of dry land between points of debarkation and the high bluffs. These were fortified and defended at all points. The rebel position was impregnable against any force that could be brought against its front. Sherman could not use one-fourth of his force. His efforts to capture the city, or the high ground north of it, were necessarily unavailing.

Sherman's attack was very unfortunate, but I had no opportunity of communicating with him after the destruction of the road and telegraph to my rear on the 20th. He did not know but what I was in the rear of the enemy and depending on him to open a new base of supplies for the troops with me. I had, before he started from Memphis, directed him to take with him a few small steamers suitable for the navigation of the Yazoo, not knowing but that I might want them to supply me after cutting loose from my base at Grenada.

On the 23d I removed my headquarters back to Holly Springs. The troops were drawn back gradually, but without haste or confusion, finding supplies abundant and no enemy following. The road was not damaged south of Holly Springs by Van Dorn, at least not to an extent to cause any delay. As I had resolved to move headquarters to Memphis, and to repair the road to that point, I remained at Holly Springs until this work was completed.

On the 10th of January, the work on the road from Holly Springs to Grand Junction and thence to Memphis being completed, I moved my headquarters to the latter place. During the campaign here described, the losses (mostly captures) were about equal, crediting the rebels with their Holly Springs capture, which they could not hold.

When Sherman started on his expedition down the river he had 20,000 men, taken from Memphis, and was reinforced by 12,000 more at Helena, Arkansas. The troops on the west bank of the river had previously been assigned to my command. McClernand having received the orders for his assignment reached the mouth of the Yazoo on the 2d of January, and immediately assumed command of all the troops with Sherman, being a part of his own corps, the 13th, and all of Sherman's, the 15th. Sherman, and Admiral Porter with the fleet, had withdrawn from the Yazoo. After consultation they decided that neither the army nor navy could render service to the cause where they were, and learning that I had withdrawn from the interior of Mississippi, they determined to return to the Arkansas River and to attack Arkansas Post, about fifty miles up that stream and garrisoned by about five or six thousand men. Sherman had learned of the existence of this force through a man who had been captured by the enemy with a steamer loaded with ammunition and other supplies intended for his command. The man had made his escape. McClernand approved this move reluctantly, as Sherman says. No obstacle was encountered until the gunboats and transports were within range of the fort. After three days' bombardment by the navy an assault was made by the troops and marines, resulting in the capture of the place, and in taking 5,000 prisoners and 17 guns. I was at first disposed to disapprove of this move as an unnecessary side movement having no especial bearing upon the work before us; but when the result was understood I regarded it as very important. Five thousand Confederate troops left in the rear might have caused us much trouble and loss of property while navigating the Mississippi.

Immediately after the reduction of Arkansas Post and the capture of the garrison, McClernand returned with his entire force to Napoleon, at the mouth of the Arkansas River. From here I received messages from both Sherman and Admiral Porter, urging me to come and take command in person, and expressing their distrust of McClernand's ability and fitness for so important and intricate an expedition.

On the 17th I visited McClernand and his command at Napoleon. It was here made evident to me that both the army and navy were so distrustful of McClernand's fitness to command that, while they would do all they could to insure success, this distrust was an element of weakness. It would have been criminal to send troops under these circumstances into such danger. By this time I had received authority to relieve McClernand, or to assign any person else to the command of the river expedition, or to assume command in person. I felt great embarrassment about McClernand. He was the senior major-general after myself within the department. It would not do, with his rank and ambition, to assign a junior over him. Nothing was left, therefore, but to assume the command myself. I would have been glad to put Sherman in command, to give him an opportunity to accomplish what he had failed in the December before; but there seemed no other way out of the difficulty, for he was junior to McClernand. Sherman's failure needs no apology.

On the 20th I ordered General McClernand with the entire command, to Young's Point and Milliken's Bend, while I returned to Memphis to make all the necessary preparation for leaving the territory behind me secure. General Hurlbut with the 16th corps was left in command. The Memphis and Charleston railroad was held, while the Mississippi Central was given up. Columbus was the only point between Cairo and Memphis, on the river, left with a garrison. All the troops and guns from the posts on the abandoned railroad and river were sent to the front.

On the 29th of January I arrived at Young's Point and assumed command the following day. General McClernand took exception in a most characteristic way — for him. His correspondence with me on the subject was more in the nature of a reprimand than a protest. It was highly insubordinate, but I overlooked it, as I believed, for the good of the service. General McClernand was a politician of very considerable prominence in his State; he was a member of Congress when the secession war broke out; he belonged to that political party which furnished all the opposition there was to a vigorous prosecution of the war for saving the Union; there was no delay in his declaring himself for the Union at all hazards, and there was no uncertain sound in his declaration of where he stood in the contest before the country. He also gave up his seat in Congress to take the field in defense of the principles he had proclaimed.

The real work of the campaign and siege of Vicksburg now began. The problem was to secure a footing upon dry ground on the east side of the river from which the troops could operate against Vicksburg. The Mississippi River, from Cairo south, runs through a rich alluvial valley of many miles in width, bound on the east by land running from eighty up to two or more hundred feet above the river. On the west side the highest land, except in a few places, is but little above the highest water. Through this valley the river meanders in the most tortuous way, varying in direction to all points of the compass. At places it runs to the very foot of the bluffs. After leaving Memphis, there are no such highlands coming to the water's edge on the east shore until Vicksburg is reached.

The intervening land is cut up by bayous filled from the river in high water — many of them navigable for steamers. All of them would be, except for overhanging trees, narrowness and tortuous course, making it impossible to turn the bends with vessels of any considerable length. Marching across this country in the face of an enemy was impossible; navigating it proved equally impracticable. The strategical way according to the rule, therefore, would have been to go back to Memphis; establish that as a base of supplies; fortify it so that the storehouses could be held by a small garrison, and move from there along the line of railroad, repairing as we advanced, to the Yallabusha, or to Jackson, Mississippi. At this time the North had become very much discouraged. Many strong Union men believed that the war must prove a failure. The elections of 1862 had gone against the party which was for the prosecution of the war to save the Union if it took the last man and the last dollar. Voluntary enlistments had ceased throughout the greater part of the North, and the draft had been resorted to to fill up our ranks. It was my judgment at the time that to make a backward movement as long as that from Vicksburg to Memphis, would be interpreted, by many of those yet full of hope for the preservation of the Union, as a defeat, and that the draft would be resisted, desertions ensue and the power to capture and punish deserters lost. There was nothing left to be done but to go *forward to a decisive victory*. This was in my mind from the moment I took command in person at Young's Point.

The winter of 1862-3 was a noted one for continuous high water in the Mississippi and for heavy rains along the lower river. To get dry land, or rather land above the water, to encamp the troops upon, took many miles of riverfront. We had to occupy the levees and the ground immediately behind. This was so limited that one corps, the 17th, under General McPherson, was at Lake Providence, seventy miles above Vicksburg.

It was in January the troops took their position opposite Vicksburg. The water was very high and the rains were incessant. There seemed no possibility of a land movement before the end of March or later, and it would not do to lie idle all this time. The effect would be demoralizing to the troops and injurious to their health. Friends in the North would have grown more and more discouraged, and enemies in the same section more and more insolent in their gibes and denunciation of the cause and those engaged in it.

I always admired the South, as bad as I thought their cause, for the boldness with which they silenced all opposition and all croaking, by press or by individuals, within their control. War at all times, whether a civil war between sections of a common country or between nations, ought to be avoided, if possible with honor. But, once entered into, it is too much for human nature to tolerate an enemy within their ranks to give aid and comfort to the armies of the opposing section or nation.

Vicksburg, as stated before, is on the first high land coming to the river's edge, below that on which Memphis stands. The bluff, or high land, follows the left bank of the Yazoo for some distance and continues in a southerly direction to the Mississippi River, thence it runs along the Mississippi to Warrenton, six miles below. The Yazoo River leaves the high land a short distance below Haines' Bluff and empties into the Mississippi nine miles above Vicksburg. Vicksburg is built on this high land where the Mississippi washes the base of the hill. Haines' Bluff, eleven miles from Vicksburg, on the Yazoo River, was strongly fortified. The whole distance from there to Vicksburg and thence to Warrenton was also entrenched, with batteries at suitable distances and rifle-pits connecting them.

From Young's Point the Mississippi turns in a northeasterly direction to a point just above the city, when it again turns and runs southwesterly, leaving vessels, which might attempt to run the blockade, exposed to the fire of batteries six miles below the city before they were in range of the upper batteries. Since then the river has made a cut-off, leaving what was the peninsula in front of the city, an island. North of the Yazoo was all a marsh, heavily timbered, cut up with bayous, and much overflowed. A front attack was therefore impossible, and was never contemplated; certainly not by me. The problem then became, how to secure a landing on high ground east of the Mississippi without an apparent retreat. Then commenced a series of experiments to consume time, and to divert the attention of the enemy, of my troops and of the public generally. I, myself, never felt great confidence that any of the experiments resorted to would prove successful. Nevertheless I was always prepared to take advantage of them in case they did.

In 1862 General Thomas Williams had come up from New Orleans and cut a ditch ten or twelve feet wide and about as deep, straight across from Young's Point to the river below. The distance across was a little over a mile. It was Williams' expectation that when the river rose it would cut a navigable channel through; but the canal started in an eddy from both ends, and, of course, it only filled up with water on the rise without doing any execution in the way of cutting. Mr. Lincoln had navigated the Mississippi in his younger days and understood well its tendency to change its channel, in places, from time to time. He set much store accordingly by this canal. General McClernand had been, therefore, directed before I went to Young's Point to push the work of widening and deepening this canal. After my arrival the work was diligently pushed with about 4,000 men — as many as could be used to advantage — until interrupted by a sudden rise in the river that broke a dam at the upper end, which had been put there to keep the water out until the excavation was completed. This was on the 8th of March.

Even if the canal had proven a success, so far as to be navigable for steamers, it could not have been of much advantage to us. It runs in a direction almost perpendicular to the line of bluffs on the opposite side, or east bank, of the river. As soon as the enemy discovered what we were doing he established a battery commanding the canal throughout its length. This battery soon drove out our dredges, two in number, which were doing the work of thousands of men. Had the canal been completed it might have proven of some use in running transports through, under the cover of night, to use below; but they would yet have to run batteries, though for a much shorter distance.

While this work was progressing we were busy in other directions, trying to find an available landing on high ground on the east bank of the river, or to make water-ways to get below the city, avoiding the batteries.

On the 30th of January, the day after my arrival at the front, I ordered General McPherson, stationed with his corps at Lake Providence, to cut the levee at that point. If successful in opening a channel for navigation by this route, it would carry us to the Mississippi River through the mouth of the Red River, just above Port Hudson and four hundred miles below Vicksburg by the river.

Lake Providence is a part of the old bed of the Mississippi, about a mile from the present channel. It is six miles long and has its outlet through Bayou Baxter, Bayou Macon, and the Tensas, Washita and Red Rivers. The last three are navigable streams at all seasons. Bayous Baxter and Macon are narrow and tortuous, and the banks are covered with dense forests overhanging the channel. They were also filled with fallen timber, the accumulation of years. The land along the Mississippi River, from Memphis down, is in all instances highest next to the river, except where the river washes the bluffs which form the boundary of the valley through which it winds. Bayou Baxter, as it reaches lower land, begins to spread out and disappears entirely in a cypress swamp before it reaches the Macon. There was about two feet of water in this swamp at the time. To get through it, even with vessels of the lightest draft, it was necessary to clear off a belt of heavy timber wide enough to make a passage way. As the trees would have to be cut close to the bottom — under water — it was an undertaking of great magnitude.

On the 4th of February I visited General McPherson, and remained with him several days. The work had not progressed so far as to admit the water from the river into the lake, but the troops had succeeded in drawing a small steamer, of probably not over thirty tons' capacity, from the river into the lake. With this we were able to explore the lake and bayou as far as cleared. I saw then that there was scarcely a chance of this ever becoming a practicable route for moving troops through an enemy's country. The distance from Lake Providence to the point where vessels going by that route would enter the Mississippi again, is about four hundred and seventy miles by the main river. The distance would probably be greater by the tortuous bayous through which this new route would carry us. The enemy held Port Hudson, below where the Red River debouches, and all the Mississippi above to Vicksburg. The Red River, Washita and Tensas were, as has been said, all navigable streams, on which the enemy could throw small bodies of men to obstruct our passage and pick off our troops with their sharpshooters. I let the work go on, believing employment was better than idleness for the men. Then, too, it served as a cover for other efforts which gave a better prospect of success. This work was abandoned after the canal proved a failure.

Lieutenant-Colonel Wilson of my staff was sent to Helena, Arkansas, to examine and open a way through Moon Lake and the Yazoo Pass if possible. Formerly there was a route by way of an inlet from the Mississippi River into Moon Lake, a mile east of the river, thence east through Yazoo Pass to Coldwater, along the latter to the Tallahatchie, which joins the Yallabusha about two hundred and fifty miles below Moon Lake and forms the Yazoo River. These were formerly navigated by steamers trading with the rich plantations along their banks; but the State of Mississippi had built a strong levee across the inlet some years before, leaving the only entrance for vessels into this rich region the one by way of the mouth of the Yazoo several hundreds of miles below.

On the 2d of February this dam, or levee, was cut. The river being high the rush of water through the cut was so great that in a very short time the entire obstruction was washed away. The bayous were soon filled and much of the country was overflowed. This pass leaves the Mississippi River but a few miles below Helena. On the 24th General Ross, with his brigade of about 4,500 men on transports, moved into this new water-way. The rebels had obstructed the navigation of Yazoo Pass and the Coldwater by felling trees into them. Much of the timber in this region being of greater specific gravity than water, and being of great size, their removal was a matter of great labor; but it was finally accomplished, and on the 11th of March Ross found himself, accompanied by two gunboats under the command of Lieutenant-Commander Watson Smith, confronting a fortification at Greenwood, where the Tallahatchie and Yallabusha unite and the Yazoo begins. The bends of the rivers are such at this point as to almost form an island, scarcely above water at that stage of the river. This island was fortified and manned. It was named Fort Pemberton after the commander at Vicksburg. No land approach was accessible. The troops, therefore, could render no assistance towards an assault further than to establish a battery on a little piece of ground which was discovered above water. The gunboats, however, attacked on the 11th and again on the 13th of March. Both efforts were failures and were not renewed. One gunboat was disabled and we lost six men killed and twenty-five wounded. The loss of the enemy was less.

Fort Pemberton was so little above the water that it was thought that a rise of two feet would drive the enemy out. In hope of enlisting the elements on our side, which had been so much against us up to this time, a second cut was made in the Mississippi levee, this time directly opposite Helena, or six miles above the former cut. It did not accomplish the desired result, and Ross, with his fleet, started back. On the 22d he met Quinby with a brigade at Yazoo Pass. Quinby was the senior of Ross, and assumed command. He was not satisfied with returning to his former position without seeing for himself whether anything could be accomplished. Accordingly Fort Pemberton was revisited by our troops; but an inspection was sufficient this time without an attack. Quinby, with his command, returned with but little delay. In the meantime I was much exercised for the safety of Ross, not knowing that Quinby had been able to join him. Reinforcements were of no use in a country covered with water, as they would have to remain on board of their transports. Relief had to come from another quarter. So I determined to get into the Yazoo below Fort Pemberton.

Steel's Bayou empties into the Yazoo River between Haines' Bluff and its mouth. It is narrow, very tortuous, and fringed with a very heavy growth of timber, but it is deep. It approaches to within one mile of the Mississippi at Eagle Bend, thirty miles above Young's Point. Steel's Bayou connects with Black Bayou, Black Bayou with Deer Creek, Deer Creek with Rolling Fork, Rolling Fork with the Big Sunflower River, and the Big Sunflower with the Yazoo River about ten miles above Haines' Bluff in a right line but probably twenty or twenty-five miles by the winding of the river. All these waterways are of about the same nature so far as navigation is concerned, until the Sunflower is reached; this affords free navigation.

Admiral Porter explored this waterway as far as Deer Creek on the 14th of March, and reported it navigable. On the next day he started with five gunboats and four mortar-boats. I went with him for some distance. The heavy overhanging timber retarded progress very much, as did also the short turns in so narrow a stream. The gunboats, however, plowed their way through without other damage than to their appearance. The transports did not fare so well although they followed behind. The road was somewhat cleared for them by the gunboats. In the evening I returned to headquarters to hurry up reinforcements. Sherman went in person on the 16th, taking with him Stuart's division of the 15th corps. They took large river transports to Eagle Bend on the Mississippi, where they debarked and marched across to Steel's Bayou, where they re-embarked on the transports. The river steamers, with their tall smoke-stacks and light guards extending out, were so much impeded that the gunboats got far ahead. Porter, with his fleet, got within a few hundred yards of where the sailing would have been clear and free from the obstructions caused by felling trees into the water, when he encountered rebel sharp-shooters, and his progress was delayed by obstructions in his front. He could do nothing with gunboats against sharpshooters. The rebels, learning his route, had sent in about 4,000 men — many more than there were sailors in the fleet.

Sherman went back, at the request of the admiral, to clear out Black Bayou and to hurry up reinforcements, which were far behind. On the night of the 19th he received notice from the admiral that he had been attacked by sharp-shooters and was in imminent peril. Sherman at once returned through Black Bayou in a canoe, and passed on until he met a steamer, with the last of the reinforcements he had, coming up. They tried to force their way through Black Bayou with their steamer, but, finding it slow and tedious work, debarked and pushed forward on foot. It was night when they landed, and intensely dark. There was but a narrow strip of land above water, and that was grown up with underbrush or cane. The troops lighted their way through this with candles carried in their hands for a mile and a half, when they came to an open plantation. Here the troops rested until morning. They made twenty-one miles from this resting-place by noon the next day, and were in time to rescue the fleet. Porter had fully made up his mind to blow up the gunboats rather than have them fall into the hands of the enemy. More welcome visitors he probably never met than the "boys in blue" on this occasion. The vessels were backed out and returned to their rendezvous on the Mississippi; and thus ended in failure the fourth attempt to get in rear of Vicksburg.

Chapter XXXII

THE BAYOUS WEST OF THE MISSISSIPPI — CRITICISMS OF THE NORTHERN PRESS — RUNNING THE BATTERIES — LOSS OF THE INDIANOLA — DISPOSITION OF THE TROOPS

The original canal scheme was also abandoned on the 27th of March. The effort to make a waterway through Lake Providence and the connecting bayous was abandoned as wholly impracticable about the same time.

At Milliken's Bend, and also at Young's Point, bayous or channels start, which connecting with other bayous passing Richmond, Louisiana, enter the Mississippi at Carthage twenty-five or thirty miles above Grand Gulf. The Mississippi levee cuts the supply of water off from these bayous or channels, but all the rainfall behind the levee, at these points, is carried through these same channels to the river below. In case of a crevasse in this vicinity, the water escaping would find its outlet through the same channels. The dredges and laborers from the canal having been driven out by overflow and the enemy's batteries, I determined to open these other channels, if possible. If successful the effort would afford a route, away from the enemy's batteries, for our transports. There was a good road back of the levees, along these bayous, to carry the troops, artillery and wagon trains over whenever the water receded a little, and after a few days of dry weather. Accordingly, with the abandonment of all the other plans for reaching a base heretofore described, this new one was undertaken.

As early as the 4th of February I had written to Halleck about this route, stating that I thought it much more practicable than the other undertaking (the Lake Providence route), and that it would have been accomplished with much less labor if commenced before the water had got all over the country.

The upper end of these bayous being cut off from a water supply, further than the rainfall back of the levees, was grown up with dense timber for a distance of several miles from their source. It was necessary, therefore, to clear this out before letting in the water from the river. This work was continued until the waters of the river began to recede and the road to Richmond, Louisiana, emerged from the water. One small steamer and some barges were got through this channel, but no further use could be made of it because of the fall in the river. Beyond this it was no more successful than the other experiments with which the winter was whiled away. All these failures would have been very discouraging if I had expected much from the efforts; but I had not. From the first the most I hoped to accomplish was the passage of transports, to be used below Vicksburg, without exposure to the long line of batteries defending that city.

This long, dreary and, for heavy and continuous rains and high water, unprecedented winter was one of great hardship to all engaged about Vicksburg. The river was higher than its natural banks from December, 1862, to the following April. The war had suspended peaceful pursuits in the South, further than the production of army supplies, and in consequence the levees were neglected and broken in many places and the whole country was covered with water. Troops could scarcely find dry ground on which to pitch their tents. Malarial fevers broke out among the men. Measles and smallpox also attacked them. The hospital arrangements and medical attendance were so perfect, however, that the loss of life was much less than might have been expected. Visitors to the camps went home with dismal stories to relate; Northern papers came back to the soldiers with these stories exaggerated. Because I would not divulge my ultimate plans to visitors, they pronounced me idle, incompetent and unfit to command men in an emergency, and clamored for my removal. They were not to be satisfied, many of them, with my simple removal, but named who my successor should be. McClernand, Fremont, Hunter and McClellan were all mentioned in this connection. I took no steps to answer these complaints, but continued to do my duty, as I understood it, to the best of my ability. Everyone has his superstitions. One of mine is that in positions of great responsibility everyone should do his duty to the best of his ability where assigned by competent authority, without application or the use of influence to change his position. While at Cairo I had watched with very great interest the operations of the Army of the Potomac, looking upon that as the main field of the war. I had no idea, myself, of ever having any large command, nor did I suppose that I was equal to one; but I had the vanity to think that as a cavalry officer I might succeed very well in the command of a brigade. On one occasion, in talking about this to my staff officers, all of whom were civilians without any military education whatever, I said that I would give anything if I were commanding a brigade of cavalry in the Army of the Potomac and I believed I could do some good. Captain Hillyer spoke up and suggested that I make application to be transferred there to command the cavalry. I then told him that I would cut my right arm off first, and mentioned this superstition.

In time of war the President, being by the Constitution Commander-in-chief of the Army and Navy, is responsible for the selection of commanders. He should not be embarrassed in making his selections. I having been selected, my responsibility ended with my doing the best I knew how. If I had sought the place, or obtained it through personal or political influence, my belief is that I would have feared to undertake any plan of my own conception, and would probably have awaited direct orders from my distant superiors. Persons obtaining important commands by application or political influence are apt to keep a written record of complaints and predictions of defeat, which are shown in case of disaster. Somebody must be responsible for their failures.

With all the pressure brought to bear upon them, both President Lincoln and General Halleck stood by me to the end of the campaign. I had never met Mr. Lincoln, but his support was constant.

At last the waters began to recede; the roads crossing the peninsula behind the levees of the bayous, were emerging from the waters; the troops were all concentrated from distant points at Milliken's Bend preparatory to a final move which was to crown the long, tedious and discouraging labors with success.

I had had in contemplation the whole winter the movement by land to a point below Vicksburg from which to operate, subject only to the possible but not expected success of someone of the expedients resorted to for the purpose of giving us a different base. This could not be undertaken until the waters receded. I did not therefore communicate this plan, even to an officer of my staff, until it was necessary to make preparations for the start. My recollection is that Admiral Porter was the first one to whom I mentioned it. The co-operation of the navy was absolutely essential to the success (even to the contemplation) of such an enterprise. I had no more authority to command Porter than he had to command me. It was necessary to have part of his fleet below Vicksburg if the troops went there. Steamers to use as ferries were also essential. The navy was the only escort and protection for these steamers, all of which in getting below had to run about fourteen miles of batteries. Porter fell into the plan at once, and suggested that he had better superintend the preparation of the steamers selected to run the batteries, as sailors would probably understand the work better than soldiers. I was glad to accept his proposition, not only because I admitted his argument, but because it would enable me to keep from the enemy a little longer our designs. Porter's fleet was on the east side of the river above the mouth of the Yazoo, entirely concealed from the enemy by the dense forests that intervened. Even spies could not get near him, on account of the undergrowth and overflowed lands. Suspicions of some mysterious movements were aroused. Our river guards discovered one day a small skiff moving quietly and mysteriously up the river near the east shore, from the direction of Vicksburg, towards the fleet. On overhauling the boat they found a small white flag, not much larger than a handkerchief, set up in the stern, no doubt intended as a flag of truce in case of discovery. The boat, crew and passengers were brought ashore to me. The chief personage aboard proved to be Jacob Thompson, Secretary of the Interior under the administration of President Buchanan. After a pleasant conversation of half an hour or more I allowed the boat and crew, passengers and all, to return to Vicksburg, without creating a suspicion that there was a doubt in my mind as to the good faith of Mr. Thompson and his flag.

Admiral Porter proceeded with the preparation of the steamers for their hazardous passage of the enemy's batteries. The great essential was to protect the boilers from the enemy's shot, and to conceal the fires under the boilers from view. This he accomplished by loading the steamers, between the guards and boilers on the boiler deck up to the deck above, with bales of hay and cotton, and the deck in front of the boilers in the same way, adding sacks of grain. The hay and grain would be wanted below, and could not be transported in sufficient quantity by the muddy roads over which we expected to march.

Before this I had been collecting, from St. Louis and Chicago, yawls and barges to be used as ferries when we got below. By the 16th of April Porter was ready to start on his perilous trip. The advance, flagship Benton, Porter commanding, started at ten o'clock at night, followed at intervals of a few minutes by the Lafayette with a captured steamer, the Price, lashed to her side, the Louisville, Mound City, Pittsburgh and Carondelet — all of these being naval vessels. Next came the transports — Forest Queen, Silver Wave and Henry Clay, each towing barges loaded with coal to be used as fuel by the naval and transport steamers when below the batteries. The gunboat Tuscumbia brought up the rear. Soon after the start a battery between Vicksburg and Warrenton opened fire across the intervening peninsula, followed by the upper batteries, and then by batteries all along the line. The gunboats ran up close under the bluffs, delivering their fire in return at short distances, probably without much effect. They were under fire for more than two hours and every vessel was struck many times, but with little damage to the gunboats. The transports did not fare so well. The Henry Clay was disabled and deserted by her crew. Soon after a shell burst in the cotton packed about the boilers, set the vessel on fire and burned her to the water's edge. The burning mass, however, floated down to Carthage before grounding, as did also one of the barges in tow.

The enemy were evidently expecting our fleet, for they were ready to light up the river by means of bonfires on the east side and by firing houses on the point of land opposite the city on the Louisiana side. The sight was magnificent, but terrible. I witnessed it from the deck of a river transport, run out into the middle of the river and as low down as it was prudent to go. My mind was much relieved when I learned that no one on the transports had been killed and but few, if any, wounded. During the running of the batteries men were stationed in the holds of the transports to partially stop with cotton shot-holes that might be made in the hulls. All damage was afterwards soon repaired under the direction of Admiral Porter.

The experiment of passing batteries had been tried before this, however, during the war. Admiral Farragut had run the batteries at Port Hudson with the flagship Hartford and one iron-clad and visited me from below Vicksburg. The 13th of February Admiral Porter had sent the gunboat Indianola, Lieutenant-Commander George Brown commanding, below. She met Colonel Ellet of the Marine brigade below Natchez on a captured steamer. Two of the Colonel's fleet had previously run the batteries, producing the greatest consternation among the people along the Mississippi from Vicksburg* to the Red River.

The Indianola remained about the mouth of the Red River some days, and then started up the Mississippi. The Confederates soon raised the Queen of the West,* and repaired her. With this vessel and the ram Webb, which they had had for some time in the Red River, and two other steamers, they followed the Indianola. The latter was encumbered with barges of coal in tow, and consequently could make but little speed against the rapid current of the Mississippi. The Confederate fleet overtook her just above Grand Gulf, and attacked her after dark on the 24th of February. The Indianola was superior to all the others in armament, and probably would have destroyed them or driven them away, but for her encumbrance. As it was she fought them for an hour and a half, but, in the dark, was struck seven or eight times by the ram and other vessels, and was finally disabled and reduced to a sinking condition. The armament was thrown overboard and the vessel run ashore. Officers and crew then surrendered.

I had started McClernand with his corps of four divisions on the 29th of March, by way of Richmond, Louisiana, to New Carthage, hoping that he might capture Grand Gulf before the balance of the troops could get there; but the roads were very bad, scarcely above water yet. Some miles from New Carthage the levee to Bayou Vidal was broken in several places, overflowing the roads for the distance of two miles. Boats were collected from the surrounding bayous, and some constructed on the spot from such material as could be collected, to transport the troops across the overflowed interval. By the 6th of April McClernand had reached New Carthage with one division and its artillery, the latter ferried through the woods by these boats. On the 17th I visited New Carthage in person, and saw that the process of getting troops through in the way we were doing was so tedious that a better method must be devised. The water was falling, and in a few days there would not be depth enough to use boats; nor would the land be dry enough to march over. McClernand had already found a new route from Smith's plantation where the crevasse occurred, to Perkins' plantation, eight to twelve miles below New Carthage. This increased the march from Milliken's Bend from twenty-seven to nearly forty miles. Four bridges had to be built across bayous, two of them each over six

---

‡ Colonel Ellet reported having attacked a Confederate battery on the Red River two days before with one of his boats, the De Soto. Running aground, he was obliged to abandon his vessel. However, he reported that he set fire to her and blew her up. Twenty of his men fell into the hands of the enemy. With the balance he escaped on the small captured steamer, the New Era, and succeeded in passing the batteries at Grand Gulf and reaching the vicinity of Vicksburg.

* One of Colonel Ellet's vessels which had run the blockade on February the 2d and been sunk in the Red River.

hundred feet long, making about two thousand feet of bridging in all. The river falling made the current in these bayous very rapid, increasing the difficulty of building and permanently fastening these bridges; but the ingenuity of the "Yankee soldier" was equal to any emergency. The bridges were soon built of such material as could be found near by, and so substantial were they that not a single mishap occurred in crossing all the army with artillery, cavalry and wagon trains, except the loss of one siege gun (a thirty-two pounder). This, if my memory serves me correctly, broke through the only pontoon bridge we had in all our march across the peninsula. These bridges were all built by McClernand's command, under the supervision of Lieutenant Hains of the Engineer Corps.

I returned to Milliken's Bend on the 18th or 19th, and on the 20th issued the following final order for the movement of troops:

HEADQUARTERS DEPARTMENT OF THE TENNESSEE,
MILLIKEN'S BEND, LOUISIANA,
April 20, 1863.

Special Orders, No. 110.

* * * * * * *

VIII. The following orders are published for the information and guidance of the "Army in the Field," in its present movement to obtain a foothold on the east bank of the Mississippi River, from which Vicksburg can be approached by practicable roads.

First. — The Thirteenth army corps, Major-General John A. McClernand commanding, will constitute the right wing.

Second. — The Fifteenth army corps, Major-General W.T. Sherman commanding, will constitute the left wing.

Third. — The Seventeenth army corps, Major-General James B. McPherson commanding, will constitute the center.

Fourth. — The order of march to New Carthage will be from right to left.

Fifth. — Reserves will be formed by divisions from each army corps; or, an entire army corps will be held as a reserve, as necessity may require. When the reserve is formed by divisions, each division will remain under the immediate command of its respective corps commander, unless otherwise specially ordered for a particular emergency.

Sixth. — Troops will be required to bivouac, until proper facilities can be afforded for the transportation of camp equipage.

Seventh. — In the present movement, one tent will be allowed to each company for the protection of rations from rain; one wall tent for each regimental headquarters; one wall tent for each brigade headquarters;

and one wall tent for each division headquarters; corps commanders having the books and blanks of their respective commands to provide for, are authorized to take such tents as are absolutely necessary, but not to exceed the number allowed by General Orders No. 160, A.G.O., series of 1862.

Eighth. — All the teams of the three army corps, under the immediate charge of the quartermasters bearing them on their returns, will constitute a train for carrying supplies and ordnance and the authorized camp equipage of the army.

Ninth. — As fast as the Thirteenth army corps advances, the Seventeenth army corps will take its place; and it, in turn, will be followed in like manner by the Fifteenth army corps.

Tenth. — Two regiments from each army corps will be detailed by corps commanders, to guard the lines from Richmond to New Carthage.

Eleventh. — General hospitals will be established by the medical director between Duckport and Milliken's Bend. All sick and disabled soldiers will be left in these hospitals. Surgeons in charge of hospitals will report convalescents as fast as they become fit for duty. Each corps commander will detail an intelligent and good drill officer, to remain behind and take charge of the convalescents of their respective corps; officers so detailed will organize the men under their charge into squads and companies, without regard to the regiments they belong to; and in the absence of convalescent commissioned officers to command them, will appoint non-commissioned officers or privates. The force so organized will constitute the guard of the line from Duckport to Milliken's Bend. They will furnish all the guards and details required for general hospitals, and with the contrabands that may be about the camps, will furnish all the details for loading and unloading boats.

Twelfth. — The movement of troops from Milliken's Bend to New Carthage will be so conducted as to allow the transportation of ten days' supply of rations, and one-half the allowance of ordnance, required by previous orders.

Thirteenth. — Commanders are authorized and enjoined to collect all the beef cattle, corn and other necessary supplies on the line of march; but wanton destruction of property, taking of articles useless for military purposes, insulting citizens, going into and searching houses without proper orders from division commanders, are positively prohibited. All such irregularities must be summarily punished.

Fourteenth. — Brigadier-General J.C. Sullivan is appointed to the command of all the forces detailed for the protection of the line from here to New Carthage. His particular attention is called to General

Orders, No. 69, from Adjutant-General's Office, Washington, of date March 20, 1863.

By order of Major-General U.S. Grant

McClernand was already below on the Mississippi. Two of McPherson's divisions were put upon the march immediately. The third had not yet arrived from Lake Providence; it was on its way to Milliken's Bend and was to follow on arrival.

Sherman was to follow McPherson. Two of his divisions were at Duckport and Young's Point, and the third under Steele was under orders to return from Greenville, Mississippi, where it had been sent to expel a rebel battery that had been annoying our transports.

It had now become evident that the army could not be rationed by a wagon train over the single narrow and almost impassable road between Milliken's Bend and Perkins' plantation. Accordingly six more steamers were protected as before, to run the batteries, and were loaded with supplies. They took twelve barges in tow, loaded also with rations. On the night of the 22d of April they ran the batteries, five getting through more or less disabled while one was sunk. About half the barges got through with their needed freight.

When it was first proposed to run the blockade at Vicksburg with river steamers there were but two captains or masters who were willing to accompany their vessels, and but one crew. Volunteers were called for from the army, men who had had experience in any capacity in navigating the western rivers. Captains, pilots, mates, engineers and deckhands enough presented themselves to take five times the number of vessels we were moving through this dangerous ordeal. Most of them were from Logan's division, composed generally of men from the southern part of Illinois and from Missouri. All but two of the steamers were commanded by volunteers from the army, and all but one so manned. In this instance, as in all others during the war, I found that volunteers could be found in the ranks and among the commissioned officers to meet every call for aid whether mechanical or professional. Colonel W.S. Oliver was master of transportation on this occasion by special detail.

Chapter XXXIII

ATTACK ON GRAND GULF — OPERATIONS BELOW VICKSBURG

On the 24th my headquarters were with the advance at Perkins' plantation. Reconnaissances were made in boats to ascertain whether there was high land on the east shore of the river where we might land above Grand Gulf. There was none practicable. Accordingly the troops were set in motion for Hard Times, twenty-two miles farther down the river and nearly opposite Grand Gulf. The loss of two steamers and six barges reduced our transportation so that only 10,000 men could be moved by water. Some of the steamers that had got below were injured in their machinery, so that they were only useful as barges towed by those less severely injured. All the troops, therefore, except what could be transported in one trip, had to march. The road lay west of Lake St. Joseph. Three large bayous had to be crossed. They were rapidly bridged in the same manner as those previously encountered.*

On the 27th McClernand's corps was all at Hard Times, and McPherson's was following closely. I had determined to make the attempt to effect a landing on the east side of the river as soon as possible. Accordingly, on the morning of the 29th, McClernand was directed to embark all the troops from his corps that our transports and barges could carry. About 10,000 men were so embarked. The plan was to have the navy silence the guns at Grand Gulf, and to have as many men as possible ready to debark in the shortest possible time under cover of the fire of the navy and carry the works by storm. The following order was issued:

PERKINS PLANTATION, LA.,
APRIL 27, 1863

---

* *Note.* — On this occasion Governor Richard Yates, of Illinois, happened to be on a visit to the army and accompanied me to Carthage. I furnished an ambulance for his use and that of some of the State officers who accompanied him.

MAJOR-GENERAL J.A. McCLERNAND, Commanding 13th A.C.

Commence immediately the embarkation of your corps, or so much of it as there is transportation for. Have put aboard the artillery and every article authorized in orders limiting baggage, except the men, and hold them in readiness, with their places assigned, to be moved at a moment's warning.

All the troops you may have, except those ordered to remain behind, send to a point nearly opposite Grand Gulf, where you see, by special orders of this date, General McPherson is ordered to send one division.

The plan of the attack will be for the navy to attack and silence all the batteries commanding the river. Your corps will be on the river, ready to run to and debark on the nearest eligible land below the promontory first brought to view passing down the river. Once on shore, have each commander instructed beforehand to form his men the best the ground will admit of, and take possession of the most commanding points, but avoid separating your command so that it cannot support itself. The first object is to get a foothold where our troops can maintain themselves until such time as preparations can be made and troops collected for a forward movement.

Admiral Porter has proposed to place his boats in the position indicated to you a few days ago, and to bring over with them such troops as may be below the city after the guns of the enemy are silenced.

It may be that the enemy will occupy positions back from the city, out of range of the gunboats, so as to make it desirable to run past Grand Gulf and land at Rodney. In case this should prove the plan, a signal will be arranged and you duly informed, when the transports are to start with this view. Or, it may be expedient for the boats to run past, but not the men. In this case, then, the transports would have to be brought back to where the men could land and move by forced marches to below Grand Gulf, re-embark rapidly and proceed to the latter place. There will be required, then, three signals; one, to indicate that the transports can run down and debark the troops at Grand Gulf; one, that the transports can run by without the troops; and the last, that the transports can run by with the troops on board.

Should the men have to march, all baggage and artillery will be left to run the blockade.

If not already directed, require your men to keep three days' rations in their haversacks, not to be touched until a movement commences.

U.S. GRANT, Major-General

At 8 o'clock A.M., 29th, Porter made the attack with his entire strength present, eight gunboats. For nearly five and a half hours the attack was kept up without silencing a single gun of the enemy. All this time McClernand's 10,000 men were huddled together on the transports in the stream ready to attempt a landing if signaled. I occupied a tug from which I could see the effect of the battle on both sides, within range of the enemy's guns; but a small tug, without armament, was not calculated to attract the fire of batteries while they were being assailed themselves. About half-past one the fleet withdrew, seeing their efforts were entirely unavailing. The enemy ceased firing as soon as we withdrew. I immediately signaled the Admiral and went aboard his ship. The navy lost in this engagement eighteen killed and fifty-six wounded. A large proportion of these were of the crew of the flagship, and most of those from a single shell which penetrated the ship's side and exploded between decks where the men were working their guns. The sight of the mangled and dying men which met my eye as I boarded the ship was sickening.

Grand Gulf is on a high bluff where the river runs at the very foot of it. It is as defensible upon its front as Vicksburg and, at that time, would have been just as impossible to capture by a front attack. I therefore requested Porter to run the batteries with his fleet that night, and to take charge of the transports, all of which would be wanted below.

There is a long tongue of land from the Louisiana side extending towards Grand Gulf, made by the river running nearly east from about three miles above and nearly in the opposite direction from that point for about the same distance below. The land was so low and wet that it would not have been practicable to march an army across but for a levee. I had had this explored before, as well as the east bank below to ascertain if there was a possible point of debarkation north of Rodney. It was found that the top of the levee afforded a good road to march upon.

Porter, as was always the case with him, not only acquiesced in the plan, but volunteered to use his entire fleet as transports. I had intended to make this request, but he anticipated me. At dusk, when concealed from the view of the enemy at Grand Gulf, McClernand landed his command on the west bank. The navy and transports ran the batteries successfully. The troops marched across the point of land under cover of night, unobserved. By the time it was light the enemy saw our whole fleet, ironclads, gunboats, river steamers and barges, quietly moving down the river three miles below them, black, or rather blue, with National troops.

When the troops debarked, the evening of the 29th, it was expected that we would have to go to Rodney, about nine miles below, to find a landing; but that night a colored man came in who informed me that a good landing would be found at Bruinsburg, a few miles above

Rodney, from which point there was a good road leading to Port Gibson some twelve miles in the interior. The information was found correct, and our landing was effected without opposition.

Sherman had not left his position above Vicksburg yet. On the morning of the 27th I ordered him to create a diversion by moving his corps up the Yazoo and threatening an attack on Haines' Bluff.

My object was to compel Pemberton to keep as much force about Vicksburg as I could, until I could secure a good footing on high land east of the river. The move was eminently successful and, as we afterwards learned, created great confusion about Vicksburg and doubts about our real design. Sherman moved the day of our attack on Grand Gulf, the 29th, with ten regiments of his command and eight gunboats which Porter had left above Vicksburg.

He debarked his troops and apparently made every preparation to attack the enemy while the navy bombarded the main forts at Haines' Bluff. This move was made without a single casualty in either branch of the service. On the first of May Sherman received orders from me (sent from Hard Times the evening of the 29th of April) to withdraw from the front of Haines' Bluff and follow McPherson with two divisions as fast as he could.

I had established a depot of supplies at Perkins' plantation. Now that all our gunboats were below Grand Gulf it was possible that the enemy might fit out boats in the Big Black with improvised armament and attempt to destroy these supplies. McPherson was at Hard Times with a portion of his corps, and the depot was protected by a part of his command. The night of the 29th I directed him to arm one of the transports with artillery and send it up to Perkins' plantation as a guard; and also to have the siege guns we had brought along moved there and put in position.

The embarkation below Grand Gulf took place at De Shroon's, Louisiana, six miles above Bruinsburg, Mississippi. Early on the morning of 30th of April McClernand's corps and one division of McPherson's corps were speedily landed.

When this was effected I felt a degree of relief scarcely ever equaled since. Vicksburg was not yet taken it is true, nor were its defenders demoralized by any of our previous moves. I was now in the enemy's country, with a vast river and the stronghold of Vicksburg between me and my base of supplies. But I was on dry ground on the same side of the river with the enemy. All the campaigns, labors, hardships and exposures from the month of December previous to this time that had been made and endured, were for the accomplishment of this one object.

I had with me the 13th corps, General McClernand commanding, and two brigades of Logan's division of the 17th corps, General McPherson commanding — in all not more than twenty thousand men to commence the campaign with. These were soon reinforced by the remaining brigade of Logan's division and Crocker's division of the 17th corps. On the 7th of May I was further reinforced by Sherman with two divisions of his, the 15th corps. My total force was then about thirty-three thousand men.

The enemy occupied Grand Gulf, Haines' Bluff and Jackson with a force of nearly sixty thousand men. Jackson is fifty miles east of Vicksburg and is connected with it by a railroad. My first problem was to capture Grand Gulf to use as a base.

Bruinsburg is two miles from high ground. The bottom at that point is higher than most of the low land in the valley of the Mississippi, and a good road leads to the bluff. It was natural to expect the garrison from Grand Gulf to come out to meet us and prevent, if they could, our reaching this solid base. Bayou Pierre enters the Mississippi just above Bruinsburg and, as it is a navigable stream and was high at the time, in order to intercept us they had to go by Port Gibson, the nearest point where there was a bridge to cross upon. This more than doubled the distance from Grand Gulf to the high land back of Bruinsburg. No time was to be lost in securing this foothold. Our transportation was not sufficient to move all the army across the river at one trip, or even two; but the landing of the 13th corps and one division of the 17th was effected during the day, April 30th, and early evening. McClernand was advanced as soon as ammunition and two days' rations (to last five) could be issued to his men. The bluffs were reached an hour before sunset and McClernand was pushed on, hoping to reach Port Gibson and save the bridge spanning the Bayou Pierre before the enemy could get there; for crossing a stream in the presence of an enemy is always difficult. Port Gibson, too, is the starting point of roads to Grand Gulf, Vicksburg and Jackson.

McClernand's advance met the enemy about five miles west of Port Gibson at Thompson's plantation. There was some firing during the night, but nothing rising to the dignity of a battle until daylight. The enemy had taken a strong natural position with most of the Grand Gulf garrison, numbering about seven or eight thousand men, under General Bowen. His hope was to hold me in check until reinforcements under Loring could reach him from Vicksburg; but Loring did not come in time to render much assistance south of Port Gibson. Two brigades of McPherson's corps followed McClernand as fast as rations and ammunition could be issued, and were ready to take position upon the battlefield whenever the 13th corps could be got out of the way.

The country in this part of Mississippi stands on edge, as it were, the roads running along the ridges except when they occasionally pass from one ridge to another. Where there are no clearings the sides of the hills are covered with a very heavy growth of timber and with undergrowth, and the ravines are filled with vines and canebrakes, almost impenetrable. This makes it easy for an inferior force to delay, if not defeat, a far superior one.

Near the point selected by Bowen to defend, the road to Port Gibson divides, taking two ridges which do not diverge more than a mile or two at the widest point. These roads unite just outside the town. This made it necessary for McClernand to divide his force. It was not only divided, but it was separated by a deep ravine of the character above described. One flank could not reinforce the other except by marching back to the junction of the roads. McClernand put the divisions of Hovey, Carr and A.J. Smith upon the right-hand branch and Osterhaus on the left. I was on the field by ten A.M., and inspected both flanks in person. On the right the enemy, if not being pressed back, was at least not repulsing our advance. On the left, however, Osterhaus was not faring so well. He had been repulsed with some loss. As soon as the road could be cleared of McClernand's troops I ordered up McPherson, who was close upon the rear of the 13th corps, with two brigades of Logan's division. This was about noon. I ordered him to send one brigade (General John E. Smith's was selected) to support Osterhaus, and to move to the left and flank the enemy out of his position. This movement carried the brigade over a deep ravine to a third ridge and, when Smith's troops were seen well through the ravine, Osterhaus was directed to renew his front attack. It was successful and unattended by heavy loss. The enemy was sent in full retreat on their right, and their left followed before sunset. While the movement to our left was going on, McClernand, who was with his right flank, sent me frequent requests for reinforcements, although the force with him was not being pressed. I had been upon the ground and knew it did not admit of his engaging all the men he had. We followed up our victory until night overtook us about two miles from Port Gibson; then the troops went into bivouac for the night.

Chapter XXXIV

CAPTURE OF PORT GIBSON — GRIERSON'S RAID — OCCUPATION OF GRAND GULF — MOVEMENT UP THE BIG BLACK — BATTLE OF RAYMOND

*W*e started next morning for Port Gibson as soon as it was light enough to see the road. We were soon in the town, and I was delighted to find that the enemy had not stopped to contest our crossing further at the bridge, which he had burned. The troops were set to work at once to construct a bridge across the South Fork of the Bayou Pierre. At this time the water was high and the current rapid. What might be called a raft-bridge was soon constructed from material obtained from wooden buildings, stables, fences, etc., which sufficed for carrying the whole army over safely. Colonel J.H. Wilson, a member of my staff, planned and superintended the construction of this bridge, going into the water and working as hard as anyone engaged. Officers and men generally joined in this work. When it was finished the army crossed and marched eight miles beyond to the North Fork that day. One brigade of Logan's division was sent down the stream to occupy the attention of a rebel battery, which had been left behind with infantry supports to prevent our repairing the burned railroad bridge. Two of his brigades were sent up the bayou to find a crossing and reach the North Fork to repair the bridge there. The enemy soon left when he found we were building a bridge elsewhere. Before leaving Port Gibson we were reinforced by Crocker's division, McPherson's corps, which had crossed the Mississippi at Bruinsburg and come up without stopping except to get two days' rations. McPherson still had one division west of the Mississippi River, guarding the road from Milliken's Bend to the river below until Sherman's command should relieve it.

On leaving Bruinsburg for the front I left my son Frederick, who had joined me a few weeks before, on board one of the gunboats asleep, and hoped to get away without him until after Grand Gulf should fall into our hands; but on waking up he learned that I had gone, and being guided by the sound of the battle raging at Thompson's Hill — called the Battle of Port Gibson — found his way to where I was. He had no horse to ride at the time, and I had no facilities for even preparing a meal. He, therefore, foraged around the best he could until we reached Grand Gulf. Mr. C.A. Dana, then an officer of the War Department, accompanied me on the Vicksburg campaign and through a portion of the siege. He was in the same situation as Fred so far as transportation and mess arrangements were concerned. The first time I call to mind seeing either of them, after the battle, they were mounted on two enormous horses, grown white from age, each equipped with dilapidated saddles and bridles.

Our trains arrived a few days later, after which we were all perfectly equipped.

My son accompanied me throughout the campaign and siege, and caused no anxiety either to me or to his mother, who was at home. He looked out for himself and was in every battle of the campaign. His age, then not quite thirteen, enabled him to take in all he saw, and to retain a recollection of it that would not be possible in more mature years.

When the movement from Bruinsburg commenced we were without a wagon train. The train still west of the Mississippi was carried around with proper escort, by a circuitous route from Milliken's Bend to Hard Times seventy or more miles below, and did not get up for some days after the battle of Port Gibson. My own horses, headquarters' transportation, servants, mess chest, and everything except what I had on, was with this train. General A.J. Smith happened to have an extra horse at Bruinsburg which I borrowed, with a saddle-tree without upholstering further than stirrups. I had no other for nearly a week.

It was necessary to have transportation for ammunition. Provisions could be taken from the country; but all the ammunition that can be carried on the person is soon exhausted when there is much fighting. I directed, therefore, immediately on landing that all the vehicles and draft animals, whether horses, mules, or oxen, in the vicinity should be collected and loaded to their capacity with ammunition. Quite a train was collected during the 30th, and a motley train it was. In it could be found fine carriages, loaded nearly to the top with boxes of cartridges that had been pitched in promiscuously, drawn by mules with plow, harness, straw collars, rope-lines, etc.; long-coupled wagons, with racks for carrying cotton bales, drawn by oxen, and everything that could be found in the way of transportation on a plantation, either for use or pleasure. The making out of provision returns was stopped for the time.

No formalities were to retard our progress until a position was secured when the time could be spared to observe them.

It was at Port Gibson I first heard through a Southern paper of the complete success of Colonel Grierson, who was making a raid through central Mississippi. He had started from La Grange April 17th with three regiments of about 1,700 men. On the 21st he had detached Colonel Hatch with one regiment to destroy the railroad between Columbus and Macon and then return to La Grange. Hatch had a sharp fight with the enemy at Columbus and retreated along the railroad, destroying it at Okalona and Tupelo, and arriving in La Grange April 26. Grierson continued his movement with about 1,000 men, breaking the Vicksburg and Meridian railroad and the New Orleans and Jackson railroad, arriving at Baton Rouge May 2d. This raid was of great importance, for Grierson had attracted the attention of the enemy from the main movement against Vicksburg.

During the night of the 2d of May the bridge over the North Fork was repaired, and the troops commenced crossing at five the next morning. Before the leading brigade was over it was fired upon by the enemy from a commanding position; but they were soon driven off. It was evident that the enemy was covering a retreat from Grand Gulf to Vicksburg. Every commanding position from this (Grindstone) crossing to Hankinson's ferry over the Big Black was occupied by the retreating foe to delay our progress. McPherson, however, reached Hankinson's ferry before night, seized the ferry boat, and sent a detachment of his command across and several miles north on the road to Vicksburg. When the junction of the road going to Vicksburg with the road from Grand Gulf to Raymond and Jackson was reached, Logan with his division was turned to the left towards Grand Gulf. I went with him a short distance from this junction. McPherson had encountered the largest force yet met since the battle of Port Gibson and had a skirmish nearly approaching a battle; but the road Logan had taken enabled him to come up on the enemy's right flank, and they soon gave way. McPherson was ordered to hold Hankinson's ferry and the road back to Willow Springs with one division; McClernand, who was now in the rear, was to join in this as well as to guard the line back down the bayou. I did not want to take the chances of having an enemy lurking in our rear.

On the way from the junction to Grand Gulf, where the road comes into the one from Vicksburg to the same place six or seven miles out, I learned that the last of the enemy had retreated past that place on their way to Vicksburg. I left Logan to make the proper disposition of his troops for the night, while I rode into the town with an escort of about twenty cavalry. Admiral Porter had already arrived with his fleet. The enemy had abandoned his heavy guns and evacuated the place.

When I reached Grand Gulf May 3d I had not been with my baggage since the 27th of April and consequently had had no change of under-clothing, no meal except such as I could pick up sometimes at other headquarters, and no tent to cover me. The first thing I did was to get a bath, borrow some fresh underclothing from one of the naval officers and get a good meal on the flag-ship. Then I wrote letters to the general-in-chief informing him of our present position, dispatches to be telegraphed from Cairo, orders to General Sullivan commanding above Vicksburg, and gave orders to all my corps commanders. About twelve o'clock at night I was through my work and started for Hankin-son's ferry, arriving there before daylight. While at Grand Gulf I heard from Banks, who was on the Red River, and who said that he could not be at Port Hudson before the 10th of May and then with only 15,000 men. Up to this time my intention had been to secure Grand Gulf, as a base of supplies, detach McClernand's corps to Banks and co-operate with him in the reduction of Port Hudson.

The news from Banks forced upon me a different plan of campaign from the one intended. To wait for his co-operation would have detained me at least a month. The reinforcements would not have reached ten thousand men after deducting casualties and necessary river guards at all high points close to the river for over three hundred miles. The enemy would have strengthened his position and been reinforced by more men than Banks could have brought. I therefore determined to move inde-pendently of Banks, cut loose from my base, destroy the rebel force in rear of Vicksburg and invest or capture the city.

Grand Gulf was accordingly given up as a base and the authorities at Washington were notified. I knew well that Halleck's caution would lead him to disapprove of this course; but it was the only one that gave any chance of success. The time it would take to communicate with Washington and get a reply would be so great that I could not be interfered with until it was demonstrated whether my plan was practi-cable. Even Sherman, who afterwards ignored bases of supplies other than what were afforded by the country while marching through four States of the Confederacy with an army more than twice as large as mine at this time, wrote me from Hankinson's ferry, advising me of the impossibility of supplying our army over a single road. He urged me to "stop all troops till your army is partially supplied with wagons, and then act as quick as possible; for this road will be jammed, as sure as life." To this I replied: "I do not calculate upon the possibility of supplying the army with full rations from Grand Gulf. I know it will be impossible without constructing additional roads. What I do expect is to get up what rations of hard bread, coffee and salt we can, and make the country furnish the balance." We started from Bruinsburg with an average of about two days' rations, and received no more from our own supplies for some days; abundance was found in the meantime. A delay would give the enemy time to reinforce and fortify.

McClernand's and McPherson's commands were kept substantially as they were on the night of the 2d, awaiting supplies sufficient to give them three days' rations in haversacks. Beef, mutton, poultry and forage were found in abundance. Quite a quantity of bacon and molasses was also secured from the country, but bread and coffee could not be obtained in quantity sufficient for all the men. Every plantation, however, had a run of stone, propelled by mule power, to grind corn for the owners and their slaves. All these were kept running while we were stopping, day and night, and when we were marching, during the night, at all plantations covered by the troops. But the product was taken by the troops nearest by, so that the majority of the command was destined to go without bread until a new base was established on the Yazoo above Vicksburg.

While the troops were awaiting the arrival of rations I ordered reconnaissances made by McClernand and McPherson, with the view of leading the enemy to believe that we intended to cross the Big Black and attack the city at once.

On the 6th Sherman arrived at Grand Gulf and crossed his command that night and the next day. Three days' rations had been brought up from Grand Gulf for the advanced troops and were issued. Orders were given for a forward movement the next day. Sherman was directed to order up Blair, who had been left behind to guard the road from Milliken's Bend to Hard Times with two brigades.

The quartermaster at Young's Point was ordered to send two hundred wagons with Blair, and the commissary was to load them with hard bread, coffee, sugar, salt and one hundred thousand pounds of salt meat.

On the 3d Hurlbut, who had been left at Memphis, was ordered to send four regiments from his command to Milliken's Bend to relieve Blair's division, and on the 5th he was ordered to send Lauman's division in addition, the latter to join the army in the field. The four regiments were to be taken from troops near the river so that there would be no delay.

During the night of the 6th McPherson drew in his troops north of the Big Black and was off at an early hour on the road to Jackson, via Rocky Springs, Utica and Raymond. That night he and McClernand were both at Rocky Springs ten miles from Hankinson's ferry. McPherson remained there during the 8th, while McClernand moved to Big Sandy and Sherman marched from Grand Gulf to Hankinson's ferry. The 9th, McPherson moved to a point within a few miles west of Utica; McClernand and Sherman remained where they were. On the 10th McPherson moved to Utica, Sherman to Big Sandy; McClernand was still at Big Sandy. The 11th, McClernand was at Five Mile Creek; Sherman at Auburn; McPherson five miles advanced from Utica. May 12th, McClernand was at Fourteen Mile Creek; Sherman at Fourteen Mile Creek; McPherson at Raymond after a battle.

After McPherson crossed the Big Black at Hankinson's ferry Vicksburg could have been approached and besieged by the south side. It is not probable, however, that Pemberton would have permitted a close besiegement. The broken nature of the ground would have enabled him to hold a strong defensible line from the river south of the city to the Big Black, retaining possession of the railroad back to that point. It was my plan, therefore, to get to the railroad east of Vicksburg, and approach from that direction. Accordingly, McPherson's troops that had crossed the Big Black were withdrawn and the movement east to Jackson commenced.

As has been stated before, the country is very much broken and the roads generally confined to the tops of the hills. The troops were moved one (sometimes two) corps at a time to reach designated points out parallel to the railroad and only from six to ten miles from it. McClernand's corps was kept with its left flank on the Big Black guarding all the crossings. Fourteen Mile Creek, a stream substantially parallel with the railroad, was reached and crossings effected by McClernand and Sherman with slight loss. McPherson was to the right of Sherman, extending to Raymond. The cavalry was used in this advance in reconnoitering to find the roads: to cover our advances and to find the most practicable routes from one command to another so they could support each other in case of an attack. In making this move I estimated Pemberton's movable force at Vicksburg at about eighteen thousand men, with smaller forces at Haines' Bluff and Jackson. It would not be possible for Pemberton to attack me with all his troops at one place, and I determined to throw my army between his and fight him in detail. This was done with success, but I found afterwards that I had entirely under-estimated Pemberton's strength.

Up to this point our movements had been made without serious opposition. My line was now nearly parallel with the Jackson and Vicksburg railroad and about seven miles south of it. The right was at Raymond eighteen miles from Jackson, McPherson commanding; Sherman in the center on Fourteen Mile Creek, his advance thrown across;

McClernand to the left, also on Fourteen Mile Creek, advance across, and his pickets within two miles of Edward's station, where the enemy had concentrated a considerable force and where they undoubtedly expected us to attack. McClernand's left was on the Big Black. In all our moves, up to this time, the left had hugged the Big Black closely, and all the ferries had been guarded to prevent the enemy throwing a force on our rear.

McPherson encountered the enemy, five thousand strong with two batteries under General Gregg, about two miles out of Raymond. This was about two P.M. Logan was in advance with one of his brigades. He deployed and moved up to engage the enemy. McPherson ordered the road in rear to be cleared of wagons, and the balance of Logan's division, and Crocker's, which was still farther in rear, to come forward with all dispatch. The order was obeyed with alacrity. Logan got his division in position for assault before Crocker could get up, and attacked with vigor, carrying the enemy's position easily, sending Gregg flying from the field not to appear against our front again until we met at Jackson.

In this battle McPherson lost 66 killed, 339 wounded, and 37 missing — nearly or quite all from Logan's division. The enemy's loss was 100 killed, 305 wounded, besides 415 taken prisoners.

I regarded Logan and Crocker as being as competent division commanders as could be found in or out of the army and both equal to a much higher command. Crocker, however, was dying of consumption when he volunteered. His weak condition never put him on the sick report when there was a battle in prospect, as long as he could keep on his feet. He died not long after the close of the rebellion.

Chapter XXXV

MOVEMENT AGAINST JACKSON — FALL OF
JACKSON — INTERCEPTING THE ENEMY —
BATTLE OF CHAMPION'S HILL

*W*hen the news reached me of McPherson's victory at Raymond about sundown my position was with Sherman. I decided at once to turn the whole column towards Jackson and capture that place without delay.

Pemberton was now on my left, with, as I supposed, about 18,000 men; in fact, as I learned afterwards, with nearly 50,000. A force was also collecting on my right, at Jackson, the point where all the railroads communicating with Vicksburg connect. All the enemy's supplies of men and stores would come by that point. As I hoped in the end to besiege Vicksburg I must first destroy all possibility of aid. I therefore determined to move swiftly towards Jackson, destroy or drive any force in that direction and then turn upon Pemberton. But by moving against Jackson, I uncovered my own communication. So I finally decided to have none — to cut loose altogether from my base and move my whole force eastward. I then had no fears for my communications, and if I moved quickly enough could turn upon Pemberton before he could attack me in the rear.

Accordingly, all previous orders given during the day for movements on the 13th were annulled by new ones. McPherson was ordered at daylight to move on Clinton, ten miles from Jackson; Sherman was notified of my determination to capture Jackson and work from there westward. He was ordered to start at four in the morning and march to Raymond. McClernand was ordered to march with three divisions by Dillon's to Raymond. One was left to guard the crossing of the Big Black.

On the 10th I had received a letter from Banks, on the Red River, asking reinforcements. Porter had gone to his assistance with a part of his fleet on the 3d, and I now wrote to him describing my position and declining to send any troops. I looked upon side movements as long as the enemy held Port Hudson and Vicksburg as a waste of time and material.

General Joseph E. Johnston arrived at Jackson in the night of the 13th from Tennessee, and immediately assumed command of all the Confederate troops in Mississippi. I knew he was expecting reinforcements from the south and east. On the 6th I had written to General Halleck: "Information from the other side leaves me to believe the enemy are bringing forces from Tullahoma."

Up to this time my troops had been kept in supporting distances of each other, as far as the nature of the country would admit. Reconnaissances were constantly made from each corps to enable them to acquaint themselves with the most practicable routes from one to another in case a union became necessary.

McPherson reached Clinton with the advance early on the 13th and immediately set to work destroying the railroad. Sherman's advance reached Raymond before the last of McPherson's command had got out of the town. McClernand withdrew from the front of the enemy, at Edward's station, with much skill and without loss, and reached his position for the night in good order. On the night of the 13th, McPherson was ordered to march at early dawn upon Jackson, only fifteen miles away. Sherman was given the same order; but he was to move by the direct road from Raymond to Jackson, which is south of the road McPherson was on and does not approach within two miles of it at the point where it crossed the line of entrenchments which, at that time, defended the city. McClernand was ordered to move one division of his command to Clinton, one division a few miles beyond Mississippi Springs following Sherman's line, and a third to Raymond. He was also directed to send his siege guns, four in number with the troops going by Mississippi Springs. McClernand's position was an advantageous one in any event. With one division at Clinton he was in position to reinforce McPherson, at Jackson, rapidly if it became necessary; the division beyond Mississippi Springs was equally available to reinforce Sherman; the one at Raymond could take either road. He still had two other divisions farther back now that Blair had come up, available within a day at Jackson. If this last command should not be wanted at Jackson, they were already one day's march from there on their way to Vicksburg and on three different roads leading to the latter city. But the most important consideration in my mind was to have a force confronting Pemberton if he should come out to attack my rear. This I expected him to do; as shown further on, he was directed by Johnston to make this very move.

I notified General Halleck that I should attack the State capital on the 14th. A courier carried the dispatch to Grand Gulf through an unprotected country.

Sherman and McPherson communicated with each other during the night and arranged to reach Jackson at about the same hour. It rained in torrents during the night of the 13th and the fore part of the day of the 14th. The roads were intolerable, and in some places on Sherman's line, where the land was low, they were covered more than a foot deep with water. But the troops never murmured. By nine o'clock Crocker, of McPherson's corps, who was now in advance, came upon the enemy's pickets and speedily drove them in upon the main body. They were outside of the entrenchments in a strong position, and proved to be the troops that had been driven out of Raymond. Johnston had been reinforced; during the night by Georgia and South Carolina regiments, so that his force amounted to eleven thousand men, and he was expecting still more.

Sherman also came upon the rebel pickets some distance out from the town, but speedily drove them in. He was now on the south and southwest of Jackson confronting the Confederates behind their breastworks, while McPherson's right was nearly two miles north, occupying a line running north and south across the Vicksburg railroad. Artillery was brought up and reconnaissances made preparatory to an assault. McPherson brought up Logan's division while he deployed Crocker's for the assault. Sherman made similar dispositions on the right. By eleven A.M. both were ready to attack. Crocker moved his division forward, preceded by a strong skirmish line. These troops at once encountered the enemy's advance and drove it back on the main body, when they returned to their proper regiment and the whole division charged, routing the enemy completely and driving him into this main line. This stand by the enemy was made more than two miles outside of his main fortifications. McPherson followed up with his command until within range of the guns of the enemy from their entrenchments, when he halted to bring his troops into line and reconnoiter to determine the next move. It was now about noon.

While this was going on Sherman was confronting a rebel battery which enfiladed the road on which he was marching — the Mississippi Springs road — and commanded a bridge spanning a stream over which he had to pass. By detaching right and left the stream was forced and the enemy flanked and speedily driven within the main line. This brought our whole line in front of the enemy's line of works, which was continuous on the north, west and south sides from the Pearl River north of the city to the same river south. I was with Sherman. He was confronted by a force sufficient to hold us back. Appearances did not justify an assault where we were. I had directed Sherman to send a force to the right, and to reconnoiter as far as to the Pearl River. This force, Tuttle's division, not returning I rode to the right with my staff, and soon found that the enemy had left that part of the line. Tuttle's movement or McPherson's pressure had no doubt led Johnston to order a retreat, leaving only the men at the guns to retard us while he was getting away. Tuttle had seen this and, passing through the lines without resistance, came up in the rear of the artillerists confronting Sherman and captured them with ten pieces of artillery. I rode immediately to the State House, where I was soon followed by Sherman. About the same time McPherson discovered that the enemy was leaving his front, and advanced Crocker, who was so close upon the enemy that they could not move their guns or destroy them. He captured seven guns and, moving on, hoisted the National flag over the rebel capital of Mississippi. Stevenson's brigade was sent to cut off the rebel retreat, but was too late or not expeditious enough.

Our loss in this engagement was: McPherson, 37 killed, 228 wounded; Sherman, 4 killed and 21 wounded and missing. The enemy lost 845 killed, wounded and captured. Seventeen guns fell into our hands, and the enemy destroyed by fire their store-houses, containing a large amount of commissary stores.

On this day Blair reached New Auburn and joined McClernand's 4th division. He had with him two hundred wagons loaded with rations, the only commissary supplies received during the entire campaign.

I slept that night in the room that Johnston was said to have occupied the night before.

About four in the afternoon I sent for the corps commanders and directed the dispositions to be made of their troops. Sherman was to remain in Jackson until he destroyed that place as a railroad center, and manufacturing city of military supplies. He did the work most effectually. Sherman and I went together into a manufactory which had not ceased work on account of the battle nor for the entrance of Yankee troops. Our presence did not seem to attract the attention of either the manager or the operatives, most of whom were girls. We looked on for a while to see the tent cloth which they were making roll out of the looms, with "C.S.A." woven in each bolt. There was an immense amount of cotton, in bales, stacked outside. Finally I told Sherman I thought they had done work enough. The operatives were told they could leave and take with them what cloth they could carry. In a few minutes cotton and factory were in a blaze. The proprietor visited Washington while I was President to get his pay for this property, claiming that it was private.

He asked me to give him a statement of the fact that his property had been destroyed by National troops, so that he might use it with Congress where he was pressing, or proposed to press, his claim. I declined.

On the night of the 13th Johnston sent the following dispatch to Pemberton at Edward's station: "I have lately arrived, and learn that Major-General Sherman is between us with four divisions at Clinton. It is important to establish communication, that you may be reinforced. If practicable, come up in his rear at once. To beat such a detachment would be of immense value. All the troops you can quickly assemble should be brought. Time is all-important." This dispatch was sent in triplicate, by different messengers. One of the messengers happened to be a loyal man who had been expelled from Memphis some months before by Hurlbut for uttering disloyal and threatening sentiments. There was a good deal of parade about his expulsion, ostensibly as a warning to those who entertained the sentiments he expressed; but Hurlbut and the expelled man understood each other. He delivered his copy of Johnston's dispatch to McPherson who forwarded it to me.

Receiving this dispatch on the 14th I ordered McPherson to move promptly in the morning back to Bolton, the nearest point where Johnston could reach the road. Bolton is about twenty miles west of Jackson. I also informed McClernand of the capture of Jackson and sent him the following order: "It is evidently the design of the enemy to get north of us and cross the Big Black, and beat us into Vicksburg. We must not allow them to do this. Turn all your forces towards Bolton station, and make all dispatch in getting there. Move troops by the most direct road from wherever they may be on the receipt of this order."

And to Blair I wrote: "Their design is evidently to cross the Big Black and pass down the peninsula between the Big Black and Yazoo rivers. We must beat them. Turn your troops immediately to Bolton; take all the trains with you. Smith's division, and any other troops now with you, will go to the same place. If practicable, take parallel roads, so as to divide your troops and train."

Johnston stopped on the Canton road only six miles north of Jackson, the night of the 14th. He sent from there to Pemberton dispatches announcing the loss of Jackson, and the following order:

"As soon as the reinforcements are all up, they must be united to the rest of the army. I am anxious to see a force assembled that may be able to inflict a heavy blow upon the enemy. Can Grant supply himself from the Mississippi? Can you not cut him off from it, and above all, should he be compelled to fall back for want of supplies, beat him."

The concentration of my troops was easy, considering the character of the country. McPherson moved along the road parallel with and near the railroad. McClernand's command was, one division (Hovey's) on the road McPherson had to take, but with a start of four miles. One (Osterhaus) was at Raymond, on a converging road that intersected the other near Champion's Hill; one (Carr's) had to pass over the same road with Osterhaus, but being back at Mississippi Springs, would not be detained by it; the fourth (Smith's) with Blair's division, was near Auburn with a different road to pass over. McClernand faced about and moved promptly. His cavalry from Raymond seized Bolton by half-past nine in the morning, driving out the enemy's pickets and capturing several men.

The night of the 15th Hovey was at Bolton; Carr and Osterhaus were about three miles south, but abreast, facing west; Smith was north of Raymond with Blair in his rear.

McPherson's command, with Logan in front, had marched at seven o'clock, and by four reached Hovey and went into camp; Crocker bivouacked just in Hovey's rear on the Clinton road. Sherman with two divisions, was in Jackson, completing the destruction of roads, bridges and military factories. I rode in person out to Clinton. On my arrival I ordered McClernand to move early in the morning on Edward's station, cautioning him to watch for the enemy and not bring on an engagement unless he felt very certain of success.

I naturally expected that Pemberton would endeavor to obey the orders of his superior, which I have shown were to attack us at Clinton. This, indeed, I knew he could not do; but I felt sure he would make the attempt to reach that point. It turned out, however, that he had decided his superior's plans were impracticable, and consequently determined to move south from Edward's station and get between me and my base. I, however, had no base, having abandoned it more than a week before. On the 15th Pemberton had actually marched south from Edward's station, but the rains had swollen Baker's Creek, which he had to cross so much that he could not ford it, and the bridges were washed away. This brought him back to the Jackson road, on which there was a good bridge over Baker's Creek. Some of his troops were marching until midnight to get there. Receiving here early on the 16th a repetition of his order to join Johnston at Clinton, he concluded to obey, and sent a dispatch to his chief, informing him of the route by which he might be expected.

About five o'clock in the morning (16th) two men, who had been employed on the Jackson and Vicksburg railroad, were brought to me. They reported that they had passed through Pemberton's army in the night, and that it was still marching east. They reported him to have eighty regiments of infantry and ten batteries; in all, about twenty-five thousand men.

I had expected to leave Sherman at Jackson another day in order to complete his work; but getting the above information I sent him orders to move with all dispatch to Bolton, and to put one division with an ammunition train on the road at once, with directions to its commander to march with all possible speed until he came up to our rear. Within an hour after receiving this order Steele's division was on the road. At the same time I dispatched to Blair, who was near Auburn, to move with all speed to Edward's station. McClernand was directed to embrace Blair in his command for the present. Blair's division was a part of the 15th army corps (Sherman's); but as it was on its way to join its corps, it naturally struck our left first, now that we had faced about and were moving west. The 15th corps, when it got up, would be on our extreme right. McPherson was directed to get his trains out of the way of the troops, and to follow Hovey's division as closely as possible. McClernand had two roads about three miles apart, converging at Edward's station, over which to march his troops. Hovey's division of his corps had the advance on a third road (the Clinton) still farther north. McClernand was directed to move Blair's and A.J. Smith's divisions by the southernmost of these roads, and Osterhaus and Carr by the middle road. Orders were to move cautiously with skirmishers to the front to feel for the enemy.

Smith's division on the most southern road was the first to encounter the enemy's pickets, who were speedily driven in. Osterhaus, on the middle road, hearing the firing, pushed his skirmishers forward, found the enemy's pickets and forced them back to the main line. About the same time Hovey encountered the enemy on the northern or direct wagon road from Jackson to Vicksburg. McPherson was hastening up to join Hovey, but was embarrassed by Hovey's trains occupying the roads. I was still back at Clinton. McPherson sent me word of the situation, and expressed the wish that I was up. By half-past seven I was on the road and proceeded rapidly to the front, ordering all trains that were in front of troops off the road. When I arrived Hovey's skirmishing amounted almost to a battle.

McClernand was in person on the middle road and had a shorter distance to march to reach the enemy's position than McPherson. I sent him word by a staff officer to push forward and attack. These orders were repeated several times without apparently expediting McClernand's advance.

Champion's Hill, where Pemberton had chosen his position to receive us, whether taken by accident or design, was well selected. It is one of the highest points in that section, and commanded all the ground in range. On the east side of the ridge, which is quite precipitous, is a ravine running first north, then westerly, terminating at Baker's Creek. It was grown up thickly with large trees and undergrowth, making it difficult to penetrate with troops, even when not defended. The ridge occupied by the enemy terminated abruptly where the ravine turns westerly. The left of the enemy occupied the north end of this ridge. The Bolton and Edward's station wagon-road turns almost due south at this point and ascends the ridge, which it follows for about a mile; then turning west, descends by a gentle declivity to Baker's Creek, nearly a mile away. On the west side the slope of the ridge is gradual and is cultivated from near the summit to the creek. There was, when we were there, a narrow belt of timber near the summit west of the road.

From Raymond there is a direct road to Edward's station, some three miles west of Champion's Hill. There is one also to Bolton. From this latter road there is still another, leaving it about three and a half miles before reaching Bolton and leads direct to the same station. It was along these two roads that three divisions of McClernand's corps, and Blair of Sherman's, temporarily under McClernand, were moving. Hovey of McClernand's command was with McPherson, farther north on the road from Bolton direct to Edward's station. The middle road comes into the northern road at the point where the latter turns to the west and descends to Baker's Creek; the southern road is still several miles south and does not intersect the others until it reaches Edward's station. Pemberton's lines covered all these roads, and faced east. Hovey's line, when it first drove in the enemy's pickets, was formed parallel to that of the enemy and confronted his left.

By eleven o'clock the skirmishing had grown into a hard-contested battle. Hovey alone, before other troops could be got to assist him, had captured a battery of the enemy. But he was not able to hold his position and had to abandon the artillery. McPherson brought up his troops as fast as possible, Logan in front, and posted them on the right of Hovey and across the flank of the enemy. Logan reinforced Hovey with one brigade from his division; with his other two he moved farther west to make room for Crocker, who was coming up as rapidly as the roads would admit. Hovey was still being heavily pressed, and was calling on me for more reinforcements. I ordered Crocker, who was now coming up, to send one brigade from his division. McPherson ordered two batteries to be stationed where they nearly enfiladed the enemy's line, and they did good execution.

From Logan's position now a direct forward movement carried him over open fields, in rear of the enemy and in a line parallel with them.

He did make exactly this move, attacking, however, the enemy through the belt of woods covering the west slope of the hill for a short distance. Up to this time I had kept my position near Hovey where we were the most heavily pressed; but about noon I moved with a part of my staff by our right around, until I came up with Logan himself. I found him near the road leading down to Baker's Creek. He was actually in command of the only road over which the enemy could retreat; Hovey, reinforced by two brigades from McPherson's command, confronted the enemy's left; Crocker, with two brigades, covered their left flank; McClernand two hours before, had been within two miles and a half of their center with two divisions, and the two divisions, Blair's and A.J. Smith's, were confronting the rebel right; Ransom, with a brigade of McArthur's division of the 17th corps (McPherson's), had crossed the river at Grand Gulf a few days before, and was coming up on their right flank. Neither Logan nor I knew that we had cut off the retreat of the enemy. Just at this juncture a messenger came from Hovey, asking for more reinforcements. There were none to spare. I then gave an order to move McPherson's command by the left flank around to Hovey. This uncovered the rebel line of retreat, which was soon taken advantage of by the enemy.

During all this time, Hovey, reinforced as he was by a brigade from Logan and another from Crocker, and by Crocker gallantly coming up with two other brigades on his right, had made several assaults, the last one about the time the road was opened to the rear. The enemy fled precipitately. This was between three and four o'clock. I rode forward, or rather back, to where the middle road intersects the north road, and found the skirmishers of Carr's division just coming in. Osterhaus was farther south and soon after came up with skirmishers advanced in like manner. Hovey's division, and McPherson's two divisions with him, had marched and fought from early dawn, and were not in the best condition to follow the retreating foe. I sent orders to Osterhaus to pursue the enemy, and to Carr, whom I saw personally, I explained the situation and directed him to pursue vigorously as far as the Big Black, and to cross it if he could; Osterhaus to follow him. The pursuit was continued until after dark.

The battle of Champion's Hill lasted about four hours, hard fighting, preceded by two or three hours of skirmishing, some of which almost rose to the dignity of battle. Every man of Hovey's division and of McPherson's two divisions was engaged during the battle. No other part of my command was engaged at all, except that as described before. Osterhaus's and A.J. Smith's divisions had encountered the rebel advanced pickets as early as half-past seven. Their positions were admirable for advancing upon the enemy's line. McClernand, with two divisions, was within a few miles of the battlefield long before noon and in easy hearing. I sent him repeated orders by staff officers fully competent to explain to him the situation. These traversed the wood separating us, without escort, and directed him to push forward; but he did not come. It is true, in front of McClernand there was a small force of the enemy and posted in a good position behind a ravine obstructing his advance; but if he had moved to the right by the road my staff officers had followed the enemy must either have fallen back or been cut off. Instead of this he sent orders to Hovey, who belonged to his corps, to join on to his right flank. Hovey was bearing the brunt of the battle at the time. To obey the order he would have had to pull out from the front of the enemy and march back as far as McClernand had to advance to get into battle and substantially over the same ground. Of course I did not permit Hovey to obey the order of his intermediate superior.

We had in this battle about 15,000 men absolutely engaged. This excludes those that did not get up, all of McClernand's command except Hovey. Our loss was 410 killed, 1,844 wounded and 187 missing. Hovey alone lost 1,200 killed, wounded and missing — more than one-third of his division.

Had McClernand come up with reasonable promptness, or had I known the ground as I did afterwards, I cannot see how Pemberton could have escaped with any organized force. As it was he lost over three thousand killed and wounded and about three thousand captured in battle and in pursuit. Loring's division, which was the right of Pemberton's line, was cut off from the retreating army and never got back into Vicksburg. Pemberton himself fell back that night to the Big Black River. His troops did not stop before midnight and many of them left before the general retreat commenced, and no doubt a good part of them returned to their homes. Logan alone captured 1,300 prisoners and eleven guns. Hovey captured 300 under fire and about 700 in all, exclusive of 500 sick and wounded whom he paroled, thus making 1,200.

McPherson joined in the advance as soon as his men could fill their cartridge-boxes, leaving one brigade to guard our wounded. The pursuit was continued as long as it was light enough to see the road. The night of the 16th of May found McPherson's command bivouacked from two to six miles west of the battlefield, along the line of the road to Vicksburg. Carr and Osterhaus were at Edward's station, and Blair was about three miles southeast; Hovey remained on the field where his troops had fought so bravely and bled so freely. Much war material abandoned by the enemy was picked up on the battlefield, among it thirty pieces of artillery. I pushed through the advancing column with my staff and kept in advance until after night. Finding ourselves alone we stopped and took possession of a vacant house. As no troops came up we moved back a mile or more until we met the head of the column just going into bivouac on the road. We had no tents, so we occupied the porch of a house which had been taken for a rebel hospital and which was filled with wounded and dying who had been brought from the battlefield we had just left.

While a battle is raging one can see his enemy mowed down by the thousand, or the ten thousand, with great composure; but after the battle these scenes are distressing, and one is naturally disposed to do as much to alleviate the suffering of an enemy as a friend.

Chapter XXXVI

BATTLE OF BLACK RIVER BRIDGE — CROSSING THE BIG BLACK — INVESTMENT OF VICKSBURG — ASSAULTING THE WORKS

We were now assured of our position between Johnston and Pemberton, without a possibility of a junction of their forces. Pemberton might have made a night march to the Big Black, crossed the bridge there and, by moving north on the west side, have eluded us and finally returned to Johnston. But this would have given us Vicksburg. It would have been his proper move, however, and the one Johnston would have made had he been in Pemberton's place. In fact it would have been in conformity with Johnston's orders to Pemberton.

Sherman left Jackson with the last of his troops about noon on the 16th and reached Bolton, twenty miles west, before halting. His rear guard did not get in until two A.M. the 17th, but renewed their march by daylight. He paroled his prisoners at Jackson, and was forced to leave his own wounded in care of surgeons and attendants. At Bolton he was informed of our victory. He was directed to commence the march early next day, and to diverge from the road he was on to Bridgeport on the Big Black River, some eleven miles above the point where we expected to find the enemy. Blair was ordered to join him there with the pontoon train as early as possible.

This movement brought Sherman's corps together, and at a point where I hoped a crossing of the Big Black might be effected and Sherman's corps used to flank the enemy out of his position in our front, thus opening a crossing for the remainder of the army. I informed him that I would endeavor to hold the enemy in my front while he crossed the river.

The advance division, Carr's (McClernand's corps), resumed the pursuit at half-past three A.M. on the 17th, followed closely by Oster-haus, McPherson bringing up the rear with his corps. As I expected, the enemy was found in position on the Big Black. The point was only six miles from that where my advance had rested for the night, and was reached at an early hour. Here the river makes a turn to the west, and has washed close up to the high land; the east side is a low bottom, sometimes overflowed at very high water, but was cleared and in culti-vation. A bayou runs irregularly across this low land, the bottom of which, however, is above the surface of the Big Black at ordinary stages. When the river is full water runs through it, converting the point of land into an island. The bayou was grown up with timber, which the enemy had felled into the ditch. At this time there was a foot or two of water in it. The rebels had constructed a parapet along the inner bank of this bayou by using cotton bales from the plantation close by and throwing dirt over them. The whole was thoroughly commanded from the height west of the river. At the upper end of the bayou there was a strip of uncleared land which afforded a cover for a portion of our men. Carr's division was deployed on our right, Lawler's brigade forming his extreme right and reaching through these woods to the river above. Osterhaus' division was deployed to the left of Carr and covered the enemy's entire front. McPherson was in column on the road, the head close by, ready to come in wherever he could be of assistance.

While the troops were standing as here described an officer from Banks' staff came up and presented me with a letter from General Halleck, dated the 11th of May. It had been sent by the way of New Orleans to Banks to be forwarded to me. It ordered me to return to Grand Gulf and to co-operate from there with Banks against Port Hudson, and then to return with our combined forces to besiege Vicksburg. I told the officer that the order came too late, and that Halleck would not give it now if he knew our position. The bearer of the dispatch insisted that I ought to obey the order, and was giving arguments to support his position when I heard great cheering to the right of our line and, looking in that direction, saw Lawler in his shirt sleeves leading a charge upon the enemy. I immediately mounted my horse and rode in the direction of the charge, and saw no more of the officer who delivered the dispatch; I think not even to this day.

The assault was successful. But little resistance was made. The enemy fled from the west bank of the river, burning the bridge behind him and leaving the men and guns on the east side to fall into our hands. Many tried to escape by swimming the river. Some succeeded and some were drowned in the attempt. Eighteen guns were captured and 1,751 prisoners. Our loss was 39 killed, 237 wounded and 3 missing. The enemy probably lost but few men except those captured and drowned. But for the successful and complete destruction of the bridge, I have but little doubt that we should have followed the enemy so closely as to prevent his occupying his defenses around Vicksburg.

As the bridge was destroyed and the river was high, new bridges had to be built. It was but little after nine o'clock A.M. when the capture took place. As soon as work could be commenced, orders were given for the construction of three bridges. One was taken charge of by Lieutenant Hains, of the Engineer Corps, one by General McPherson himself and one by General Ransom, a most gallant and intelligent volunteer officer. My recollection is that Hains built a raft bridge; McPherson a pontoon, using cotton bales in large numbers, for pontoons; and that Ransom felled trees on opposite banks of the river, cutting only on one side of the tree, so that they would fall with their tops interlacing in the river, without the trees being entirely severed from their stumps. A bridge was then made with these trees to support the roadway. Lumber was taken from buildings, cotton gins and wherever found, for this purpose. By eight o'clock in the morning of the 18th all three bridges were complete and the troops were crossing.

Sherman reached Bridgeport about noon of the 17th and found Blair with the pontoon train already there. A few of the enemy were entrenched on the west bank, but they made little resistance and soon surrendered. Two divisions were crossed that night and the third the following morning.

On the 18th I moved along the Vicksburg road in advance of the troops and as soon as possible joined Sherman. My first anxiety was to secure a base of supplies on the Yazoo River above Vicksburg. Sherman's line of march led him to the very point on Walnut Hills occupied by the enemy the December before when he was repulsed. Sherman was equally anxious with myself. Our impatience led us to move in advance of the column and well up with the advanced skirmishers. There were some detached works along the crest of the hill. These were still occupied by the enemy, or else the garrison from Haines' Bluff had not all got past on their way to Vicksburg. At all events the bullets of the enemy whistled by thick and fast for a short time. In a few minutes Sherman had the pleasure of looking down from the spot coveted so much by him the December before on the ground where his command had lain so helpless for offensive action. He turned to me, saying that up to this minute he had felt no positive assurance of success. This, however, he said was the end of one of the greatest campaigns in history and I ought to make a report of it at once. Vicksburg was not yet captured, and there was no telling what might happen before it was taken; but whether captured or not, this was a complete and successful campaign. I do not claim to quote Sherman's language; but the substance only. My reason for mentioning this incident will appear further on.

McPherson, after crossing the Big Black, came into the Jackson and Vicksburg road which Sherman was on, but to his rear. He arrived at night near the lines of the enemy, and went into camp. McClernand moved by the direct road near the railroad to Mount Albans, and then turned to the left and put his troops on the road from Baldwin's ferry to Vicksburg. This brought him south of McPherson. I now had my three corps up the works built for the defense of Vicksburg, on three roads — one to the north, one to the east and one to the southeast of the city. By the morning of the 19th the investment was as complete as my limited number of troops would allow. Sherman was on the right, and covered the high ground from where it overlooked the Yazoo as far southeast as his troops would extend. McPherson joined on to his left, and occupied ground on both sides of the Jackson road. McClernand took up the ground to his left and extended as far towards Warrenton as he could, keeping a continuous line.

On the 19th there was constant skirmishing with the enemy while we were getting into better position. The enemy had been much demoralized by his defeats at Champion's Hill and the Big Black, and I believed he would not make much effort to hold Vicksburg. Accordingly, at two o'clock I ordered an assault. It resulted in securing more advanced positions for all our troops where they were fully covered from the fire of the enemy.

The 20th and 21st were spent in strengthening our position and in making roads in rear of the army, from Yazoo River or Chickasaw Bayou. Most of the army had now been for three weeks with only five days' rations issued by the commissary. They had an abundance of food, however, but began to feel the want of bread. I remember that in passing around to the left of the line on the 21st, a soldier, recognizing me, said in rather a low voice, but yet so that I heard him, "Hard tack." In a moment the cry was taken up all along the line, "Hard tack! Hard tack!" I told the men nearest to me that we had been engaged ever since the arrival of the troops in building a road over which to supply them with everything they needed. The cry was instantly changed to cheers. By the night of the 21st all the troops had full rations issued to them. The bread and coffee were highly appreciated.

I now determined on a second assault. Johnston was in my rear, only fifty miles away, with an army not much inferior in numbers to the one I had with me, and I knew he was being reinforced. There was danger of his coming to the assistance of Pemberton, and after all he might defeat my anticipations of capturing the garrison if, indeed, he did not prevent the capture of the city. The immediate capture of Vicksburg would save sending me the reinforcements which were so much wanted elsewhere, and would set free the army under me to drive Johnston from the State. But the first consideration of all was — the troops believed they could carry the works in their front, and would not have worked so patiently in the trenches if they had not been allowed to try.

The attack was ordered to commence on all parts of the line at ten o'clock A.M. on the 22d with a furious cannonade from every battery in position. All the corps commanders set their time by mine so that all might open the engagement at the same minute. The attack was gallant, and portions of each of the three corps succeeded in getting up to the very parapets of the enemy and in planting their battle flags upon them; but at no place were we able to enter. General McClernand reported that he had gained the enemy's entrenchments at several points, and wanted reinforcements. I occupied a position from which I believed I could see as well as he what took place in his front, and I did not see the success he reported. But his request for reinforcements being repeated I could not ignore it, and sent him Quinby's division of the 17th corps. Sherman and McPherson were both ordered to renew their assaults as a diversion in favor of McClernand. This last attack only served to increase our casualties without giving any benefit whatever. As soon as it was dark our troops that had reached the enemy's line and been obliged to remain there for security all day, were withdrawn; and thus ended the last assault upon Vicksburg.

Chapter *XXXVII*

SIEGE OF VICKSBURG

I now determined upon a regular siege — to "out-camp the enemy," as it were, and to incur no more losses. The experience of the 22d convinced officers and men that this was best, and they went to work on the defenses and approaches with a will. With the navy holding the river, the investment of Vicksburg was complete. As long as we could hold our position the enemy was limited in supplies of food, men and munitions of war to what they had on hand. These could not last always.

The crossing of troops at Bruinsburg commenced April 30th. On the 18th of May the army was in rear of Vicksburg. On the 19th, just twenty days after the crossing, the city was completely invested and an assault had been made: five distinct battles (besides continuous skirmishing) had been fought and won by the Union forces; the capital of the State had fallen and its arsenals, military manufactories and everything useful for military purposes had been destroyed; an average of about one hundred and eighty miles had been marched by the troops engaged; but five days' rations had been issued, and no forage; over six thousand prisoners had been captured, and as many more of the enemy had been killed or wounded; twenty-seven heavy cannon and sixty-one field-pieces had fallen into our hands; and four hundred miles of the river, from Vicksburg to Port Hudson, had become ours. The Union force that had crossed the Mississippi River up to this time was less than forty-three thousand men. One division of these, Blair's, only arrived in time to take part in the battle of Champion's Hill, but was not engaged there; and one brigade, Ransom's of McPherson's corps, reached the field after the battle. The enemy had at Vicksburg, Grand Gulf, Jackson, and on the roads between these places, over sixty thousand men. They were in their own country, where no rear guards were necessary. The country is admirable for defense, but difficult for the conduct of an offensive campaign. All their troops had to be met. We were fortunate, to say the least, in meeting them in detail: at Port Gibson seven or eight thousand;

at Raymond, five thousand; at Jackson, from eight to eleven thousand; at Champion's Hill, twenty-five thousand; at the Big Black, four thousand. A part of those met at Jackson were all that was left of those encountered at Raymond. They were beaten in detail by a force smaller than their own, upon their own ground. Our loss up to this time was:

	KILLED	WOUNDED	MISSING
Port Gibson 131		719	25
South Fork Bayou Pierre 1			
Skirmishes, May 3 1		9	
Fourteen Mile Creek 6		24	
Raymond 66		339	39
Jackson 42		251	7
Champion's Hill 410		1,844	187
Big Black 39		237	3
Bridgeport 1			
Total	695	3,425	259

Of the wounded many were but slightly so, and continued on duty. Not half of them were disabled for any length of time.

After the unsuccessful assault of the 22d the work of the regular siege began. Sherman occupied the right starting from the river above Vicksburg, McPherson the center (McArthur's division now with him) and McClernand the left, holding the road south to Warrenton. Lauman's division arrived at this time and was placed on the extreme left of the line.

In the interval between the assaults of the 19th and 22d, roads had been completed from the Yazoo River and Chickasaw Bayou, around the rear of the army, to enable us to bring up supplies of food and ammunition; ground had been selected and cleared on which the troops were to be encamped, and tents and cooking utensils were brought up. The troops had been without these from the time of crossing the Mississippi up to this time. All was now ready for the pick and spade. Prentiss and Hurlbut were ordered to send forward every man that could be spared. Cavalry especially was wanted to watch the fords along the Big Black, and to observe Johnston. I knew that Johnston was receiving reinforcements from Bragg, who was confronting Rosecrans in Tennessee. Vicksburg was so important to the enemy that I believed he would make the most strenuous efforts to raise the siege, even at the risk of losing ground elsewhere.

My line was more than fifteen miles long, extending from Haines' Bluff to Vicksburg, thence to Warrenton. The line of the enemy was about seven. In addition to this, having an enemy at Canton and Jackson, in our rear, who was being constantly reinforced, we required a second line of defense facing the other way. I had not troops enough under my command to man these. General Halleck appreciated the situation and, without being asked, forwarded reinforcements with all possible dispatch.

The ground about Vicksburg is admirable for defense. On the north it is about two hundred feet above the Mississippi River at the highest point and very much cut up by the washing rains; the ravines were grown up with cane and underbrush, while the sides and tops were covered with a dense forest. Farther south the ground flattens out somewhat, and was in cultivation. But here, too, it was cut up by ravines and small streams. The enemy's line of defense followed the crest of a ridge from the river north of the city eastward, then southerly around to the Jackson road, full three miles back of the city; thence in a southwesterly direction to the river. Deep ravines of the description given lay in front of these defenses. As there is a succession of gullies, cut out by rains along the side of the ridge, the line was necessarily very irregular. To follow each of these spurs with entrenchments, so as to command the slopes on either side, would have lengthened their line very much. Generally therefore, or in many places, their line would run from near the head of one gully nearly straight to the head of another, and an outer work triangular in shape, generally open in the rear, was thrown up on the point; with a few men in this outer work they commanded the approaches to the main line completely.

The work to be done, to make our position as strong against the enemy as his was against us, was very great. The problem was also complicated by our wanting our line as near that of the enemy as possible. We had but four engineer officers with us. Captain Prime, of the Engineer Corps, was the chief, and the work at the beginning was mainly directed by him. His health soon gave out, when he was succeeded by Captain Comstock, also of the Engineer Corps. To provide assistants on such a long line I directed that all officers who had graduated at West Point, where they had necessarily to study military engineering, should in addition to their other duties assist in the work.

The chief quartermaster and the chief commissary were graduates. The chief commissary, now the Commissary-General of the Army, begged off, however, saying that there was nothing in engineering that he was good for unless he would do for a sap-roller. As soldiers require rations while working in the ditches as well as when marching and fighting, and as we would be sure to lose him if he was used as a sap-roller, I let him off. The general is a large man; weighs two hundred and twenty pounds, and is not tall.

We had no siege guns except six thirty-two pounders, and there were none at the West to draw from. Admiral Porter, however, supplied us with a battery of navy-guns of large caliber, and with these, and the field artillery used in the campaign, the siege began. The first thing to do was to get the artillery in batteries where they would occupy commanding positions; then establish the camps, under cover from the fire of the enemy but as near up as possible; and then construct rifle-pits and covered ways, to connect the entire command by the shortest route. The enemy did not harass us much while we were constructing our batteries. Probably their artillery ammunition was short; and their infantry was kept down by our sharpshooters, who were always on the alert and ready to fire at a head whenever it showed itself above the rebel works.

In no place were our lines more than six hundred yards from the enemy. It was necessary, therefore, to cover our men by something more than the ordinary parapet. To give additional protection sand bags, bullet-proof, were placed along the tops of the parapets far enough apart to make loopholes for musketry. On top of these, logs were put. By these means the men were enabled to walk about erect when off duty, without fear of annoyance from sharpshooters. The enemy used in their defense explosive musket-balls, no doubt thinking that, bursting over our men in the trenches, they would do some execution; but I do not remember a single case where a man was injured by a piece of one of these shells. When they were hit and the ball exploded, the wound was terrible. In these cases a solid ball would have hit as well. Their use is barbarous, because they produce increased suffering without any corresponding advantage to those using them.

The enemy could not resort to our method to protect their men, because we had an inexhaustible supply of ammunition to draw upon and used it freely. Splinters from the timber would have made havoc among the men behind.

There were no mortars with the besiegers, except what the navy had in front of the city; but wooden ones were made by taking logs of the toughest wood that could be found, boring them out for six or twelve pound shells and binding them with strong iron bands. These answered as cochorns, and shells were successfully thrown from them into the trenches of the enemy.

The labor of building the batteries and entrenching was largely done by the pioneers, assisted by Negroes who came within our lines and who were paid for their work; but details from the troops had often to be made. The work was pushed forward as rapidly as possible, and when an advanced position was secured and covered from the fire of the enemy the batteries were advanced. By the 30th of June there were two hundred and twenty guns in position, mostly light field-pieces, besides a battery of heavy guns belonging to, manned and commanded by the navy. We were now as strong for defense against the garrison of Vicksburg as they were against us; but I knew that Johnston was in our rear, and was receiving constant reinforcements from the east. He had at this time a larger force than I had had at any time prior to the battle of Champion's Hill.

As soon as the news of the arrival of the Union army behind Vicksburg reached the North, floods of visitors began to pour in. Some came to gratify curiosity; some to see sons or brothers who had passed through the terrible ordeal; members of the Christian and Sanitary Associations came to minister to the wants of the sick and the wounded. Often those coming to see a son or brother would bring a dozen or two of poultry. They did not know how little the gift would be appreciated. Many of the soldiers had lived so much on chickens, ducks and turkeys without bread during the march, that the sight of poultry, if they could get bacon, almost took away their appetite. But the intention was good.

Among the earliest arrivals was the Governor of Illinois, with most of the State officers. I naturally wanted to show them what there was of most interest. In Sherman's front the ground was the most broken and most wooded, and more was to be seen without exposure. I therefore took them to Sherman's headquarters and presented them. Before start-ing out to look at the lines — possibly while Sherman's horse was being saddled — there were many questions asked about the late campaign, about which the North had been so imperfectly informed. There was a little knot around Sherman and another around me, and I heard Sherman repeating, in the most animated manner, what he had said to me when we first looked down from Walnut Hills upon the land below on the 18th of May, adding: "Grant is entitled to every bit of the credit for the campaign; I opposed it. I wrote him a letter about it." But for this speech it is not likely that Sherman's opposition would have ever been heard of. His untiring energy and great efficiency during the campaign entitle him to a full share of all the credit due for its success. He could not have done more if the plan had been his own.*

---

* *Note.* — When General Sherman first learned of the move I proposed to make, he called to see me about it. I recollect that I had transferred my headquarters from a boat in the river to a house a short distance back from the levee. I was seated on the piazza engaged in conversation with my staff when Sherman came up. After a few moments' conversation he said that he would like to see me alone. We passed into the house together and shut the door after us. Sherman then expressed his alarm at the move I had ordered, saying that I was putting myself in a position voluntarily which an enemy would be glad to maneuver a year — or a long time — to get me in. I was going into the enemy's country, with a large river behind me

On the 26th of May I sent Blair's division up the Yazoo to drive out a force of the enemy supposed to be between the Big Black and the Yazoo. The country was rich and full of supplies of both food and forage. Blair was instructed to take all of it. The cattle were to be driven in for the use of our army, and the food and forage to be consumed by our troops or destroyed by fire; all bridges were to be destroyed, and the roads rendered as nearly impassable as possible. Blair went forty-five miles and was gone almost a week. His work was effectually done. I requested Porter at this time to send the marine brigade, a floating nondescript force which had been assigned to his command and which proved very useful, up to Haines' Bluff to hold it until reinforcements could be sent.

On the 26th I also received a letter from Banks, asking me to reinforce him with ten thousand men at Port Hudson. Of course I could not

---

and the enemy holding points strongly fortified above and below. He said that it was an axiom in war that when any great body of troops moved against an enemy they should do so from a base of supplies, which they would guard as they would the apple of the eye, etc. He pointed out all the difficulties that might be encountered in the campaign proposed, and stated in turn what would be the true campaign to make. This was, in substance, to go back until high ground could be reached on the east bank of the river; fortify there and establish a depot of supplies, and move from there, being always prepared to fall back upon it in case of disaster. I said this would take us back to Memphis. Sherman then said that was the very place he would go to, and would move by railroad from Memphis to Grenada, repairing the road as we advanced. To this I replied, the country is already disheartened over the lack of success on the part of our armies; the last election went against the vigorous prosecution of the war, voluntary enlistments had ceased throughout most of the North and conscription was already resorted to, and if we went back so far as Memphis it would discourage the people so much that bases of supplies would be of no use: neither men to hold them nor supplies to put in them would be furnished. The problem for us was to move forward to a decisive victory, or our cause was lost. No progress was being made in any other field, and we had to go on.

Sherman wrote to my adjutant general, Colonel J. A. Rawlins, embodying his views of the campaign that should be made, and asking him to advise me to at least get the views of my generals upon the subject. Colonel Rawlins showed me the letter, but I did not see any reason for changing my plans. The letter was not answered and the subject was not subsequently mentioned between Sherman and myself to the end of the war, that I remember of. I did not regard the letter as official, and consequently did not preserve it. General Sherman furnished a copy himself to General Badeau, who printed it in his history of my campaigns. I did not regard either the conversation between us or the letter to my adjutant-general as protests, but simply friendly advice which the relations between us fully justified. Sherman gave the same energy to make the campaign a success that he would or could have done if it had been ordered by himself. I make this statement here to correct an impression which was circulated at the close of the war to Sherman's prejudice, and for which there was no fair foundation.

comply with his request, nor did I think he needed them. He was in no danger of an attack by the garrison in his front, and there was no army organizing in his rear to raise the siege.

On the 3d of June a brigade from Hurlbut's command arrived, General Kimball commanding. It was sent to Mechanicsburg, some miles northeast of Haines' Bluff and about midway between the Big Black and the Yazoo. A brigade of Blair's division and twelve hundred cavalry had already, on Blair's return from the Yazoo, been sent to the same place with instructions to watch the crossings of the Big Black River, to destroy the roads in his (Blair's) front, and to gather or destroy all supplies.

On the 7th of June our little force of colored and white troops across the Mississippi, at Milliken's Bend, were attacked by about 3,000 men from Richard Taylor's trans-Mississippi command. With the aid of the gunboats they were speedily repelled. I sent Mower's brigade over with instructions to drive the enemy beyond the Tensas Bayou; and we had no further trouble in that quarter during the siege. This was the first important engagement of the war in which colored troops were under fire. These men were very raw, having all been enlisted since the beginning of the siege, but they behaved well.

On the 8th of June a full division arrived from Hurlbut's command, under General Sooy Smith. It was sent immediately to Haines' Bluff, and General C.C. Washburn was assigned to the general command at that point.

On the 11th a strong division arrived from the Department of the Missouri under General Herron, which was placed on our left. This cut off the last possible chance of communication between Pemberton and Johnston, as it enabled Lauman to close up on McClernand's left while Herron entrenched from Lauman to the water's edge. At this point the water recedes a few hundred yards from the high land. Through this opening no doubt the Confederate commanders had been able to get messengers under cover of night.

On the 14th General Parke arrived with two divisions of Burnside's corps, and was immediately dispatched to Haines' Bluff. These latter troops — Herron's and Parke's — were the reinforcements already spoken of sent by Halleck in anticipation of their being needed. They arrived none too soon.

I now had about seventy-one thousand men. More than half were disposed across the peninsula, between the Yazoo at Haines' Bluff and the Big Black, with the division of Osterhaus watching the crossings of the latter river farther south and west from the crossing of the Jackson road to Baldwin's ferry and below.

There were eight roads leading into Vicksburg, along which and their immediate sides, our work was specially pushed and batteries advanced; but no commanding point within range of the enemy was neglected.

On the 17th I received a letter from General Sherman and one on the 18th from General McPherson, saying that their respective commands had complained to them of a fulsome, congratulatory order published by General McClernand to the 13th corps, which did great injustice to the other troops engaged in the campaign. This order had been sent North and published, and now papers containing it had reached our camps. The order had not been heard of by me, and certainly not by troops outside of McClernand's command until brought in this way. I at once wrote to McClernand, directing him to send me a copy of this order. He did so, and I at once relieved him from the command of the 13th army corps and ordered him back to Springfield, Illinois. The publication of his order in the press was in violation of War Department orders and also of mine.

Chapter XXXVIII

JOHNSTON'S MOVEMENTS — FORTIFICATIONS AT HAINES' BLUFF — EXPLOSION OF THE MINE — EXPLOSION OF THE SECOND MINE — PREPARING FOR THE ASSAULT — THE FLAG OF TRUCE — MEETING WITH PEMBERTON — NEGOTIATIONS FOR SURRENDER — ACCEPTING THE TERMS — SURRENDER OF VICKSBURG

On the 22d of June positive information was received that Johnston had crossed the Big Black River for the purpose of attacking our rear, to raise the siege and release Pemberton. The correspondence between Johnston and Pemberton shows that all expectation of holding Vicksburg had by this time passed from Johnston's mind. I immediately ordered Sherman to the command of all the forces from Haines' Bluff to the Big Black River. This amounted now to quite half the troops about Vicksburg. Besides these, Herron and A.J. Smith's divisions were ordered to hold themselves in readiness to reinforce Sherman. Haines' Bluff had been strongly fortified on the land side, and on all commanding points from there to the Big Black at the railroad crossing batteries had been constructed. The work of connecting by rifle-pits where this was not already done, was an easy task for the troops that were to defend them.

We were now looking west, besieging Pemberton, while we were also looking east to defend ourselves against an expected siege by Johnston. But as against the garrison of Vicksburg we were as substantially protected as they were against us. Where we were looking east and north we were strongly fortified, and on the defensive. Johnston evidently took in the situation and wisely, I think, abstained from making an assault on us because it would simply have inflicted loss on both sides without accomplishing any result. We were strong enough to have taken the offensive against him; but I did not feel disposed to take any risk of losing our hold upon Pemberton's army, while I would have rejoiced at the opportunity of defending ourselves against an attack by Johnston.

From the 23d of May the work of fortifying and pushing forward our position nearer to the enemy had been steadily progressing. At three points on the Jackson road, in front of Leggett's brigade, a sap was run up to the enemy's parapet, and by the 25th of June we had it undermined and the mine charged. The enemy had countermined, but did not succeed in reaching our mine. At this particular point the hill on which the rebel work stands rises abruptly. Our sap ran close up to the outside of the enemy's parapet. In fact this parapet was also our protection. The soldiers of the two sides occasionally conversed pleasantly across this barrier; sometimes they exchanged the hard bread of the Union soldiers for the tobacco of the Confederates; at other times the enemy threw over hand-grenades, and often our men, catching them in their hands, returned them.

Our mine had been started some distance back down the hill; consequently when it had extended as far as the parapet it was many feet below it. This caused the failure of the enemy in his search to find and destroy it. On the 25th of June at three o'clock, all being ready, the mine was exploded. A heavy artillery fire all along the line had been ordered to open with the explosion. The effect was to blow the top of the hill off and make a crater where it stood. The breach was not sufficient to enable us to pass a column of attack through. In fact, the enemy having failed to reach our mine had thrown up a line farther back, where most of the men guarding that point were placed. There were a few men, however, left at the advance line, and others working in the countermine, which was still being pushed to find ours. All that were there were thrown into the air, some of them coming down on our side, still alive. I remember one colored man, who had been underground at work when the explosion took place, who was thrown to our side. He was not much hurt, but terribly frightened. Someone asked him how high he had gone up. "Dun no, massa, but t'ink 'bout t'ree mile," was his reply. General Logan commanded at this point and took this colored man to his quarters, where he did service to the end of the siege.

As soon as the explosion took place the crater was seized by two regiments of our troops who were near by, under cover, where they had been placed for the express purpose. The enemy made a desperate effort to expel them, but failed, and soon retired behind the new line. From here, however, they threw hand-grenades, which did some execution. The compliment was returned by our men, but not with so much effect. The enemy could lay their grenades on the parapet, which alone divided the contestants, and roll them down upon us; while from our side they had to be thrown over the parapet, which was at considerable elevation. During the night we made efforts to secure our position in the crater against the missiles of the enemy, so as to run trenches along the outer base of their parapet, right and left; but the enemy continued throwing their grenades, and brought boxes of field ammunition (shells), the fuses of which they would light with portfires, and throw them by hand into our ranks. We found it impossible to continue this work. Another mine was consequently started which was exploded on the 1st of July, destroying an entire rebel redan, killing and wounding a considerable number of its occupants and leaving an immense chasm where it stood. No attempt to charge was made this time, the experience of the 25th admonishing us. Our loss in the first affair was about thirty killed and wounded. The enemy must have lost more in the two explosions than we did in the first. We lost none in the second.

From this time forward the work of mining and pushing our position nearer to the enemy was prosecuted with vigor, and I determined to explode no more mines until we were ready to explode a number at different points and assault immediately after. We were up now at three different points, one in front of each corps, to where only the parapet of the enemy divided us.

At this time an intercepted dispatch from Johnston to Pemberton informed me that Johnston intended to make a determined attack upon us in order to relieve the garrison at Vicksburg. I knew the garrison would make no formidable effort to relieve itself. The picket lines were so close to each other — where there was space enough between the lines to post pickets — that the men could converse. On the 21st of June I was informed, through this means, that Pemberton was preparing to escape, by crossing to the Louisiana side under cover of night; that he had employed workmen in making boats for that purpose; that the men had been canvassed to ascertain if they would make an assault on the "Yankees" to cut their way out; that they had refused, and almost mutinied, because their commander would not surrender and relieve their sufferings, and had only been pacified by the assurance that boats enough would be finished in a week to carry them all over. The rebel pickets also said that houses in the city had been pulled down to get material to build these boats with. Afterwards this story was verified: on entering the city we found a large number of very rudely constructed boats.

All necessary steps were at once taken to render such an attempt abortive. Our pickets were doubled; Admiral Porter was notified, so that the river might be more closely watched; material was collected on the west bank of the river to be set on fire and light up the river if the attempt was made; and batteries were established along the levee crossing the peninsula on the Louisiana side. Had the attempt been made the garrison of Vicksburg would have been drowned, or made prisoners on the Louisiana side. General Richard Taylor was expected on the west bank to co-operate in this movement, I believe, but he did not come, nor could he have done so with a force sufficient to be of service. The Mississippi was now in our possession from its source to its mouth, except in the immediate front of Vicksburg and of Port Hudson. We had nearly exhausted the country, along a line drawn from Lake Providence to opposite Bruinsburg. The roads west were not of a character to draw supplies over for any considerable force.

By the 1st of July our approaches had reached the enemy's ditch at a number of places. At ten points we could move under cover to within from five to one hundred yards of the enemy. Orders were given to make all preparations for assault on the 6th of July. The debouches were ordered widened to afford easy egress, while the approaches were also to be widened to admit the troops to pass through four abreast. Plank, and bags filled with cotton packed in tightly, were ordered prepared, to enable the troops to cross the ditches.

On the night of the 1st of July Johnston was between Brownsville and the Big Black, and wrote Pemberton from there that about the 7th of the month an attempt would be made to create a diversion to enable him to cut his way out. Pemberton was a prisoner before this message reached him.

On July 1st Pemberton, seeing no hope of outside relief, addressed the following letter to each of his four division commanders:

"Unless the siege of Vicksburg is raised, or supplies are thrown in, it will become necessary very shortly to evacuate the place. I see no prospect of the former, and there are many great, if not insuperable obstacles in the way of the latter. You are, therefore, requested to inform me with as little delay as possible, as to the condition of your troops and their ability to make the marches and undergo the fatigues necessary to accomplish a successful evacuation."

Two of his generals suggested surrender, and the other two practically did the same. They expressed the opinion that an attempt to evacuate would fail. Pemberton had previously got a message to Johnston suggesting that he should try to negotiate with me for a release of the garrison with their arms. Johnston replied that it would be a confession of weakness for him to do so; but he authorized Pemberton to use his name in making such an arrangement.

On the 3d about ten o'clock A.M. white flags appeared on a portion of the rebel works. Hostilities along that part of the line ceased at once. Soon two persons were seen coming towards our lines bearing a white flag. They proved to be General Bowen, a division commander, and Colonel Montgomery, aide-de-camp to Pemberton, bearing the following letter to me:

"I have the honor to propose an armistice for — hours, with the view to arranging terms for the capitulation of Vicksburg. To this end, if agreeable to you, I will appoint three commissioners, to meet a like number to be named by yourself at such place and hour today as you may find convenient. I make this proposition to save the further effusion of blood, which must otherwise be shed to a frightful extent, feeling myself fully able to maintain my position for a yet indefinite period. This communication will be handed you under a flag of truce, by Major-General John S. Bowen."

It was a glorious sight to officers and soldiers on the line where these white flags were visible, and the news soon spread to all parts of the command. The troops felt that their long and weary marches, hard fighting, ceaseless watching by night and day, in a hot climate, exposure to all sorts of weather, to diseases and, worst of all, to the gibes of many Northern papers that came to them saying all their suffering was in vain, that Vicksburg would never be taken, were at last an end and the Union sure to be saved.

Bowen was received by General A.J. Smith, and asked to see me. I had been a neighbor of Bowen's in Missouri, and knew him well and favorably before the war; but his request was refused. He then suggested that I should meet Pemberton. To this I sent a verbal message saying that, if Pemberton desired it, I would meet him in front of McPherson's corps at three o'clock that afternoon. I also sent the following written reply to Pemberton's letter:

"Your note of this date is just received, proposing an armistice for several hours, for the purpose of arranging terms of capitulation through commissioners, to be appointed, etc. The useless effusion of blood you propose stopping by this course can be ended at any time you may choose, by the unconditional surrender of the city and garrison. Men who have shown so much endurance and courage as those now in Vicksburg, will always challenge the respect of an adversary, and I can assure you will be treated with all the respect due to prisoners of war. I do not favor the proposition of appointing commissioners to arrange the terms of capitulation, because I have no terms other than those indicated above."

At three o'clock Pemberton appeared at the point suggested in my verbal message, accompanied by the same officers who had borne his letter of the morning. Generals Ord, McPherson, Logan and A.J. Smith, and several officers of my staff, accompanied me. Our place of meeting was on a hillside within a few hundred feet of the rebel lines. Near by stood a stunted oak tree, which was made historical by the event. It was but a short time before the last vestige of its body, root and limb had disappeared, the fragments taken as trophies. Since then the same tree has furnished as many cords of wood, in the shape of trophies, as "The True Cross."

Pemberton and I had served in the same division during part of the Mexican War. I knew him very well therefore, and greeted him as an old acquaintance. He soon asked what terms I proposed to give his army if it surrendered. My answer was the same as proposed in my reply to his letter. Pemberton then said, rather snappishly, "The conference might as well end," and turned abruptly as if to leave. I said, "Very well." General Bowen, I saw, was very anxious that the surrender should be consummated. His manner and remarks while Pemberton and I were talking, showed this. He now proposed that he and one of our generals should have a conference. I had no objection to this, as nothing could be made binding upon me that they might propose. Smith and Bowen accordingly had a conference, during which Pemberton and I, moving a short distance away towards the enemy's lines were in conversation. After a while Bowen suggested that the Confederate army should be allowed to march out with the honors of war, carrying their small arms and field artillery. This was promptly and unceremoniously rejected.

The interview here ended, I agreeing, however, to send a letter giving final terms by ten o'clock that night.

Word was sent to Admiral Porter soon after the correspondence with Pemberton commenced, so that hostilities might be stopped on the part of both army and navy. It was agreed on my paging with Pemberton that they should not be renewed until our correspondence ceased.

When I returned to my headquarters I sent for all the corps and division commanders with the army immediately confronting Vicksburg. Half the army was from eight to twelve miles off, waiting for Johnston. I informed them of the contents of Pemberton's letters, of my reply and the substance of the interview, and that I was ready to hear any suggestion; but would hold the power of deciding entirely in my own hands. This was the nearest approach to a "council of war" I ever held. Against the general, and almost unanimous judgment of the council I sent the following letter:

"In conformity with agreement of this afternoon, I will submit the following proposition for the surrender of the City of Vicksburg, public stores, etc. On your accepting the terms proposed, I will march in one division as a guard, and take possession at eight A.M. tomorrow. As soon as rolls can be made out, and paroles be signed by officers and men, you will be allowed to march out of our lines, the officers taking with them their side-arms and clothing, and the field, staff and cavalry officers one horse each. The rank and file will be allowed all their clothing, but no other property. If these conditions are accepted, any amount of rations you may deem necessary can be taken from the stores you now have, and also the necessary cooking utensils for preparing them. Thirty wagons also, counting two two-horse or mule teams as one, will be allowed to transport such articles as cannot be carried along. The same conditions will be allowed to all sick and wounded officers and soldiers as fast as they become able to travel. The paroles for these latter must be signed, however, whilst officers present are authorized to sign the roll of prisoners."

By the terms of the cartel then in force, prisoners captured by either army were required to be forwarded as soon as possible to either Aiken's landing below Dutch Gap on the James River, or to Vicksburg, there to be exchanged, or paroled until they could be exchanged. There was a Confederate commissioner at Vicksburg, authorized to make the exchange. I did not propose to take him a prisoner, but to leave him free to perform the functions of his office. Had I insisted upon an unconditional surrender there would have been over thirty thousand men to transport to Cairo, very much to the inconvenience of the army on the Mississippi. Thence the prisoners would have had to be transported by rail to Washington or Baltimore; thence again by steamer to Aiken's — all at very great expense. At Aiken's they would have had to be paroled, because the Confederates did not have Union prisoners to give in exchange. Then again Pemberton's army was largely composed of men whose homes were in the Southwest; I knew many of them were tired of the war and would get home just as soon as they could. A large number of them had voluntarily come into our lines during the siege, and requested to be sent north where they could get employment until the war was over and they could go to their homes.

Late at night I received the following reply to my last letter:

"I have the honor to acknowledge the receipt of your communication of this date, proposing terms of capitulation for this garrison and post. In the main your terms are accepted; but, in justice both to the honor and spirit of my troops manifested in the defense of Vicksburg, I have to submit the following amendments, which, if acceded to by you, will perfect the agreement between us. At ten o'clock A.M. tomorrow, I propose to evacuate the works in and around Vicksburg, and to surrender the city and garrison under my command, by marching out with my colors and arms, stacking them in front of my present lines. After which you will take possession. Officers to retain their side-arms and personal property, and the rights and property of citizens to be respected."

This was received after midnight. My reply was as follows:

"I have the honor to acknowledge the receipt of your communication of 3d July. The amendment proposed by you cannot be acceded to in full. It will be necessary to furnish every officer and man with a parole signed by himself, which, with the completion of the roll of prisoners, will necessarily take some time. Again, I can make no stipulations with regard to the treatment of citizens and their private property. While I do not propose to cause them any undue annoyance or loss, I cannot consent to leave myself under any restraint by stipulations. The property which officers will be allowed to take with them will be as stated in my proposition of last evening; that is, officers will be allowed their private baggage and side-arms, and mounted officers one horse each. If you mean by your proposition for each brigade to march to the front of the lines now occupied by it, and stack arms at ten o'clock A.M., and then return to the inside and there remain as prisoners until properly paroled, I will make no objection to it. Should no notification be received of your acceptance of my terms by nine o'clock A.M. I shall regard them as having been rejected, and shall act accordingly. Should these terms be accepted, white flags should be displayed along your lines to prevent such of my troops as may not have been notified, from firing upon your men."

Pemberton promptly accepted these terms.

During the siege there had been a good deal of friendly sparring between the soldiers of the two armies, on picket and where the lines were close together. All rebels were known as "Johnnies," all Union troops as "Yanks." Often "Johnny" would call: "Well, Yank, when are you coming into town?" The reply was sometimes: "We propose to celebrate the 4th of July there." Sometimes it would be: "We always treat our prisoners with kindness and do not want to hurt them;" or, "We are holding you as prisoners of war while you are feeding yourselves." The garrison, from the commanding general down, undoubtedly expected an assault on the fourth. They knew from the temper of their men it would be successful when made; and that would be a greater humiliation than to surrender. Besides it would be attended with severe loss to them.

The Vicksburg paper, which we received regularly through the courtesy of the rebel pickets, said prior to the fourth, in speaking of the "Yankee" boast that they would take dinner in Vicksburg that day, that the best receipt for cooking a rabbit was "First ketch your rabbit." The paper at this time and for some time previous was printed on the plain side of wall paper. The last number was issued on the fourth and announced that we had "caught our rabbit."

I have no doubt that Pemberton commenced his correspondence on the third with a two-fold purpose: first, to avoid an assault, which he knew would be successful, and second, to prevent the capture taking place on the great national holiday, the anniversary of the Declaration of American Independence. Holding out for better terms as he did he defeated his aim in the latter particular.

At the appointed hour the garrison of Vicksburg marched out of their works and formed line in front, stacked arms and marched back in good order. Our whole army present witnessed this scene without cheering. Logan's division, which had approached nearest the rebel works, was the first to march in; and the flag of one of the regiments of his division was soon floating over the court-house. Our soldiers were no sooner inside the lines than the two armies began to fraternize. Our men had had full rations from the time the siege commenced, to the close. The enemy had been suffering, particularly towards the last. I myself saw our men taking bread from their haversacks and giving it to the enemy they had so recently been engaged in starving out. It was accepted with avidity and with thanks.

Pemberton says in his report:

"If it should be asked why the 4th of July was selected as the day for surrender, the answer is obvious. I believed that upon that day I should obtain better terms. Well aware of the vanity of our foe, I knew they would attach vast importance to the entrance on the 4th of July into the stronghold of the great river, and that, to gratify their national vanity, they would yield then what could not be extorted from them at any other time."

This does not support my view of his reasons for selecting the day he did for surrendering. But it must be recollected that his first letter asking terms was received about 10 o'clock A.M., July 3d. It then could hardly be expected that it would take twenty-four hours to effect a surrender. He knew that Johnston was in our rear for the purpose of raising the siege, and he naturally would want to hold out as long as he could. He knew his men would not resist an assault, and one was expected on the fourth. In our interview he told me he had rations enough to hold out for some time — my recollection is two weeks. It was this statement that induced me to insert in the terms that he was to draw rations for his men from his own supplies.

On the 4th of July General Holmes, with an army of eight or nine thousand men belonging to the trans-Mississippi department, made an attack upon Helena, Arkansas. He was totally defeated by General Prentiss, who was holding Helena with less than forty-two hundred soldiers. Holmes reported his loss at 1,636, of which 173 were killed; but as Prentiss buried 400, Holmes evidently understated his losses. The Union loss was 57 killed, 127 wounded, and between 30 and 40 missing. This was the last effort on the part of the Confederacy to raise the siege of Vicksburg.

On the third, as soon as negotiations were commenced, I notified Sherman and directed him to be ready to take the offensive against Johnston, drive him out of the State and destroy his army if he could. Steele and Ord were directed at the same time to be in readiness to join Sherman as soon as the surrender took place. Of this Sherman was notified.

I rode into Vicksburg with the troops, and went to the river to exchange congratulations with the navy upon our joint victory. At that time I found that many of the citizens had been living underground. The ridges upon which Vicksburg is built, and those back to the Big Black, are composed of a deep yellow clay of great tenacity. Where roads and streets are cut through, perpendicular banks are left and stand as well as if composed of stone. The magazines of the enemy were made by running passage-ways into this clay at places where there were deep cuts. Many citizens secured places of safety for their families by carving out rooms in these embankments. A door-way in these cases would be cut in a high bank, starting from the level of the road or street, and after running in a few feet a room of the size required was carved out of the clay, the dirt being removed by the door-way. In some instances I saw where two rooms were cut out, for a single family, with a door-way in the clay wall separating them. Some of these were carpeted and furnished with considerable elaboration. In these the occupants were fully secure from the shells of the navy, which were dropped into the city night and day without intermission.

I returned to my old headquarters outside in the afternoon, and did not move into the town until the sixth. On the afternoon of the fourth I sent Captain Wm. M. Dunn of my staff to Cairo, the nearest point where the telegraph could be reached, with a dispatch to the general-in-chief. It was as follows:

"The enemy surrendered this morning. The only terms allowed is their parole as prisoners of war. This I regard as a great advantage to us at this moment. It saves, probably, several days in the capture, and leaves troops and transports ready for immediate service. Sherman, with a large force, moves immediately on Johnston, to drive him from the State. I will send troops to the relief of Banks, and return the 9th army corps to Burnside."

This news, with the victory at Gettysburg won the same day, lifted a great load of anxiety from the minds of the President, his Cabinet and the loyal people all over the North. The fate of the Confederacy was sealed when Vicksburg fell. Much hard fighting was to be done afterwards and many precious lives were to be sacrificed; but the *morale* was with the supporters of the Union ever after.

I at the same time wrote to General Banks informing him of the fall and sending him a copy of the terms; also saying I would send him all the troops he wanted to insure the capture of the only foothold the enemy now had on the Mississippi River. General Banks had a number of copies of this letter printed, or at least a synopsis of it, and very soon a copy fell into the hands of General Gardner, who was then in command of Port Hudson. Gardner at once sent a letter to the commander of the National forces saying that he had been informed of the surrender of Vicksburg and telling how the information reached him. He added that if this was true, it was useless for him to hold out longer. General Banks gave him assurances that Vicksburg had been surrendered, and General Gardner surrendered unconditionally on the 9th of July. Port Hudson with nearly 6,000 prisoners, 51 guns, 5,000 small-arms and other stores fell into the hands of the Union forces: from that day to the close of the rebellion the Mississippi River, from its source to its mouth, remained in the control of the National troops.

Pemberton and his army were kept in Vicksburg until the whole could be paroled. The paroles were in duplicate, by organization (one copy for each, Federals and Confederates), and signed by the commanding officers of the companies or regiments. Duplicates were also made for each soldier and signed by each individually, one to be retained by the soldier signing and one to be retained by us. Several hundred refused to sign their paroles, preferring to be sent to the North as prisoners to being sent back to fight again. Others again kept out of the way, hoping to escape either alternative.

Pemberton appealed to me in person to compel these men to sign their paroles, but I declined. It also leaked out that many of the men who had signed their paroles, intended to desert and go to their homes as soon as they got out of our lines. Pemberton hearing this, again appealed to me to assist him. He wanted arms for a battalion, to act as guards in keeping his men together while being marched to a camp of instruction, where he expected to keep them until exchanged. This request was also declined. It was precisely what I expected and hoped that they would do. I told him, however, that I would see that they marched beyond our lines in good order. By the eleventh, just one week after the surrender, the paroles were completed and the Confederate garrison marched out. Many deserted, and fewer of them were ever returned to the ranks to fight again than would have been the case had the surrender been unconditional and the prisoners sent to the James River to be paroled.

As soon as our troops took possession of the city guards were established along the whole line of parapet, from the river above to the river below. The prisoners were allowed to occupy their old camps behind the entrenchments. No restraint was put upon them, except by their own commanders. They were rationed about as our own men, and from our supplies. The men of the two armies fraternized as if they had been fighting for the same cause. When they passed out of the works they had so long and so gallantly defended, between lines of their late antagonists, not a cheer went up, not a remark was made that would give pain. Really, I believe there was a feeling of sadness just then in the breasts of most of the Union soldiers at seeing the dejection of their late antagonists.

The day before the departure the following order was issued:

"Paroled prisoners will be sent out of here tomorrow. They will be authorized to cross at the railroad bridge, and move from there to Edward's Ferry,* and on by way of Raymond. Instruct the commands to be orderly and quiet as these prisoners pass, to make no offensive remarks, and not to harbor any who fall out of ranks after they have passed."

Chapter XXXIX

RETROSPECT OF THE CAMPAIGN — SHERMAN'S MOVEMENTS — PROPOSED MOVEMENT UPON MOBILE — A PAINFUL ACCIDENT — ORDERED TO REPORT AT CAIRO

The capture of Vicksburg, with its garrison, ordnance and ordnance stores, and the successful battles fought in reaching them, gave new spirit to the loyal people of the North. New hopes for the final success of the cause of the Union were inspired. The victory gained at Gettysburg, upon the same day, added to their hopes. Now the Mississippi River was entirely in the possession of the National troops; for the fall of Vicksburg gave us Port Hudson at once. The army of northern Virginia was driven out of Pennsylvania and forced back to about the same ground it occupied in 1861. The Army of the Tennessee united with the Army of the Gulf, dividing the Confederate States completely.

The first dispatch I received from the government after the fall of Vicksburg was in these words:

"I fear your paroling the prisoners at Vicksburg, without actual delivery to a proper agent as required by the seventh article of the cartel, may be construed into an absolute release, and that the men will immediately be placed in the ranks of the enemy. Such has been the case elsewhere. If these prisoners have not been allowed to depart, you will detain them until further orders."

---

‡ Meant Edward's Station.

Halleck did not know that they had already been delivered into the hands of Major Watts, Confederate commissioner for the exchange of prisoners.

At Vicksburg 31,600 prisoners were surrendered, together with 172 cannon about 60,000 muskets and a large amount of ammunition. The small-arms of the enemy were far superior to the bulk of ours. Up to this time our troops at the West had been limited to the old United States flint-lock muskets changed into percussion, or the Belgian musket imported early in the war — almost as dangerous to the person firing it as to the one aimed at — and a few new and improved arms. These were of many different calibers, a fact that caused much trouble in distributing ammunition during an engagement. The enemy had generally new arms which had run the blockade and were of uniform caliber. After the surrender I authorized all colonels whose regiments were armed with inferior muskets, to place them in the stack of captured arms and replace them with the latter. A large number of arms turned in to the Ordnance Department as captured, were thus arms that had really been used by the Union army in the capture of Vicksburg.

In this narrative I have not made the mention I should like of officers, dead and alive, whose services entitle them to special mention. Neither have I made that mention of the navy which its services deserve. Suffice it to say, the close of the siege of Vicksburg found us with an army unsurpassed, in proportion to its numbers, taken as a whole of officers and men. A military education was acquired which no other school could have given. Men who thought a company was quite enough for them to command properly at the beginning, would have made good regimental or brigade commanders; most of the brigade commanders were equal to the command of a division, and one, Ransom, would have been equal to the command of a corps at least. Logan and Crocker ended the campaign fitted to command independent armies.

General F.P. Blair joined me at Milliken's Bend a full-fledged general, without having served in a lower grade. He commanded a division in the campaign. I had known Blair in Missouri, where I had voted against him in 1858 when he ran for Congress. I knew him as a frank, positive and generous man, true to his friends even to a fault, but always a leader. I dreaded his coming; I knew from experience that it was more difficult to command two generals desiring to be leaders than it was to command one army officered intelligently and with subordination. It affords me the greatest pleasure to record now my agreeable disappointment in respect to his character. There was no man braver than he, nor was there any who obeyed all orders of his superior in rank with more unquestioning alacrity. He was one man as a soldier, another as a politician.

The navy under Porter was all it could be, during the entire campaign. Without its assistance the campaign could not have been successfully made with twice the number of men engaged. It could not have been made at all, in the way it was, with any number of men without such assistance. The most perfect harmony reigned between the two arms of the service. There never was a request made, that I am aware of, either of the flag-officer or any of his subordinates, that was not promptly complied with.

The campaign of Vicksburg was suggested and developed by circumstances. The elections of 1862 had gone against the prosecution of the war. Voluntary enlistments had nearly ceased and the draft had been resorted to; this was resisted, and a defeat or backward movement would have made its execution impossible. A forward movement to a decisive victory was necessary. Accordingly I resolved to get below Vicksburg, unite with Banks against Port Hudson, make New Orleans a base and, with that base and Grand Gulf as a starting point, move our combined forces against Vicksburg. Upon reaching Grand Gulf, after running its batteries and fighting a battle, I received a letter from Banks informing me that he could not be at Port Hudson under ten days, and then with only fifteen thousand men. The time was worth more than the reinforcements; I therefore determined to push into the interior of the enemy's country.

With a large river behind us, held above and below by the enemy, rapid movements were essential to success. Jackson was captured the day after a new commander had arrived, and only a few days before large reinforcements were expected. A rapid movement west was made; the garrison of Vicksburg was met in two engagements and badly defeated, and driven back into its stronghold and there successfully besieged. It looks now as though Providence had directed the course of the campaign while the Army of the Tennessee executed the decree.

Upon the surrender of the garrison of Vicksburg there were three things that required immediate attention. The first was to send a force to drive the enemy from our rear, and out of the State. The second was to send reinforcements to Banks near Port Hudson, if necessary, to complete the triumph of opening the Mississippi from its source to its mouth to the free navigation of vessels bearing the Stars and Stripes. The third was to inform the authorities at Washington and the North of the good news, to relieve their long suspense and strengthen their confidence in the ultimate success of the cause they had so much at heart.

Soon after negotiations were opened with General Pemberton for the surrender of the city, I notified Sherman, whose troops extended from

Haines' Bluff on the left to the crossing of the Vicksburg and Jackson road over the Big Black on the right, and directed him to hold his command in readiness to advance and drive the enemy from the State as soon as Vicksburg surrendered. Steele and Ord were directed to be in readiness to join Sherman in his move against General Johnston, and Sherman was advised of this also. Sherman moved promptly, crossing the Big Black at three different points with as many columns, all concentrating at Bolton, twenty miles west of Jackson.

Johnston heard of the surrender of Vicksburg almost as soon as it occurred, and immediately fell back on Jackson. On the 8th of July Sherman was within ten miles of Jackson and on the 11th was close up to the defenses of the city and shelling the town. The siege was kept up until the morning of the 17th, when it was found that the enemy had evacuated during the night. The weather was very hot, the roads dusty and the water bad. Johnston destroyed the roads as he passed and had so much the start that pursuit was useless; but Sherman sent one division, Steele's, to Brandon, fourteen miles east of Jackson.

The National loss in the second capture of Jackson was less than one thousand men, killed, wounded and missing. The Confederate loss was probably less, except in captured. More than this number fell into our hands as prisoners.

Medicines and food were left for the Confederate wounded and sick who had to be left behind. A large amount of rations was issued to the families that remained in Jackson. Medicine and food were also sent to Raymond for the destitute families as well as the sick and wounded, as I thought it only fair that we should return to these people some of the articles we had taken while marching through the country. I wrote to Sherman: "Impress upon the men the importance of going through the State in an orderly manner, abstaining from taking anything not absolutely necessary for their subsistence while traveling. They should try to create as favorable an impression as possible upon the people." Provisions and forage, when called for by them, were issued to all the people, from Bruinsburg to Jackson and back to Vicksburg, whose resources had been taken for the supply of our army. Very large quantities of groceries and provisions were so issued.

Sherman was ordered back to Vicksburg, and his troops took much the same position they had occupied before — from the Big Black to Haines' Bluff. Having cleaned up about Vicksburg and captured or routed all regular Confederate forces for more than a hundred miles in all directions, I felt that the troops that had done so much should be allowed to do more before the enemy could recover from the blow he had received, and while important points might be captured without bloodshed. I suggested to the General-in-chief the idea of a campaign against Mobile, starting from Lake Pontchartrain. Halleck preferred another course. The possession of the trans-Mississippi by the Union forces seemed to possess more importance in his mind than almost any campaign east of the Mississippi. I am well aware that the President was very anxious to have a foothold in Texas, to stop the clamor of some of the foreign governments which seemed to be seeking a pretext to interfere in the war, at least so far as to recognize belligerent rights to the Confederate States. This, however, could have been easily done without wasting troops in western Louisiana and eastern Texas, by sending a garrison at once to Brownsville on the Rio Grande.

Halleck disapproved of my proposition to go against Mobile, so that I was obliged to settle down and see myself put again on the defensive as I had been a year before in west Tennessee. It would have been an easy thing to capture Mobile at the time I proposed to go there. Having that as a base of operations, troops could have been thrown into the interior to operate against General Bragg's army. This would necessarily have compelled Bragg to detach in order to meet this fire in his rear. If he had not done this the troops from Mobile could have inflicted inestimable damage upon much of the country from which his army and Lee's were yet receiving their supplies. I was so much impressed with this idea that I renewed my request later in July and again about the 1st of August, and proposed sending all the troops necessary, asking only the assistance of the navy to protect the debarkation of troops at or near Mobile. I also asked for a leave of absence to visit New Orleans, particularly if my suggestion to move against Mobile should be approved. Both requests were refused. So far as my experience with General Halleck went it was very much easier for him to refuse a favor than to grant one. But I did not regard this as a favor. It was simply in line of duty, though out of my department.

The General-in-chief having decided against me, the depletion of an army, which had won a succession of great victories, commenced, as had been the case the year before after the fall of Corinth when the army was sent where it would do the least good. By orders, I sent to Banks a force of 4,000 men; returned the 9th corps to Kentucky and, when transportation had been collected, started a division of 5,000 men to Schofield in Missouri where Price was raiding the State. I also detached a brigade under Ransom to Natchez, to garrison that place permanently. This latter move was quite fortunate as to the time when Ransom arrived there. The enemy happened to have a large number, about 5,000 head, of beef cattle there on the way from Texas to feed the Eastern armies, and also a large amount of munitions of war which had probably come through Texas from the Rio Grande and which were on the way to Lee's and other armies in the East.

The troops that were left with me around Vicksburg were very busily and unpleasantly employed in making expeditions against guerilla bands and small detachments of cavalry which infested the interior, and in destroying mills, bridges and rolling stock on the railroads. The guerillas and cavalry were not there to fight but to annoy, and therefore disappeared on the first approach of our troops.

The country back of Vicksburg was filled with deserters from Pemberton's army and, it was reported, many from Johnston's also. The men determined not to fight again while the war lasted. Those who lived beyond the reach of the Confederate army wanted to get to their homes. Those who did not, wanted to get North where they could work for their support till the war was over. Besides all this there was quite a peace feeling, for the time being, among the citizens of that part of Mississippi, but this feeling soon subsided. It is not probable that Pemberton got off with over 4,000 of his army to the camp where he proposed taking them, and these were in a demoralized condition.

On the 7th of August I further depleted my army by sending the 13th corps, General Ord commanding, to Banks. Besides this I received orders to co-operate with the latter general in movements west of the Mississippi. Having received this order I went to New Orleans to confer with Banks about the proposed movement. All these movements came to naught.

During this visit I reviewed Banks' army a short distance above Carrollton. The horse I rode was vicious and but little used, and on my return to New Orleans ran away and, shying at a locomotive in the street, fell, probably on me. I was rendered insensible, and when I regained consciousness I found myself in a hotel near by with several doctors attending me. My leg was swollen from the knee to the thigh, and the swelling, almost to the point of bursting, extended along the body up to the armpit. The pain was almost beyond endurance. I lay at the hotel something over a week without being able to turn myself in bed. I had a steamer stop at the nearest point possible, and was carried to it on a litter. I was then taken to Vicksburg, where I remained unable to move for some time afterwards.

While I was absent General Sherman declined to assume command because, he said, it would confuse the records; but he let all the orders be made in my name, and was glad to render any assistance he could. No orders were issued by my staff, certainly no important orders, except upon consultation with and approval of Sherman.

On the 13th of September, while I was still in New Orleans, Halleck telegraphed to me to send all available forces to Memphis and thence to Tuscumbia, to co-operate with Rosecrans for the relief of Chattanooga. On the 15th he telegraphed again for all available forces to go to Rosecrans. This was received on the 27th. I was still confined to my bed, unable to rise from it without assistance; but I at once ordered Sherman to send one division to Memphis as fast as transports could be provided. The division of McPherson's corps, which had got off and was on the way to join Steele in Arkansas, was recalled and sent, likewise, to report to Hurlbut at Memphis. Hurlbut was directed to forward these two divisions with two others from his own corps at once, and also to send any other troops that might be returning there. Halleck suggested that some good man, like Sherman or McPherson, should be sent to Memphis to take charge of the troops going east. On this I sent Sherman, as being, I thought, the most suitable person for an independent command, and besides he was entitled to it if it had to be given to anyone. He was directed to take with him another division of his corps. This left one back, but having one of McPherson's divisions he had still the equivalent.

Before the receipt by me of these orders the battle of Chickamauga had been fought and Rosecrans forced back into Chattanooga. The administration as well as the General-in-chief was nearly frantic at the situation of affairs there. Mr. Charles A. Dana, an officer of the War Department, was sent to Rosecrans' headquarters. I do not know what his instructions were, but he was still in Chattanooga when I arrived there at a later period.

It seems that Halleck suggested that I should go to Nashville as soon as able to move and take general direction of the troops moving from the west. I received the following dispatch dated October 3d: "It is the wish of the Secretary of War that as soon as General Grant is able he will come to Cairo and report by telegraph." I was still very lame, but started without delay. Arriving at Columbus on the 16th I reported by telegraph: "Your dispatch from Cairo of the 3d directing me to report from Cairo was received at 11:30 on the 10th. Left the same day with staff and headquarters and am here en route for Cairo."